THE DGSE

I0877098

CONCISE HISTORIES
OF INTELLIGENCE
SERIES

Series Editors
Christopher Moran, Mark Phythian, and Mark Stout

The Concise Histories of Intelligence series provides students, scholars, and general readers with accessible guides to the most important and impactful intelligence services of the past and present. The books in the series span a wide range of national contexts, facilitating comparative analysis. Each title addresses the origins and history of a service, its range of activities, its leadership, its place in its country's intelligence and political system, and its role in the country's domestic and foreign security endeavors.

Other Titles in the Series
Iran's Ministry of Intelligence: A Concise History
Steven R. Ward

Pakistan's ISI: A Concise History of the Inter-Services Intelligence Directorate
Julian Richards

The Russian FSB: A Concise History of the Federal Security Service
Kevin P. Riehle

THE DGSE

A CONCISE HISTORY OF FRANCE'S FOREIGN INTELLIGENCE SERVICE

DAMIEN VAN PUYVELDE

Georgetown University Press / Washington, DC

© 2026 Damien Van Puyvelde. All rights reserved. No part of this book may be reproduced or utilized in any form or by any means, electronic or mechanical, including photocopying and recording, or by any information storage and retrieval system, without permission in writing from the publisher.

The publisher is not responsible for third-party websites or their content. URL links were active at time of publication.

Library of Congress Cataloging-in-Publication Data

Names: Van Puyvelde, Damien, author
Title: The DGSE : a concise history of France's foreign intelligence service / Damien Van Puyvelde.
Description: Washington, DC : Georgetown University Press, [2026] | Series: Concise histories of intelligence | Includes bibliographical references and index.
Identifiers: LCCN 2025026144 (print) | LCCN 2025026145 (ebook) | ISBN 9781647127077 hardcover | ISBN 9781647127084 paperback | ISBN 9781647127091 ebook
Subjects: LCSH: France. Direction générale de la sécurité extérieure—History | Intelligence service—France—History
Classification: LCC JN2738.I58 V36 2026 (print) | LCC JN2738.I58 (ebook) | DDC 327.1244009—dc23/eng/20251118
LC record available at https://lccn.loc.gov/2025026144
LC ebook record available at https://lccn.loc.gov/2025026145

∞ This paper meets the requirements of ANSI/NISO Z39.48-1992 (Permanence of Paper).

EU GPSR Authorized Representative
Logos Europe, 9 rue Nicolas Poussin, 17000, La Rochelle, France
Email: Contact@logoseurope.eu

27 26 9 8 7 6 5 4 3 2 First printing

Printed in the United States of America

Cover design by Jeremy John Parker
Interior design by Paul Hotvedt

Contents

Figures

Acknowledgments

I owe a debt of gratitude to several colleagues who encouraged me to write a book on the DGSE. Richard Aldrich casually mentioned the idea at the end of a long conference day over a decade ago. Considering the depth and scope of his six-hundred-page book on the GCHQ, the United Kingdom's SIGINT agency, I initially found the prospect overwhelming. The challenge felt even greater due to the absence of public DGSE archives and the resulting scarcity of academic research on the agency.

The project felt more manageable when Christopher Moran, Mark Phythian, and Mark Stout, together with Don Jacobs, launched a book series that would provide concise histories of intelligence agencies. The idea of a shorter book, following a predefined outline, felt much less daunting. The opportunity to contribute to a larger body of knowledge that would facilitate comparative work in the field was very motivating.

In the early stages of this project, conversations with Peter Jackson, Pauline Blistène, Olivier Chopin, and Benjamin Oudet had a profound impact. Their research and insights shaped my thinking, leaving many traces in this book. I am also grateful to Olivier Forcade, Sébastien Laurent, and Bertrand Warusfel—the "Three Musketeers" of French intelligence studies—who were always supportive and generous with their time, providing a solid foundation on which to build this project. Rory Cormac, Mark Stout, and Mathilde von Bülow offered valuable feedback on my early work on French covert action. Paul Charon, Nikki Ikani,

Quentin Jalabert, Clément Renault, and Simon Willmetts kindly reviewed selected chapters. Dan Lomas also shared valuable insights on how to approach this book project.

Initially I hesitated to contact the DGSE regarding my research. Some colleagues advised against it, to preserve my independence. Others, and eventually I, felt writing about the DGSE without engaging the agency would be a missed opportunity. In late 2022 I submitted a request to access classified documents related to the DGSE's coverage of the Gulf War of 1990–91 and reports on the presence of weapons of mass destruction in Iraq in the lead-up to the 2003 invasion led by the coalition led by the United States. By the summer of 2024, Director General Nicolas Lerner authorized access to several documents, which are utilized in this book. I am grateful to the DGSE personnel who assisted in locating these materials and facilitating access to them, and to the director general for his support.

In an unrelated development, I was invited by the DGSE's think tank, Interaxions, to give a talk at the agency's headquarters. This event provided me the opportunity to visit the agency's in-house exhibition and engage in conversation with senior officials. These discussions deepened my understanding of the DGSE's culture. Importantly, no conditions or requests were made in exchange for these opportunities.

As a courtesy, I chose to share a copy of my manuscript with the DGSE's communications unit. Given that I had engaged with some of the agency's officers and had been granted access to DGSE material, it seemed appropriate to offer it the opportunity to raise any concerns. None were. I want to be absolutely clear that this does not make this book into an authorized or official history. Any inaccuracies, whether factual or interpretive, are solely my responsibility.

There is no doubt that interactions with practitioners in France and beyond have shaped my understanding and interpretation of intelligence, particularly regarding the DGSE's organization, activities, and culture. This book makes rigorous use of references, and I hope it provides a solid foundation for others to pursue further research on the DGSE, identify errors, and challenge my interpretations and arguments. In the spirit of academic inquiry, I welcome such critiques.

Abbreviations

AN	Assemblée Nationale
BCRA	Bureau Central de Renseignement et d'Action (Central Intelligence and Action Bureau)
BND	Bundesnachrichtendienst (Federal Intelligence Service [Germany])
CIA	Central Intelligence Agency
CNCTR	Commission Nationale de Contrôle des Techniques de Renseignement (National Commission for the Control of Intelligence Techniques)
CNR	*coordonnateur national du renseignement* (national intelligence adviser)
CNRLT	Coordination Nationale du Renseignement et de la Lutte contre le Terrorisme (National Center for Intelligence and Counterterrorism)
COMINT	communications intelligence
COS	Commandement des Opérations Spéciales (Special Operations Command)
CPEOM	Centre Parachutiste d'Entrainement aux Opérations Maritimes (Parachute Training Center for Maritime Operations)
CPES	Centre Parachutiste d'Entrainement Spécialisé (Specialized Parachute Training Center)

CPIS	Centre Parachutiste d'Instruction Spécialisé (Specialized Parachute Instruction Center)
CSE	Communications Security Establishment (Canada)
CVFS	Commission de Vérification des Fonds Spéciaux (Special Funds Audit Commission)
DA	Direction de l'Administration (Administration Directorate)
DG	director general
DGSE	Direction Générale de la Sécurité Extérieure (Directorate General for External Security)
DGSI	Direction Générale de la Sécurité Intérieure (Directorate General for Internal Security)
DGSS	Direction Générale des Services Spéciaux (Directorate General for Special Services)
DNRED	Direction Nationale du Renseignement et des Enquêtes Douanières (National Directorate for Intelligence and Customs Investigations)
DO	Direction des Opérations (Operations Directorate)
DPR	Délégation Parlementaire au Renseignement (Parliamentary Delegation to Intelligence)
DR	Direction du Renseignement (Intelligence Directorate)
DRM	Direction du Renseignement Militaire (Directorate of Military Intelligence)
DRO	Direction de la Recherche et des Opérations (Directorate for Research and Operations)
DRSD	Direction du Renseignement et de Sécurité de la Défense (Directorate for Defense Intelligence and Security)
DS	Direction de la Stratégie (Directorate for Strategy)
DST	Direction de la Surveillance du Territoire (Territorial Surveillance Directorate)
DT	Direction Technique (Technical Directorate)
DTI	Direction Technique et de l'Innovation (Technical and Innovation Directorate)
ENA	École Nationale d'Administration (National School of Administration)
EU	European Union
FBI	Federal Bureau of Investigation (United States)
FLN	Front de Libération Nationale (National Liberation Front [Algeria])

FSB	Federal'naya Sluzhba Bezopasnosti (Federal Security Service [Russia])
GCHQ	Government Communications Headquarters
GEOINT	geospatial intelligence
GIA	Groupe Islamique Armé (Armed Islamic Group [Algeria])
HUMINT	human intelligence
ICE	Intelligence College in Europe
IMINT	imagery intelligence
INTCEN	Intelligence and Situation Centre (European Union)
ISI	Inter-Services Intelligence (Pakistan)
NSA	National Security Agency (United States)
OAS	Organisation de l'Armée Secrète (Secret Army Organization)
OSS	Office of Strategic Services (United States)
OT	*officier traitant* (case officer)
PNOR	*plan national d'orientation du renseignement* (national intelligence orientation plan)
SA	Service Action
SAE	Section des Armées Étrangères (Foreign Armies Section)
SCR	Section de Centralisation du Renseignement (Intelligence Centralization Section)
SDECE	Service de Documentation Extérieure et de Contre-Espionnage (External Documentation and Counterespionage Service)
SGAS	Secrétariat Général pour l'Analyse et la Stratégie (General Secretariat for Analysis and Strategy)
SGDSN	Secrétariat Général de la Défense et de la Sécurité Nationale (General Secretariat for Defense and National Security)
SIGINT	signals intelligence
SIS	Secret Intelligence Service (United Kingdom)
SR	Service de Renseignement (Intelligence Service)
TECHINT	technical intelligence
TRACFIN	Traitement du Renseignement et Action contre les Circuits Financiers Clandestins (Intelligence Processing and Action against Clandestine Financial Circuits)
UNITA	União Nacional para a Independência Total de Angola (National Union for the Total Independence of Angola)

Introduction

This book tells the story of France's foreign intelligence service from its rebranding in 1982 as the Direction Générale de la Sécurité Extérieure (DGSE; Directorate General for External Security) to today. The DGSE is France's highest-profile intelligence agency, yet we know very little about it. Some readers will recall the *Rainbow Warrior* fiasco, when DGSE operators sank Greenpeace's flagship, causing the death of a photographer in 1985. Others will be more familiar with the popular TV show *The Bureau*, which portrays the lives of nonofficial cover DGSE officers operating in contemporary hot spots. These vignettes, just like much of the media coverage, paint a misleading portrait of the DGSE as a group of dedicated but reckless officers.

France is a middle power that matters on the world stage. Politically, it has a seat on the United Nations Security Council and drives much of European integration. Militarily, it is a nuclear power with a capable army. Economically, it has one of the largest gross domestic products in the world and is a member of the Group of Seven and the Group of Twenty. The DGSE plays an important role in informing and executing France's foreign policy, thereby influencing world affairs. Yet the extent to which this agency has adapted to support and shape French foreign and security policy is not clear.

The secretive nature of intelligence work inherently limits public knowledge about the role and activities of agencies like the DGSE.

Researchers working on France's foreign intelligence have access to a limited array of sources, many of which focus on World War II and France's wars of decolonization in Indochina (1946–54) and Algeria (1954–62). Contemporary historians have barely started to examine the role of the DGSE's predecessor, the Service de Documentation Extérieure et de Contre-Espionnage (SDECE; External Documentation and Counterespionage Service) in maintaining French power in its African sphere of influence during the Cold War.[1] The best-known history, *The French Secret Services*, stops in the early 1990s, a few years after the DGSE was established.[2] The vast majority of the French books on the agency are journalistic and lack rigor in their use of sources and concepts.[3] The dearth of academic literature on the DGSE is easily explained: With a few exceptions, its archives remain classified.

Research for this book nevertheless engaged with some archival sources. Following a presidential decision to set up a commission of inquiry on French involvement in Rwanda during the genocide against the Tutsi, dozens of DGSE reports are available at the French National Archives.[4] In 2022 I sent a request to the "missions archives" of the DGSE. Two years later, Director General Nicolas Lerner granted me access to ten classified documents: one postmortem on the DGSE's coverage of the Gulf War (1990–91) and nine "yellow notes" (intended for policymakers) about the possible presence of weapons of mass destruction in Iraq dated from December 2002 to March 2003. Taken together, these sources provide a small window into some DGSE activities. My empirical research went far beyond, using parliamentary reports and legal texts, memoirs, published collections of interviews with and publications by serving and former DGSE officials, journalistic investigations, and media coverage. Much of this material is available only in French and is therefore presented here for the first time to anglophone readers.

Together, these sources provide a foundation for writing a comprehensive—though concise and imperfect—history of the DGSE. This history moves beyond scandals and heroic feats to show how the agency adapted to changes in its environment.[5] My goal is not to provide a detailed narrative but rather to offer a concise, accessible account of the DGSE's evolution, using insights from institutionalist scholarship to underline its changing role and enduring constraints.

Institutional Adaptation

All organizations adapt, and intelligence agencies are no exception. Shifts in the political and threat environment set the stage for this evolution. The election of Socialist President François Mitterrand in 1981 ushered in an era of change for the agency. Internationally, the end of the Cold War forced Western intelligence services to reassess their missions, often triggering internal reforms. In the 1990s the growing threat of terrorism pushed French policymakers to pay more attention to intelligence. Over a decade later, it was elevated as a *politique publique* (public policy). Although the French state had long produced and used intelligence, policymakers began to frame it as a more visible and defined public function in the late 2000s. Rooted in the doctrine of *raison d'état* (literally "reason of state" but better translated as "state interest"), France's intelligence tradition emphasizes secrecy, discretion, and strong executive control; historically, intelligence was considered an exceptional realm to protect the state. The rise of a *politique publique du renseignement* (intelligence public policy) marks a shift: Intelligence is now a recognized core function of government, subject to greater legal and policy debate.[6] This shift coincided with steady investment in intelligence, reflected in the DGSE's growing budget, workforce, and improved public image.

This development paints a more positive view of intelligence adaptation in the post–Cold War era than often depicted. In his book *The French Secret Services*, historian Douglas Porch concludes that the DGSE's overly military culture, combined with the straitjacket of the French state, stifled intelligence adaptation.[7] This finding echoes a broader trend in intelligence studies and political science that underlines how bureaucratic inertia hinders adaptation.[8] Yet scholars have also shown that when conditions allow, reforms can help agencies adjust to contemporary political and security demands.[9]

While the DGSE's missions have stayed much the same since 1982, the agency itself looks very different today. Its structure, resources, capabilities, ties to policymakers, and public image have all changed—often for the better—to keep pace with environmental and political demands. How then did changes occur? Historians and political scientists identify several factors that explain how organizational change takes place.

External shocks, such as major crises and national security threats, can heighten public and political attention, thus providing an impetus for change.[10] Political alternance and the nominations of new leaders often bring fresh perspectives and expectations that can catalyze change. In democracies, public demands for transparency and accountability serve as another powerful driver, evident in parliamentary oversight and lawmaking, media scrutiny, and even cultural representations.

Not all change stems from external events and pressures. Internal developments—such as the accumulation of institutional resources, institutional learning, shifts in power among actors or groups of officials, and reinterpretation of rules—can produce gradual transformation. In intelligence studies, secrecy often obscures these subtler forms of change. Adaptation becomes more visible when new practices are institutionalized—for example, through the establishment of a new directorate, an interagency task force, or a public affairs position. Such reforms require persuasion as leaders must align broader networks of colleagues and superiors behind a shared vision.[11] Institutionalist scholarship also shows that change is not always deliberate. It may arise as an unintended by-product of internal struggles and uneven rule compliance.[12] While such dynamics are hard to capture in a concise history of a secretive agency, the idea that change happens both by design and by default provides a helpful anchor for understanding adaptation.

To further clarify how such change unfolds—and why it often remains uneven—Edgar Schein's model of organizational culture offers a valuable lens. His distinction between artifacts, espoused values, and underlying assumptions helps separate structural reforms from shifts in discourse and deeper assumptions that often resist change. Formal structures and coordination reflect artifacts: visible signs of adaptation. Evolving official discourse, such as the recognition of intelligence as a public policy rather than a tool of *raison d'état*, signals shifting espoused values. Yet deeper assumptions about secrecy, executive authority, and institutional identity often persist. These shape how change is received politically and internally and explain why some reforms embed while others remain superficial or contested. Schein's framework clarifies why adaptation is uneven and why it often provokes friction.[13]

Taken together, these factors provide a framework for understanding how the DGSE has both sought and been forced to adapt—that is, to adjust to changes in its environment. The effects of these factors are best observed over time; history offers the empirical depth needed to trace how an agency adjusts. Adaptation appears not only in laws and directives but also in shifting rhetoric and enduring cultural patterns. This framework guides an analysis of the DGSE across several fronts: internal restructuring, coordination with the broader public administration, ties to policymakers, expanded international cooperation, and public discourses from the agency, its overseers, and the media that emphasize specific missions and activities.[14] These artifacts, and the values discourses convey, expose deeper assumptions about the role of foreign intelligence. Equally revealing are signs of inertia, when adaptation stalls. These include unreformed structures, entrenched hierarchies, and policy and operational lag, where strategic shifts outpace capabilities and activities.[15] Persistent friction between directorates and partner agencies point to procedural stasis;[16] a static public image points to discursive inertia.[17] Inertia, in turn, reflects the weight of underlying assumptions about the role of foreign intelligence. Though the DGSE's history offers examples of inertia, the broader record suggests that adaptation has, on balance, prevailed.

Three main factors have enabled the DGSE's adaptation. First, the growing prominence of terrorism on the political agenda since the 1990s has highlighted the political utility of foreign intelligence in anticipating and disrupting threats. Second, from the 2000s onward, policymakers have grown more supportive of intelligence—especially the DGSE—espousing its value as a public policy tool and moving beyond the paradigm of *raison d'état*. Third, leaders used this political support to drive reforms across multiple fronts: restructuring the agency, strengthening ties with policymakers and the broader administration, expanding operational scope, broadening international cooperation, and improving public communication. These changes left a public trail that this book traces to show how the DGSE has adapted. While some limitations remain, the convergence of threat awareness, political backing, and leadership initiative has cemented the DGSE's role in French security policy.

Outline

Change and adaptation are rarely uniform. They can be sudden in some areas and progressive in others. To reflect this complexity, the book adopts a thematic approach, consistent with the Concise Histories of Intelligence series, that explores several facets of the DGSE.

All changes build on prior ground. Chapter 1 traces the historical foundation of French foreign intelligence, from its military roots in the nineteenth century to the creation of the DGSE in 1982. It examines how successive conflicts—particularly the world wars and decolonization wars—and political crises shaped not only the structure of foreign intelligence but also its more intangible traits. The chapter shows how early organizational structures that espoused values and assumptions about secrecy, authority, and missions became embedded in the agency's identity. World War II introduced civilian oversight, but Cold War realities and decolonization conflicts entrenched an operational culture steeped in secrecy and shaped by military influence. Intelligence remained a tool of executive power, more associated with operations than with informing policy. This legacy explains important facets of the DGSE's organization and culture: its civilian chain of command, its early distance from policymakers, its operational focus, and at times its tarnished reputation. These elements provide a baseline against which later adaptations can be understood.

Chapter 2 moves to a more contemporary setting and outlines the evolution and current status of the DGSE within the French intelligence community, emphasizing its role as an integrated service covering all core intelligence functions—a trait that has remained an espoused value of French foreign intelligence since its institutionalization during World War II. Over time the DGSE has become a quasi-normal part of the French administration. In a context marked by the threat of terrorism, policymakers have authorized major investments and reforms. The agency has adapted by expanding its workforce and capabilities, furthering the integration of its core functions, improving coordination with the rest of the administration, and acquiescing to increased democratic oversight. A recent reform in 2022 and a planned move to a new headquarters by 2030 signal continued efforts to meet the demands of an increasingly complex world. These changes are not merely structural—they reflect a deeper shift in the values and assumptions linked to French intelligence as it undergoes a process of "normalization."[18]

Chapter 3 focuses on leadership to examine crucial shifts in the agency's relationship with policymakers and key internal reforms. The chapter explores how new political and agency leadership brought structural reforms and supported a gradual shift that strengthened intelligence-policy relations and institutional legitimacy. Historically, directors of the SDECE all had military or paramilitary experience dating back to World War II. The establishment of the DGSE in 1982 was accompanied by the nomination of an industry leader, Pierre Marion, with a disruptive personality, who was followed by a series of experienced civil servants from the Ministry of the Interior and the Ministry of Foreign Affairs. While the DGSE initially continued to suffer from its distance from political elites, from the late 1980s onward agency leaders were able to progressively overcome this detachment. Since the presidency of Nicolas Sarkozy (2007–12), political leaders have become much more supportive of the agency. The prominence of the terrorist threat on the political agenda and the crucial role intelligence plays in anticipating and mitigating this threat largely explain this reversal. Political support acted as a sustaining condition for adaptation, empowering several directors general (DGs) to reform the agency, enhance its capabilities, and integrate them with the rest of the French administration. This adaptation, in turn, hinged not only on political support but also on the DGs and their collaborators' understanding of the French state, which shaped their ability to align the agency's procedures and values with those of the broader apparatus.

Chapter 4 provides an overview of DGSE core activities, from intelligence collection and analysis to covert action and security. The discussion highlights the agency's enduring emphasis on operations, a trait rooted in institutional legacies dating back to World War II and underlying assumptions about what constitutes intelligence. This operational focus has remained salient in the post-9/11 era, where counterterrorism has dominated intelligence agendas. While reforms have aimed to strengthen analysis, they have not reversed the agency's traditional focus on operations. The chapter also highlights the DGSE's broad geographic reach and growing adaptability, which challenge reductive portrayals of the agency. At the same time, it reveals a service stretched between strategic ambition and expanding yet limited resources and capacity.

Chapter 5 examines the DGSE's relations with its international partners. It begins with an overview of the agency's global network and traces how shifts in the threat landscape, France's political ambitions, and the rise of digital technologies have driven a broader policy of cooperation.

Counterterrorism in particular has elevated intelligence sharing and contributed to expand the DGSE's reach. The growing burden and opportunities provided by technical intelligence in the digital era have further encouraged cooperation, especially with allies such as the United States and Germany. Internally, this expansion was underpinned by reforms such as the creation of the Direction de la Stratégie (DS; Directorate of Strategy)—now called the Secrétariat Général pour l'Analyse et la Stratégie (SGAS; General Secretariat for Analysis and Strategy)—and the placement of diplomats in key posts. The chapter then explores bilateral partnerships, contrasting deep ties with liberal democracies—where shared values and strategic alignment facilitate a degree of trust—with more constrained cooperation with such countries as Pakistan and Russia. Political tensions, such as disagreements over Iraq or allegations of economic espionage, illustrate the limits of even close alliances. Multilateral cooperation, particularly in Europe, reflects both ambition and constraint. France has promoted new mechanisms for elite socialization, but persistent attachments to sovereignty and national control limit deeper integration. Across all levels of cooperation, enduring beliefs about autonomy, sovereignty, and institutional identity continue to shape how far the DGSE can—and will—go.

Chapter 6 examines the multifaceted cultural representations of foreign intelligence in France. It begins by challenging the notion—often voiced by political leaders—that France lacks an "intelligence culture." Rather than equating culture with public recognition, the chapter treats it as a set of evolving practices shaped by institutional, political, and social interactions. The first two sections analyze fiction, in both literature and screen entertainment, that casts spies as heroes or antiheroes—narratives shaped more by the need to entertain than to inform. The chapter then turns to the DGSE's efforts to shape its public image through curated communication, collaboration with media and academia, exhibitions, and selective public engagement. Insider narratives, while often seen as authoritative, reflect bias and selective storytelling. These portrayals across fiction, journalism, and institutional discourse signal evolving espoused values such as professionalism and openness, yet they also reinforce persistent assumptions about the highly secretive and operational character of the DGSE. Although public trust in the DGSE has grown, and intelligence now features more visibly in politics, public discourses, and strategic communication, deeper assumptions remain slow to shift. Competing narratives shape and contest the boundaries of acceptable intelligence practices, revealing the layered and negotiated nature of adaptation in democratic life.

The concluding chapter builds on the book's argument, using the three core factors that have driven the DGSE's adaptation—the prominence of the terrorist threat, support from policymakers, and informed leadership—to explore the agency's future. It examines recent changes in the threat environment, including the return of war to Europe, intensifying global competition, and technological disruption; proposes an extreme scenario for the intelligence-policy relationship in France; and considers the possible outcomes of the agency's latest reforms. Drawing together insights from structural changes, evolving public and elite discourse, and enduring assumptions, the chapter assesses the depth and durability of the DGSE's transformation. The book closes with a discussion of the agency's public engagement and oversight, two pillars of intelligence in a liberal democracy. It underscores that adaptation is ongoing and uneven, shaped not only by deliberate reform but also by shifting public expectations and political constraints. These expectations have cemented the DGSE's role as a core instrument of French foreign and security policy—an assumption now so well established it seems beyond doubt.

Notes

1. Bat, *La fabrique des barbouzes*; von Bülow, "Myth or Reality," 787–820.
2. Porch, *French Secret Services*.
3. See, e.g., Faligot, Guisnel, and Kauffer, *Histoire politique*; Nouzille, *Les tueurs*; Guisnel, *Histoire secrète de la DGSE*; Faure, *Aux services de la république*.
4. Commission de Recherche sur les Archives Françaises Relatives au Rwanda et au Génocide des Tutsis, *La France*.
5. On the need for such a long history, see Laurent, "Le gaullisme et la 'société du renseignement,'" 351.
6. Chopin, "Intelligence Reform," 534–47; Oudet, "D'une stratégie à une "politique publique" de renseignement," 15; Assemblée Nationale, *Loi no. 2015-912 relative au renseignement*.
7. Porch, *French Secret Services*, 469–70. See also Silberzahn, *Au coeur du secret*, 91.
8. See, e.g., Neumann, "Member State Intelligence Support," 160–64; Shedd, "Intelligence Reform," 51; Zegart, *Spying Blind*, 43–44.
9. Bruneau and Matei, "Intelligence Reform in New Democracies," 624; Lonsdale, "Intelligence Reform," 440; Durbin, *CIA and Politics of Intelligence Reform*, 258–72; Pillar, "Adapting Intelligence to Changing Issues," 157–61.

10. Warner and McDonald, *US Intelligence Community Reform*, 43; Estévez, "Comparing Intelligence Democratization," 579. On exogenous shocks as junctures and drivers of change, see Orren and Skowronek, *Search for American Political Development*, 103; Thelen, "Institutional Change," 474–75.
11. Handel, "Leaders and Intelligence," 3–39.
12. Mahoney and Thelen, "Theory of Gradual Institutional Change," 23–29.
13. Schein, *Organizational Culture and Leadership*, 23–33.
14. Orren and Skowronek, *Search for American Political Development*, 6, 20–26; Cormac, Walton, and Van Puyvelde, "What Constitutes Successful Covert Action?," 118–19.
15. Hudson, Hunter, and Peckman, "Policy Failure and the Policy-Implementation Gap," 1–14; Dahl, "Missing the Wake-Up Call," 780.
16. Dahl, *New Security for New Threats*; Zegart, "September 11 and the Adaptation Failure," 103.
17. Schmidt, "Discursive Institutionalism."
18. Chopin, "Intelligence Reform," 546–47.

1

Foundations

This chapter sheds light on the historical foundations of France's foreign intelligence capabilities, from the emergence of state intelligence power in the fifteenth century to the establishment of the DGSE in 1982. The history of French intelligence is often associated with controversial episodes such as the Dreyfus affair (1894–1906), the use of torture and assassination during the Algerian War of Independence, and covert operations in and around francophone Africa. These controversies are significant to the extent that they reveal France's struggle to effectively orient and integrate its foreign intelligence capabilities.[1] The overview that follows moves beyond the headlines to underline the long institutionalization of France's foreign intelligence apparatus.[2] The analysis highlights the catalytic effect of wars on this process and the difficult relation between foreign intelligence and policymakers in France. Drawing on organizational culture theory, it also traces the emergence of core structures, values, and assumptions that shaped French foreign intelligence.[3] In doing so, the chapter establishes a baseline for assessing how the DGSE has changed.

The first section examines the emergence of secret state intelligence capabilities. From the Franco-Prussian War in 1870 to the end of World War I, France institutionalized a military intelligence apparatus to support war efforts against one main enemy: Germany. By the end of the Great War, the Deuxième Bureau of the General Staff centralized much of

France's military intelligence capabilities. The second section highlights a period of consolidation, from the Armistice of 1918 to the end of World War II. French military intelligence capabilities were scaled back during the interwar period, but key institutions persisted before undergoing a significant expansion on all fronts to support the war effort. World War II was a turning point, prompting the establishment of an integrated foreign intelligence agency reporting to a civilian authority for the first time in France's history. This institutional arrangement—an artifact—continues to shape the DGSE's position within the state. More than a structural change, it signaled an emerging cultural shift: the idea that intelligence should serve political, not just military, leadership.

The third section starts with the establishment of the SDECE, France's Cold War foreign intelligence agency, in 1946. It places the SDECE within its broader institutional context and highlights tensions between its civilian status and military hierarchy. The wars of decolonization in Indochina and Algeria accentuated civil-military tensions in the metropole. The SDECE's role in these conflicts revealed core elements of its early organizational culture: a degree of operational autonomy, a focus on tactical effectiveness, and the perceived legitimacy of forceful covert action in what many viewed as existential crises for the French Republic. These values and assumptions shaped how officers came to understand their missions and defined part of the SDECE's organizational identity. In the wake of the Ben Barka affair (1965), the agency's oversight shifted from the prime minister to the minister of armed forces, a move that symbolized renewed military control.

The fourth section examines the SDECE activities in France's sphere of interest in Africa. Although active in the Middle East and Eastern Europe, the agency's operations remained anchored in the political and institutional legacy of French colonialism, particularly in francophone Africa. The SDECE demonstrated political utility by helping to preserve French influence in its former colonies and curtail Soviet expansion.[4] Yet the agency struggled to shed its controversial image. Public discourse and elite skepticism reflected entrenched assumptions about intelligence as a shady business. Wary of association, policymakers publicly kept the agency at arm's length. The chapter ends with arrival of Socialist candidate François Mitterrand in 1981, the first left-wing president of the Fifth Republic, ushering in a major shift in power and an era of reform. These changes began with the 1982 creation of the DGSE, which replaced the SDECE but inherited many of its cultural features.

Origins

French political and military leaders have used intelligence since at least the fifteenth century, when they pushed back the English presence to consolidate France's territory. At the time, *renseignement*—the French word for intelligence—referred to information or reports used to inform the king's military decisions. Recurrent wars and military campaigns fostered early forms of institutionalization—for example, through the Dépôt de la Guerre, which archived relevant documents and maps from 1688 onward. This military department did not produce intelligence but instead centralized information.[5] Napoleon made extensive use of intelligence to secure and extend French power. His reforms consolidated various forms of intelligence—for instance, with the establishment of a *cabinet noir* that intercepted mail within the postal service. Within the Grand Quartier Général, a dedicated bureau provided strategic intelligence to the chief of military staff, Louis-Alexandre Berthier. However, Napoleonic reforms did not establish a permanent service.[6]

The rise of a modern intelligence apparatus can be traced to the nineteenth century, an era marked by nationalism and militarism. These conditions spurred an institutionalization of the regalian functions of the state: to enforce law and order at home and to project power through diplomatic and military means. The police, military intelligence agencies, and diplomacy came to embody a form of state power that was directly attached to the core executive, thus forming what French historians Sébastien-Yves Laurent and Olivier Forcade call "the secret state."[7] The use of the term *renseignement* evolved in parallel, referring to the collection of domestic security and military information in the nineteenth century and eventually to state intelligence agencies in the twentieth.[8]

The establishment in 1853 of the Sûreté Générale, a law enforcement agency that gathered domestic intelligence, was one of the first steps in the institutionalization of French intelligence. Abroad, the conquest and then colonization of Algeria in the early nineteenth century was supported by the Bureaux Arabes (established in 1844), which gathered and processed information on native leadership and populations.[9] The military defeat during the Franco-Prussian War (1870–71) catalyzed the institutionalization of France's foreign intelligence capability. The war underlined the need for a well-organized intelligence capability and prompted a broader reorganization of the military apparatus. A Section de Statistique (1871) was established to collect intelligence and then an intelligence bureau (Deuxième Bureau, 1874) within the General Staff to synthesize and exploit intelligence.[10] In 1886 the French legislature criminalized espionage, thus reorienting some of the work of the Deuxième Bureau and the Section de Statistique toward counterespionage.[11] By the turn of the twentieth century, the Deuxième Bureau was composed of a few dozen officers, most of whom focused on the German threat. Its role within the military and foreign policy apparatus remained secondary.

Any overview of French intelligence history would be incomplete without a discussion of the Dreyfus affair. This scandal crystalized deep-running mistrust between political leaders and the French people on the one side and their intelligence agencies and spies on the other.[12] In 1894 a note containing confidential military information was found in a wastebasket at the German embassy in Paris, which triggered suspicions of espionage. The Deuxième Bureau initiated an investigation, which narrowed its focus to Alfred Dreyfus, a French Army officer whose Jewish identity made him a convenient suspect. Dreyfus's geographic origins—he was born in Alsace, a region annexed by Germany after the Franco-Prussian War—also raised suspicion about his loyalty, though not as centrally as his Jewishness. The case against Dreyfus relied on circumstantial evidence, including handwriting analysis. Yet prevailing anti-Semitic sentiments within the military establishment reinforced the belief that a Jewish officer would be more likely to betray his country. Dreyfus was arrested, tried in a military court, convicted of high treason, and sent to the Devil's Island penal colony in French Guiana. When evidence emerged that a Maj. Ferdinand Walsin Esterhazy was the actual culprit, senior officers sought to protect the military institution and their reputation and refused to acknowledge the miscarriage of justice. Dreyfus's second trial led to another wrongful conviction. It was only when a group of outsiders, including prominent French writer Émile Zola, intervened publicly that the opinion began to shift in favor of Dreyfus, eventually rallying politicians, artists, and intellectuals behind his cause. In 1906 new evidence proved Dreyfus's innocence, and he was officially exonerated. The Deuxième Bureau took most of the blame for broader issues within the military establishment and French society, and the affair durably tarnished the image of intelligence in France. Many observers use this scandal as a starting point to explain the historical distance between French leaders and their intelligence services.[13]

Following Germany's declaration of war on France, its initial military success in August 1914 took French intelligence by surprise. The Section de Statistique had collected intelligence about the existence of the Schlieffen Plan years earlier, but the Deuxième Bureau was skeptical, and senior officers discarded it.[14] The total nature of World War I accelerated the institutionalization of French military intelligence, driving its expansion on multiple fronts. The war prompted advances in technical intelligence collection and processing, most notably in direction finding to track enemy movement and cryptography to access the content of German communications.[15] The advent of aviation led to reconnaissance flights, which added a new dimension to intelligence gathering.[16] Photographic equipment enabled detailed analysis of enemy positions and guided artillery bombardment. Economic intelligence was key to understand the sustainability of the enemy's war effort and the effects of the blockade on Germany.[17] The French and their allies also ran more traditional human intelligence (HUMINT) operations in Belgium, French-occupied territories, and the Netherlands.[18] The growing volume and variety of intelligence sources required specialization and significant institutional adaptations to orient, process, exploit, and integrate intelligence into the war effort. By the end of the Great War, the Deuxième Bureau had established itself as the key entity responsible for integrating intelligence and counterintelligence.[19]

Consolidation: From the Armistice to VE Day

The Armistice of November 1918 was followed by demobilization and the dissolution of the general headquarters of the French Army. The overall intelligence structure that emerged from World War I remained largely untouched, but capabilities decreased. The Deuxième Bureau maintained its status as the largest military intelligence agency. Within it, a Section des Armées Etrangères (SAE; Foreign Armies Section) focused on foreign military capabilities and produced assessments on political, diplomatic, and economic affairs. The Service de Renseignement (SR; Intelligence Service), a relatively autonomous component of the Deuxième Bureau, maintained its control over secret intelligence collection abroad, including HUMINT and signals intelligence (SIGINT). Within the SR, the Section de Centralisation du Renseignement (SCR; Intelligence Centralization Section) oversaw counterespionage abroad. These organizations and other, smaller bureaus in the air arm and navy largely focused on monitoring and assessing German military strength, especially after Hitler's accession to power in 1933. With the Russian Revolution and Civil War (1917–22), the rise of communism became another key priority.[20]

The interwar period saw the establishment of an interministerial committee on intelligence (from 1937 onward) bringing together the Ministry of the Interior, the Ministry of Foreign Affairs, the Police Prefecture, the Sûreté, and military intelligence.[21] Despite the existence of this committee, the services were insufficiently coordinated and lacked access to civilian decision-makers.[22] The military maintained its hold over foreign intelligence and did not coordinate closely with the Foreign Ministry, which had no responsibility over intelligence matters.

World War II catalyzed institutional changes. The defeat of 1940, the humiliation of the occupation, and the political and institutional divide between the armistice government led by Marshal Phillipe Pétain in Vichy and the Free French government-in-exile led by Gen. Charles de Gaulle in London had a lasting impact on French intelligence. The armistice split the French community. Many intelligence officers remained in the Vichy army, which set up a Bureau of Antinational Activities to track opponents and Resistance efforts. Within the Vichy's intelligence services, some elements swore an oath to covertly pursue the fight against the Axis intelligence services until the liberation of France. The innocuously named Société des Travaux Ruraux (Society for Rural Works) epitomized this effort to pursue the fight against the Abwehr (the German military intelligence service). On the other side of the English Channel, the Free French government established a Service de Renseignement from scratch, eventually changing its name to the Bureau Central de Renseignement et d'Action (BCRA; Central Intelligence and Action Bureau) in 1942. The Pétain regime's collaboration with the Germans drove French intelligence agencies on either side of the Channel further apart. The Allied invasion of French North Africa in November 1942 and the subsequent German invasion of France's unoccupied zone prompted intelligence officers loyal to Vichy to flee to Algiers, where they reported to Gen. Henri Giraud, who led the French forces in North Africa.[23]

After de Gaulle became the undisputed leader of Free France, many of these capabilities were integrated in 1943 into a new agency—the Direction Générale des Services Spéciaux (DGSS; Directorate General for Special Services)—responsible for human and technical intelligence collection, analysis, and action and placed under the civilian control of a provisional government. This merger laid the groundwork for a more integrated approach to foreign intelligence but did not erase functional and ideological divisions. On the one side, the BCRA and other French personnel affiliated with the United Kingdom's Special Operations Executive and Secret Intelligence Services (SIS) were influenced by British practices and a focus on covert operations. On the other side, officers who had remained in France or relocated to North Africa were attached to prewar French practices. These divisions—rooted in divergent assumptions about the role and methods of intelligence—left a lasting imprint on French foreign intelligence.[24]

To this day DGSE officers invoke World War II to explain enduring subcultures within the agency, particularly the divide between staff working on operations and counterintelligence.[25] Functional differences provide a more convincing explanation, but the fact that practitioners continue to refer to the legacies of World War II demonstrates the weight of historical memory on internal perceptions. The DGSE's recent public communications have actively drawn on this legacy, often highlighting the heroism of the BCRA (see chapter 6). Yet institutional symbolism remains ambivalent. Until recently, the agency's main amphitheater was named after Louis Rivet, who led intelligence efforts to resist from within the Vichy apparatus. This complex legacy continues to shape competing interpretations—both inside and outside the DGSE—about the values, assumptions, and organizational outlook of French foreign intelligence.

The most significant legacy of World War II lies not in individual trajectories but in the institutional setting of the DGSS. The total nature of the conflict pushed French foreign intelligence beyond its traditional military bounds. While French foreign intelligence had mostly been limited to military matters and hierarchy, the specific conditions of Free France tied this capability to a civilian authority in 1943.[26] De Gaulle recognized the strategic value of intelligence networks and mobilized them as political instruments to support the Resistance and establish political legitimacy.[27] The Resistance, and the mythology he and many other public figures contributed to build about it, forged a powerful ideological legacy that continued to inspire subsequent generations of officers and policymakers.[28] The war laid the institutional foundation of a foreign intelligence–policy nexus. By its end, the need for a permanent, civilian-controlled foreign intelligence capability was no longer in doubt. The wartime experience embedded enduring assumptions about the political utility of intelligence and helped integrate it into the core executive.

Institutionalization in the Postwar Era

After the liberation, geopolitical and institutional shifts led de Gaulle to authorize the creation of a new foreign intelligence agency, the SDECE. André Dewavrin (code name Passy), who founded and led the Free French services in London, played a pivotal role in designing the SDECE and became its first director (see figure 1.1).[29] For the first time in modern history, France had a peacetime foreign intelligence agency that was directly attached to a civilian authority, the *président du conseil* (a type of prime minister in the Fourth Republic, 1946–58).[30] On paper the government would express requirements, leading to the adoption of plans supposed to orient intelligence collection and production.[31] In practice successive governments neglected intelligence and provided little to no orientation to the service. They also lacked administrative means to exert meaningful authority over and orient the SDECE. The SDECE thus developed in a relatively autonomous fashion.[32]

Like its predecessor the DGSS, the SDECE brought together disparate capabilities: technical and human intelligence, counterintelligence and security, and covert action. The executive order establishing this agency reflected a desire to integrate different functions and gave it two main missions: to collect foreign intelligence to inform the government and to detect foreign agents.[33] However, tensions between different strata of personnel, inherited from the DGSS and prewar services, hindered the effective integration of these missions.[34] The civil-military divide was another source of friction. Some senior officers remained skeptical about civilian

Figure 1.1: André Dewavrin in 1942 or 1943, the leader of the Free French civilian foreign intelligence agency, the BCRA. © *Musée de l'Ordre de la Libération*

control. Within the SDECE, military officers assumed most managerial functions, yet the agency was composed of a majority of civilians (from 51 percent in 1946 to 67.6 percent, or 1,645 personnel, in 1950).[35] Zooming out, the absence of clear institutional delineation also reinvigorated a counterintelligence rivalry between the SDECE and France's domestic intelligence agency, the Direction de la Surveillance du Territoire (DST; Territorial Surveillance Directorate), founded in 1944.[36]

The distance between the SDECE and senior policymakers limited its influence on French foreign and security policy. Nevertheless, the agency gained much operational experience as France addressed the breakdown of its colonial empire in Indochina and Algeria. The geographic distance that separated these conflicts from the metropole reinforced the operational autonomy of the SDECE, which played an important role in supporting France's counterinsurgency effort in Indochina (1946–54). The SDECE established a base in Saigon, and its officers collected human and signals intelligence on the Viet Minh. Its own airborne commando unit, Groupement des Commandos Mixtes Aéroportés (GCMA; Mixed Airborne Commando Group), established in 1951, conducted guerrilla and sabotage activities. By the end of the war, the missions of this group expanded to include propaganda and psychological warfare, thus covering a broad range of covert action capabilities. In a controversial move, SDECE operators infiltrated the opium trade to cut off a vital funding source for the communist maquis but also to finance their own activities.[37]

Three months after the Geneva Accords established a cease-fire and ended the Indochina War, another decolonization war emerged in Algeria. On November 1, 1954, following years of intercommunal violence, the Front de Libération Nationale (FLN; National Liberation Front) conducted a series of coordinated attacks on the French presence. France's response took the form of another extensive counterinsurgency campaign. The SDECE contributed to the surveillance of enemy activities, thus orienting the broader military effort.[38] Its officers were tasked with covertly infiltrating and disrupting FLN networks. At the lower end of the spectrum of violence, their actions sought to intoxicate these networks, enticing them to believe they had been penetrated by French sympathizers. At the higher end, paramilitary officers engaged in dozens of sabotage and homicide operations against FLN insurgents and their supporters.[39] These operations reflected assumptions about the operational utility of covert intelligence capabilities. Yet France struggled to transform tactical gains—whether from military or covert operations—into strategic and political successes.[40]

Efforts to preserve the French Empire through force poisoned political life. Civil-military relations—which had already suffered from the military defeat in 1940 and the debacle at Dien Bien Phu in 1954—reached a breaking point. The Algerian war overwhelmed the institutions of the Fourth Republic, prompting a political crisis that ended with de Gaulle's return to power. Though he initially supported the concept of a French Algeria, de Gaulle decided to grant Algeria its independence. This generated much discontent within parts of the French military and intelligence apparatus, leading several general officers to foment a coup against de Gaulle in 1961. When the "putsch of the generals" failed, disgruntled soldiers—including SDECE operators—set up a clandestine group to "defend" French Algeria by all means: the Organisation de l'Armée Secrète (OAS; Secret Army Organization). In response, the government purged, reorganized, and eventually dissolved the SDECE's paramilitary capability, the 11th Shock Parachute Regiment, in 1963.[41]

Soon another scandal, the Ben Barka affair, emerged, causing further damage to the relationship between French political leaders and their foreign intelligence apparatus. Mehdi Ben Barka was a prominent Moroccan opposition figure living in exile in France who disappeared in the heart of Paris on October 29, 1965. Many observers suspected the Moroccan services were behind his disappearance, with some degree of support from the French services. While no evidence conclusively linked the disappearance to the SDECE, the agency shouldered much of the blame both politically and in the court of public opinion.[42] In response, President de Gaulle dismissed SDECE Director Paul Jacquier and transferred the agency's tutelage from the prime minister to the Ministry of Armed Forces, a structural shift that diminished the agency's standing within the state and reinforced military oversight as a key organizational artifact. De Gaulle hoped the move would subject the SDECE to stronger military discipline. Within the cabinet of the armed forces minister, a dedicated *cabinet réservé* composed of senior military officers was tasked with supervising the agency. This arrangement reinforced the sense that senior military officers controlled key managerial positions both above and within the service.[43] The assumption that intelligence should be governed through military hierarchy constrained the maturation of the agency, not least because intelligence lacked the prestige of combat arms such as the cavalry and infantry and often failed to attract the most promising officers. Still, it would be too simplistic to conclude that military dominance doomed the SDECE to irrelevance. Under the right conditions, the agency could play a meaningful role in informing and executing French foreign policy.

Projecting Intelligence Power in Africa

De Gaulle's vision of grandeur sought to develop an independent path for France to express its own interests and power on the world stage.[44] French political priorities largely focused on Eastern Europe, the Middle East, and Africa.[45] The SDECE found more room to maneuver in the Middle East and Africa than behind the Iron Curtain. In Africa, France had a long history of colonialism that durably shaped local elites and institutions. SDECE officers could build on these historical networks to develop a broad range of collection and influence operations.[46] Importantly, the presidential adviser for African and Malagasy affairs from 1960 to 1974, Jacques Foccart, saw a role for the SDECE in projecting French power in the region. A former resistant and member of the BCRA, Foccart was a keen user of intelligence, both as a type of information and a means to covertly influence political situations in and around francophone Africa.[47]

Foccart's interest in intelligence facilitated SDECE access to the core executive, but this came at a cost. His decision-making style relied on his own networks within and beyond the state apparatus, thus challenging traditional hierarchies and procedures. Foccart directly tasked key SDECE officers such as Maurice Robert, who led the African sector of the agency. His network also extended into the Service Action (SA)—the agency's paramilitary branch—where he served as a reservist.[48] His approach fueled concern about unchecked executive control over intelligence operations. The pejorative term *barbouze* reflects a deep-seated cultural assumption that intelligence actors often served political masters rather than institutional mandates. Common in the latter half of the twentieth century and used to this day, the term refers to officers and agents working on behalf of Gaullist decision-makers rather than on the orders of French intelligence officials.[49] Its etymology—linked to the beards worn to obscure identity—captures the mistrust surrounding these figures. The expression embodies a broader critique of intelligence as opaque and politically driven, not as a neutral instrument of statecraft.

However, French historians have shown that Gaullist influence in the French intelligence community was more limited than often portrayed.[50] Though presidential adviser Foccart was influential, he was not the sole channel of executive control. Oversight varied with the scale and sensitivity of operations, involving the president, prime minister, defense minister, and senior officials including the director of the SDECE.[51] Admittedly, French intelligence governance remained underdeveloped. Rooted in the *raison d'état* tradition, it treated intelligence as an exceptional domain reserved to a select few within the core executive.[52] By default and by design, few policymakers maintained sustained interest in foreign intelligence. Still, intelligence was not out of control.

The institutionalization of French presence in its former colonies further underlines the limits of an excessively personalized reading. Following a wave of independences in the 1960s, France signed over twenty police and military cooperation agreements to accompany and control its former colonies. These agreements allowed France to maintain military bases and deploy troops and advisers to support its partners.[53] Building on these ties, the SDECE established a series of *postes de liaison et de renseignement* (PLRs; intelligence and liaison posts), which institutionalized its presence and provided a platform to develop close ties with political and security elites in partner countries. These posts provided protection to friendly regimes, supporting the emergence of local intelligence apparatuses and facilitating intelligence collection and cooperation.[54] SDECE stations in Abidjan, Dakar, and Libreville served as the control towers of French influence on the continent. From there, officers organized intelligence-gathering operations and evaluated the risk of subversion posed by neighboring countries and foreign powers.[55]

The instability of new African states and former colonies prompted dozens of French interventions—both overt and covert—to "maintain stability" or wield influence. The SDECE engaged in numerous covert actions during the Cold War, focusing mostly on Central and Equatorial Africa. Propaganda and economic, political, and paramilitary actions aimed to support friendly parties or regimes and destabilize unfriendly ones. The service was most active in its former colonies but also ventured beyond them—for example, to Nigeria and Angola.[56] In Nigeria, a former British colony, French authorities had announced an embargo following the secession of Biafra in 1967, but the SDECE covertly supplied arms to secessionist Col. Chukwuemeka Odumegwu Ojukwu.[57] During Alexandre de Marenches's directorship (1970–81), the SDECE expanded its anticommunist posture, providing covert support to a broader range of partners. In 1971 Marenches met with Jonas Savimbi as a part of a broader operation to support the leader of the União Nacional para a Independência Total de Angola (UNITA; National Union for the Total Independence of Angola) against the People's Movement for the Liberation of Angola.[58]

What to make of these operations? A common criticism frames the SDECE as the hidden hand of French neocolonialism.[59] There is no doubt that French overt and covert operations in Africa were largely self-serving. They helped to maintain France's status as a middle power and facilitated access to economic resources and networks of diplomatic partners. Yet, as Nathaniel Powell shows in the case of Chad, French presence and activities "did not easily translate into control."[60] French influence in Africa was a two-way street, with its partners reciprocally shaping French interests.

Conclusion

The DGSE did not emerge in a vacuum. Its creation in 1982 capped a long, uneven trajectory that shaped the structures, values, and assumptions underpinning France's foreign intelligence apparatus. From the institutionalization of military intelligence in the nineteenth century to the reorganizations driven by the two world wars, each phase left lasting imprints. The world wars expanded intelligence activities and underscored the need for a well-organized, integrated apparatus. Yet the Cold War–era SDECE, though formally civilian, remained steeped in military practices. It operated with substantial autonomy, particularly in the context of the colonial wars in Indochina and Algeria and later in Africa, where it helped maintain French influence through a wide array of covert actions. These operational engagements entrenched a culture that prioritized covert collection and actions over strategic analysis, secrecy over scrutiny, and executive loyalty over democratic accountability. Intelligence remained an instrument of *raison d'état*.

This culture endured even as political winds began to shift. United around de Gaulle's figure, the Center-Right dominated French politics for forty years. In 1981 François Mitterrand became the first left-wing president of the Fifth Republic. His election, and the inclusion of communist figures in his first government, unsettled the service and the transatlantic community. Socialists had expressed concern about the nature and methods of intelligence, which they linked to encroachment on the rule of law.[61] In 1977 left-wing parties had proposed a common program that recommended the abolition of the SDECE.[62] However, in the run-up to the elections, they set this idea aside and redirected their concerns toward advocating for reforms.[63] When the Socialists acceded to power, they encountered a series of governance challenges that they had scarcely considered while in the Opposition, even more so in the compartmentalized world of intelligence. Political alternance did, nevertheless, open room to push for reform, which materialized through a 1982 decree that renamed the SDECE the DGSE.[64] The change was largely symbolic, but over time the agency's structure, resources, and relationship with political leaders would evolve.

This chapter has explored the historical foundations of the DGSE, highlighting its emphasis on operations, distance from senior policymakers, and contested legitimacy. These characteristics offer a baseline from which to consider subsequent efforts at reform and adaptation.

Notes

1. Laurent, *État secret*, 75.
2. For a similar approach, see Laurent, "Politisations et politiques du renseignement," 295–307.
3. Stout, "World War I," 378–94; Schein, *Organizational Culture and Leadership*, 23–33.
4. Forcade, *La république secrète*.
5. Arboit, *Des services secrets*, 22–23, 55–58.
6. Porch, *French Secret Services*, 9–16. For a detailed study, see Arboit, *Napoléon et le renseignement*.
7. Forcade and Laurent, *Secrets d'état*, 59–72; Laurent, *Politiques de l'ombre*, 17–418; Laurent, *Le renseignement*, 9–10; Bely, *Espions et ambassadeurs*. This process is not unique to France; see Warner, *Rise and Fall of Intelligence*, 35–78.

8. Académie Française, "Renseignement"; Centre National des Resources Textuelles et Lexicales, "Renseignement."
9. Bauer, *Marianne Is Watching*, 31–33.
10. Laurent, *Le renseignement*, 10; Arboit, *Des services secrets*, chaps. 2–3.
11. Bauer, *Marianne Is Watching*, 139–49.
12. On the pejorative place of "spies" in the French opinion, see Dewerpe, *Espion*, 21–25.
13. See, e.g., Arboit, "Les services spéciaux," 11; Ferro, "Les services de renseignement français," 2.
14. Jackson and Laurent, *Intelligence in the Modern World*, chap. 4.
15. Couderc, "Renseignement technique et secret militaire," 57–72; Jackson and Laurent, *Intelligence in the Modern World*, chap. 5.
16. Finnegan, *Shooting the Front*, 25–33; Villatoux, "Le renseignement aérien," 33–48.
17. Braud, "Le renseignement économique militaire," 84–93; Bourlet, "La section économique pendant la Première Guerre Mondiale," 117–35.
18. Lahaie, "Pratiques du renseignement humain," 123–44.
19. Forcade, "Le renseignement français dans la Première Guerre Mondiale."
20. Jackson and Maiolo, "Strategic Intelligence," 421–24.
21. Forcade, *La république secrète*, 568–81.
22. Jackson, *France and the Nazi Menace*, 11–44; Forcade, *La république secrète*, 58–59; Alexander, "Did the Deuxème Bureau Work?," 293–333; Jackson and Maiolo, "Strategic Intelligence," 423–24.
23. Rivet, *Carnets du chef des services secrets*, 571; Paillole, *Services spéciaux*, 414–18.
24. Rivet, *Carnets du chef des services secrets*; Renault, *Franco-British Intelligence Cooperation*.
25. Alain Chouet in Guisnel and Korn-Brzoza, *Au service secret de la France*, 310; Cousseran and Hayez, *Leçons sur le renseignement*, 55; Martin Briens (head of the DS and later chief of staff to the French minister of defense) in Merchet, "Renseignement et capacité d'anticipation," 277.
26. Laurent, "Free French Secret Services," 19–41.
27. Albertelli, *Les services secrets du général de Gaulle*, 641.
28. For an example of the importance key figures assigned to the contribution of the resistance to the war effort, see de Gaulle, "Paris outragé."
29. Laurent, "Le gaullisme et la 'société du renseignement,'" 335–36.
30. Laurent, "Pierre Messmer," 226–27.
31. Laurent, "La gouvernance supérieure du renseignement," 475–78; Seibold, "Intelligence Requirements at the Crossroads."
32. Laurent, "La gouvernance supérieure du renseignement," 477, 480, 486; Laurent, "Pierre Messmer," 228.
33. Gouvernement Provisoire de la République Française, "Projet de décret portant création d'un Service de Documentation Extérieure et de Contre-Espionnage."
34. Laurent, "Le gaullisme et la 'société du renseignement,'" 336–38; Laurent, "Politisations et politiques du renseignement," 305.
35. Arboit, *Des services secrets*, 286; Laurent, "La gouvernance supérieure du renseignement," 477.
36. Laurent, *Les espions français parlent*, 28.

37. Le Page, *Les services secrets en Indochine*; Zervoudakis, "L'adaptation des services," 208–25; Faure, *Aux services de la république*, 221–43.
38. Archives Nationales, AG/5(F)/318: "Fiche: rôle du S.D.E.C.E. en ALGERIE," 1–2. For context, see von Bülow, *West Germany*, 189–224.
39. Van Puyvelde, "French Paramilitary Actions," 898–909; von Bülow, "Myth or Reality?," 787–820.
40. Frémeaux and Reis, "French Counterinsurgency," 73.
41. Laurent, "Pierre Messmer," 233; Laurent, "Le gaullisme et la 'société du renseignement,'" 347.
42. Faure, *Aux services de la république*, 341–63.
43. Laurent, "La gouvernance supérieure du renseignement," 477; Laurent, "Pierre Messmer," 234.
44. Vaïsse, *La grandeur*; Dalloz, *La France et le monde depuis 1945*, 151.
45. Soutou, "La stratégie du renseignement," 40–44; Soutou, "Le renseignement français des années 50 et 60," 68–69. One of the biggest successes of French counterintelligence during the Cold War—the recruitment of a senior KGB engineer code-named Farewell—originated with the DST, thus underlining the apparent shortfalls of the SDECE beyond the Iron Curtain. See Nart and Debain, *L'affaire Farewell*; and Kostine and Raynaud, *Adieu Farewell*.
46. Bruyère-Ostells, "Outil militaire," 15; Bat, *La fabrique des barbouzes*.
47. Foccart, *Tous les soirs avec de Gaulle*, 333; Turpin, "Jacques Foccart, le conseiller politique," 186–92; Bat, *Les réseaux Foccart*, 72–84.
48. Robert, *Maurice Robert*.
49. Bat, *Les réseaux Foccart*.
50. Laurent, "Politisations et politiques du renseignement," 295–307.
51. Laurent, "Foccart au miroir du SDECE," 231–37; Turpin, *Jacques Foccart*, 120–21; Forcade, "Jacques Foccart," 18.
52. Chopin, "Intelligence Reform," 535–42.
53. Bruyère-Ostells, "Outil militaire," 14.
54. Powell, *France's Wars in Chad*, 18.
55. Bat, "Le Secteur N (Afrique)," 44–45.
56. Bat, *Le syndrome Foccart*, 152–212; Bruyère-Ostells, "Outil militaire," 7; Faligot, Guisnel, and Kauffer, *Histoire politique*, 227–81.
57. Patrick Keatley, "French Arms for Lagos," *Guardian*, September 20, 1968; Desgrandchamps, "Soutien miliaire et aide humanitaire," 85–95; Monsieur X and Pesnot, *Les dessous de la Françafrique*, 29–37; Robert, *Maurice Robert*, 178–87.
58. De Marenches and Ockrent, *Dans le secret des princes*, 190–92; Bat, "Le Secteur N (Afrique)," 50–51; Bruyère-Ostells, "Outil militaire," 17.
59. Marion, *La mission impossible*, 106.
60. Powell, *France's Wars in Chad*, 22.
61. Laurent, "Face aux 'services,'" 62.
62. Programme Commun de Gouvernement de Gauche, *Propositions socialistes pour l'actualisation*, 93–94.
63. Vadillo, "L'administration à l'épreuve du politique," 588.
64. Laurent, "Face aux 'services,'" 72–73.

2

Organization

The DGSE is the largest agency in the French intelligence community. Senior officials often present it as an integrated service that, like its predecessors, handles all core intelligence functions, from HUMINT to technical intelligence (TECHINT), collection to analysis, counterintelligence to covert action. To support these activities, the agency has benefited from significant investments in recent decades, which have enabled it to grow its workforce and reinforce its role as the lead SIGINT provider of the community. In the meantime, a wave of reforms has normalized intelligence as a public policy, drawn agencies closer to the core executive, and improved their coordination. This chapter shows how, despite its unique capabilities and status, the DGSE has become a more conventional part of the French administration.

The first section sets the broader context of the French intelligence community, highlighting how recent reforms have narrowed the historical gap between intelligence and policymaking. The second section zooms in on the DGSE's organizational structure and resources. For most of the period under consideration in this book (1982 to today), the agency was organized in five directorates. A recent reform (2022), driven by shifts in threats and information technology and a push for greater efficiency, merged two of these and established mission centers to better integrate HUMINT and TECHINT, collection and analysis, and intelligence and policy. The third section examines DGSE's coordination with key partners across the French defense and security establishment, linking improvements to reform efforts. The fourth and final section turns to democratic accountability. It shows how recent changes have clarified the legal basis for DGSE activities and strengthened parliamentary oversight. Taken together, these developments point to an agency that has grown more capable and more embedded in the state's machinery. This portrayal challenges the dominant narrative, which focuses on controversies and covert operations while overlooking the DGSE's institutional evolution. The picture is broadly positive, though not without its flaws.

The French Intelligence Community

The notion of a French "intelligence community" first appeared in the white paper on defense and national security of 2008. Several years later, a ministerial decree identified the six core members of the French intelligence community, often referred to as the "first circle."[1] These agencies are the DGSE, the Direction Générale de la Sécurité Intérieure (DGSI; Directorate General for Internal Security), the Direction du Renseignement Militaire (DRM; Directorate for Military Intelligence), the Direction du Renseignement et de Sécurité de la Défense (DRSD; Directorate for Defense Intelligence and Security), the Direction Nationale du Renseignement et des Enquêtes Douanières (DNRED; National Directorate for Customs Intelligence and Investigations), and the Traitement du Renseignement et Action contre les Circuits Financiers Clandestins (TRACFIN; Unit for Combating Money Laundering and the Financing of Terrorism). The DGSE, DRM, and DRSD are part of the Ministry of Armed Forces (formerly the Ministry of Defense), the DGSI belongs to the Ministry of the Interior, and the DNRED and TRACFIN are in the Ministry of Economy and Finances. This first circle of agencies brings together around fourteen thousand employees.[2]

Together with the *coordonnateur national du renseignement et de la lutte contre le terrorisme* (national coordinator for intelligence and counterterrorism, who reports directly to the president), the Inspectorate of the Intelligence Services, and the Intelligence Academy (both of which report to the prime minister), these services form the French intelligence community (see gray boxes in figure 2.1). Besides this community, a broader range of government agencies are also entrusted with intelligence

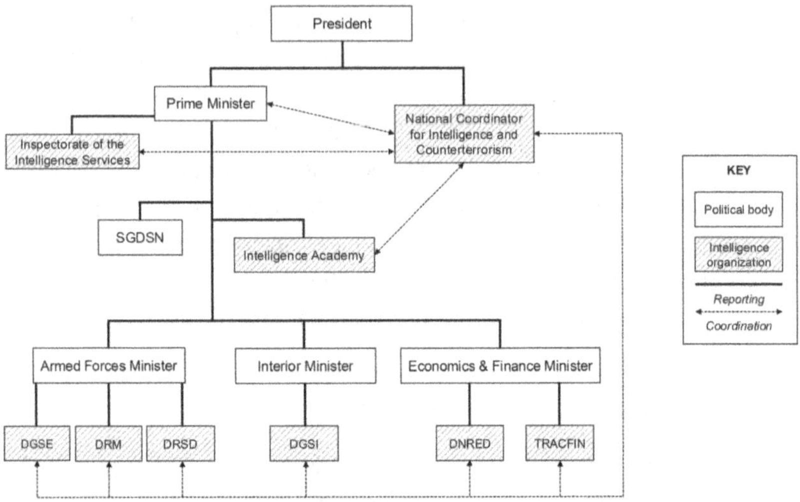

Figure 2.1: The French intelligence community

missions. The agencies forming this "second circle" include several services in the General Directorate for National Police and the Paris Police Prefecture, which belong to the Ministry of the Interior. Within the Ministry of Armed Forces, they include the research sections of the Gendarmerie and at the Ministry of Justice agencies such as the National Service for Penitentiary Intelligence.[3] The DGSE coordinates with all these agencies, though not to the same extent.

In the past two decades, changes in the threat environment and public perceptions, especially after the 2015 terrorist attacks in Paris, have prompted the government to elevate intelligence to a public policy, in the sense of a more visible and defined public function. This discursive and political shift has played a crucial role in legitimizing the intelligence community's role and operations.[4] From 2008 onward the French intelligence community and the DGSE have experienced the greatest series of reforms since the end of World War II.[5] The 2008 white paper on defense and national security made "knowledge and anticipation" a strategic function of the French defense and national security apparatus. The executive envisioned these activities as a cornerstone of foreign, military, and security policy.[6] This vision led to sustained investment in technical means and personnel to meet growing political demands and adapt to changes in information technology.[7] To reinforce coherence, President

Nicolas Sarkozy (2007–12) and his government established a position of *coordonnateur national pour le renseignement* (CNR; national coordinator for intelligence) in July 2008.[8] In 2015 Parliament passed a law that recognized intelligence as a *politique publique* (public policy), a term commentators use to underline the sense of coherence and political responsibility that had long been missing in French intelligence history.[9] From this perspective, intelligence shifted from a secretive tool of the executive to a more open and accountable policy domain, reflecting a deeper change in the underlying assumptions about its role in the French Republic. Several years later, the National Counterterrorism Center was added to the remit of the coordinator, and the institution was renamed the Coordination Nationale du Renseignement et de la Lutte contre le Terrorisme (CNRLT; National Center for Intelligence and Counterterrorism).[10]

The CNRLT is located at the Elysée Palace, which hosts the Office of the President. This positioning helped to settle historical tensions resulting from the executive diarchy between the head of state (the president) and the head of government (the prime minister) in favor of the former. In the French political system, the prime minister heads and coordinates the government and the administration. The Constitution of 1958 grants him or her responsibility for national defense (article 21). The prime minister's main instrument when it comes to intelligence and security is the Secrétariat Général de la Défense et de la Sécurité Nationale (SGDSN; General Secretariat for Defense and National Security), represented in figure 2.1 above. The president is the chief of the armed forces (article 15 of the Constitution of 1958). In matters of foreign policy, defense, and security, the president often serves as the top decision-maker. With the establishment of the CNR, the president has now a dedicated intelligence adviser, in addition to the historical roles played by his diplomatic adviser (*conseiller diplomatique*) and military adviser (*chef d'état major particulier*).

As its names indicates, the CNRLT coordinates the actions of intelligence services from the first and second circles. The head of the CNRLT acts as a transmission belt, ensuring that the services work well together in the pursuit of common objectives.[11] For instance, they control the implementation of decisions as well as the allocation of resources and mutualization of technical capabilities.[12] This is particularly relevant to the DGSE, which is France's senior SIGINT agency. DGSE SIGINT capabilities have been mutualized since 2008 and must therefore be shared with other agencies such as the DGSI.[13] The CNRLT must also ensure good coordination between the services and their respective ministries, making sure that policymakers identify clear priorities that are respected by the services. Its head reports to the Council for Defense and National Security (the equivalent of the US National Security Council) and prepares its intelligence council's configuration.

The intelligence council was established in 2008 and meets twice a year to define the strategic orientation of the community.[14] It identifies national intelligence priorities through a *plan national d'orientation du renseignement* (PNOR; national intelligence orientation plan), to which the SGDSN contributes, which supports planning and resource allocation.[15] The PNOR covers a three-year period and is updated on a yearly basis. The president chairs the national intelligence council—and therefore validates the PNOR—which brings together the prime minister, relevant ministers (armed forces, interior, justice, etc.), and the directors of the intelligence services. In July 2019 the CNRLT released, for the first time in French history, a national intelligence strategy. The PNOR is a classified document that operationalizes this strategy. The strategy identified four main priorities:

- Terrorist threats
- Anticipating crises and the risks posed by major ruptures, including international destabilizations, violent subversion operations, and crises of public order
- The defense and promotion of our economy, including the fight against fraud and lawfare
- The struggle against transnational threats, including cyber threats, foreign interferences and espionage, organized crime, and weapons proliferation[16]

The national coordinator ensures the implementation of the decisions and priorities identified during the national intelligence council meetings. In theory, the CNRLT receives all the production from the community, which allows its staff to verify that the services follow the orientations they receive.[17] The CNRLT's head uses this access to prepare a daily brief for the president and prime minister.[18] The CNRLT is also ideally positioned to work on transversal issues such as human resources and legal reforms.[19]

The rise of the CNRLT and emergence of a public policy on intelligence has addressed a long-standing need for clear political direction and a strategic vision for the French intelligence community. Centralization has helped align priorities with budgetary choices, contributing to greater coherence.[20] Yet the CNRLT is a small body, with only a few dozen staff members. Its head has no authority on specific agencies and no monopoly on access to the most senior decision-makers, the president and prime minister. The extent to which this individual effectively manages the community is debatable. Researchers point out that the role of the CNRLT remains open to interpretation. On key issues, it is unclear whether its head should advocate for the interests of the Elysée or those of the services.[21] In 2022, following the departure of Laurent Nuñez to the Paris Police Prefecture, the position was left vacant for five months. A range of circumstances explain this vacancy, yet this absence comforted critics who argue that the French community does not need a chief.

The DGSE

The DGSE is France's lead foreign intelligence agency. Though its origins can be traced back to World War II and then the SDECE, it was formally established by a presidential decree on April 2, 1982.[22] This was the first decree published in the French official journal (equivalent to the US *Federal Register*) that was dedicated to a state intelligence agency.[23] The move from a *service* (SDECE) to a *direction générale* (DGSE) was primarily cosmetic, as much of the agency's personnel remained the same and its culture, organization, and practices did not suddenly change in spring of 1982. Yet in French administrative jargon, a *direction générale* has control over its financial flow, its budget, and its recruitment. That is not the case of a *direction centrale* (e.g., the domestic intelligence service from 2008 to 2014 was a *direction centrale*) or a *direction* such as the DRM. Administratively speaking, the DGSE continued to be placed under the administrative control of the Ministry of Armed Forces. This position can give the impression that the DGSE is primarily a military agency;[24] that is not the case. The DGSE is a civilian agency that reports to political and not military authorities. The Ministry of Armed Forces administratively hosts the DGSE but does not need to know all of its activities, for which agency leaders directly report to the president and their advisers.[25]

The 1982 decree holds that the mission of the DGSE is "to research and exploit information of interest to the security of France, as well as to detect and disrupt, outside the national territory, espionage activities directed against French interests in order to prevent their consequences."[26] This mission goes well beyond the remit of the Ministry of Armed Forces. The DGSE serves governmental needs, and its consumers can be found across key offices, from the Ministry of Armed Forces to the Ministry for Europe and Foreign Affairs to the offices of the prime minister and the president.[27] On particularly sensitive operational matters, the agency reports directly to the president as head of state and chief of the armed forces. Direct access helps to maintain a short decision chain and high level of secrecy—for example, in hostage-rescue operations. On other issues, such as warrants for SIGINT intercepts, the agency reports to the prime minister.

The DGSE is an integrated service. Officials use this expression to point out that the agency engages in HUMINT, TECHINT, and "operational research"—intelligence that officers collect in the field through direct observations, document theft, and so on. The agency benefits from a national monopoly on covert HUMINT operations abroad and acts as the national lead authority on SIGINT. This differentiates the DGSE from its British counterparts (the SIS conducts HUMINT, and the Government Communications Headquarters [GCHQ] conducts SIGINT). At the DGSE, integration means *officiers traitant* (OTs; case officers) and analysts have access to in-house technical means to support their operations. Vice versa, HUMINT and operational research capacities support SIGINT—for example, by uncovering and mapping foreign networks for targeting.[28] The DGSE is also integrated in the sense that it engages in the full range of intelligence activities: from collection and analysis to dissemination (typically of processed intelligence) and covert action (which the French call *actions* or *opérations clandestines*).[29] Indeed, French law authorizes the agency "to carry out, within the framework of its attributions, *any action* that would be entrusted to it by the government."[30] This broad remit has defined the agency since the creation of the DGSS in 1943. It has become an ingrained assumption about foreign intelligence capabilities, one unlikely to be challenged successfully anytime soon.

Organization

The DGSE has long been organized into directorates, whose number has varied over the years. When DG Pierre Marion oversaw the transition of the SDECE into the DGSE in 1982, the agency was structured around an Intelligence Directorate and an Operations Directorate. Subsequent reforms in the 1980s established a Technical Directorate. In the late 1980s DG Claude Silberzahn consolidated the agency structure around five directorates. Figure 2.2 shows a simple organigram of the DGSE in 2003, which includes these five directorates.

At the top of the organigram, a group of units can be directly attached to the DG. Their existence largely depends on his preferences. DG Pierre Brochand (2002–8), for example, oversaw the establishment of the agency's situation center. This center serves a watch function, operating on a 24/7 basis to provide short-term warning to the agency's leadership. When a crisis emerges, the center establishes cells that bring together experts from across the agency—which can cause tensions with the bureaus that "lend" their personnel to the cell. The situation center can also support coordination with other partners, such as the chief of the Defense Staff (*chef d'états major des armées*) and the DRM.[31]

The security service protects the confidentiality of the agency's structures, resources, and missions.[32] Its investigators work in a relatively autonomous way to prevent and detect security breaches throughout and beyond the agency.[33] The service is in charge of personnel security, from the initial vetting process to travel authorizations for holidays abroad. The DGSE grants its own security clearances (*habilitations spéciales de sécurité*). Eight officers lost this clearance from 2015 to 2020.[34] This service also investigates contracting companies and their ability to maintain information-security standards.[35]

The General Inspectorate conducts investigations, verifications, evaluations, and studies on relevant organisms and processes within the agency. It can propose corrective measures and improvements to the DG.

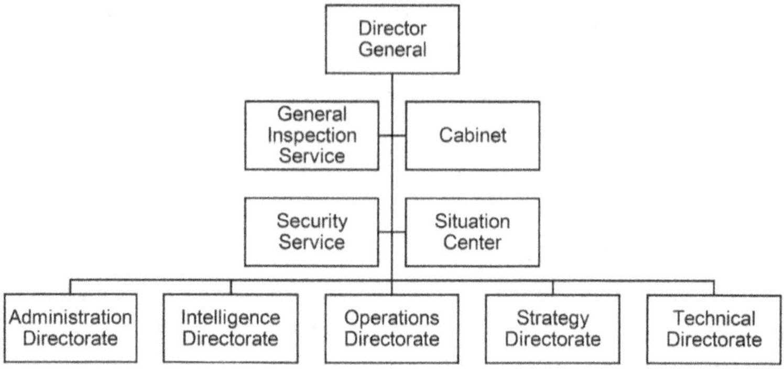

Figure 2.2: DGSE organigram, 2003. *Ministry of Defense*

The chief of the General Inspectorate also serves as a mediator.[36] This inspection service is accompanied by a permanent audit function led by a general controller.

Five directorates have structured the DGSE's activities from 1989 to 2022. The Intelligence Directorate (Direction du Renseignement, or DR) was responsible for the exploitation of all-source intelligence (technical, human, and operational means). It was widely considered the most powerful directorate and best known for overseeing HUMINT collection and analysis. DGSE case officers typically start their career with a lengthy period of training, then move to an office job, conducting analysis that will orient colleagues in the field before they are deployed there themselves.[37] In the early 2010s an internal reorganization merged these two capabilities, leading analysts to focus more exclusively on tasking intelligence collection platforms. The DR focused on a handful of core issues (organized in sectors and later in services): counterproliferation, counterterrorism, economic security, (geo)political intelligence, and counterespionage.[38] Historically, the directorate has included geographic sectors focusing on Africa, Asia-America, the Arab world, and Europe. In 2003 counterterrorism was the largest sector within the DR. This sector was further divided into a series of sections focusing on terrorist networks and their intentions, support, and means. Counterterrorism officers would evaluate the capabilities and intentions of terrorist groups that could harm French interests, anticipate and disrupt their activities abroad, and liaise with relevant services to "neutralize" the most pressing threats.[39]

The Technical Directorate (Direction Technique, or DT) benefits from the largest budget to develop the agency's technical capabilities. The DT employs around twenty-seven hundred full-time equivalents (compared to one thousand at the technical and telecommunications department of the German Federal Intelligence Service and sixty-five hundred at the British GCHQ).[40] The DGSE, and by extension the DT, is the senior SIGINT agency in the French community and thus coordinates access to capabilities across the community. The DT collects, processes, and analyzes technical intelligence, mostly SIGINT but also imagery intelligence (IMINT) and geospatial intelligence (GEOINT). It can leverage its capabilities to conduct offensive cyber operations.[41] The second key mission of the DT is to support HUMINT and the agency's covert operations. The DT also provides logistical support both at headquarters and in the field—for example, to enable covert communications.[42] In 2012 the DT was organized into three divisions focusing on information systems and support, intelligence technologies, and technical intelligence production and actions.[43]

The Operations Directorate (Direction des Opérations, or DO) conducted actions mandated by the government. It was the most militarized directorate, both in terms of its personnel (around one thousand) and procedures. Within the DO, a chief of staff ensured coordination, planning, prioritization, and after-action reporting.[44] Its most famous service was and remains the paramilitary arm of the DGSE: the SA. The SA is placed directly under the authority of the DG by delegation of the president,[45] but its personnel are managed by the military.[46] Its core missions include intelligence collection in conflict zones, support to friendly countries and movements, reconnaissance, and the identification and designation of targets. Additional missions include the protection of strategic infrastructure (e.g., embassies, factories, and airports), the protection of diplomatic and consular personnel in conflict zones, and hostage-rescue operations. At the higher end of the spectrum of violence, the SA has conducted sabotage operations—for example, targeting Greenpeace's flagship vessel the *Rainbow Warrior* in 1985 (more on this fiasco in chapters 4 and 5). The SA is also reported to engage in assassination.[47] Many of these operations likely violate the laws of target countries and are designed to be fully deniable. French authorities have the option to acknowledge them when or if they become public.[48] The SA employs several hundred operators—almost all of whom are career soldiers.[49] They are organized into three main units: Centre Parachutiste d'Instruction Spécialisé (CPIS; Specialized Parachute Instruction Center), which hosts commandos in Perpignan; Centre Parachutiste d'Entrainement Spécialisé (CPES; Specialized Parachute Training Center), which hosts covert operators in Cercottes; and combat divers at the Centre Parachutiste d'Entraînement aux Opérations Maritimes (CPEOM; Parachute Training Center for Maritime Operations), which hosts combat divers in Quélern.[50] Groupe Aérien Mixte 56 Vaucluse (GAM-56; Mixed Air Group 56) provides specialized air support to the SA. Other services within the DO include the Service Mission, a small unit that oversees covert HUMINT and operational research where the DGSE has no official presence. For example, the Service Mission sent nonofficial cover operatives to and around Rwanda in 1992 to collect intelligence and liaise with paramilitary groups.[51] The most dangerous and risky missions of the service require political approval from the highest authorities.[52] The Service Opération specializes in close surveillance and gathering intelligence in protected locations, including embassies, airports, and hotels.[53]

The Strategy Directorate (Direction de la Stratégie, or DS) was established in 1989 to better link the DGSE to other parts of the French state apparatus and "optimize the use" of intelligence.[54] Within the DS, the national liaison service communicates with French consumers to identify their needs and assess the extent to which DGSE products fulfill them.[55] While direct evidence is difficult to access, it is reasonable to assume that this service fostered a gradual rapprochement between the DGSE and the broader French administration, contributing to its normalization. Another service (Service des Liaisons Internationales) is responsible for international liaison with foreign intelligence services. In the 2010s the DS also hosted a foresight mission (*mission prospective*) that conducted outreach with academic and private-sector partners as well as an alternative analysis mission. Support for this mission has fluctuated over the past decade. As chapter 4 will show, DGSE culture has traditionally placed limited emphasis on strategic analysis.

The Administration Directorate (Direction de l'Administration, or DA) supports all the directorates, services, and centers within the agency. In 2015 the DA was structured in five services: human resources management (from recruitment to career progression, staff mobility, and career transition),[56] formation, purchases and finances, real estate, and operational support and logistics.[57]

The 2022 Reform

The division of labor across directorates inevitably created silos that—together with the strong compartmentalization that characterizes intelligence services—constrained the flow of relevant information within and between the DGSE and its consumers.[58] The most obvious divide separated the directorates specialized on a collection discipline (SIGINT for DT and HUMINT for DR) and access to policymakers and consumer (DS). Specialized directorates rarely—if ever—received direct orientation and feedback from consumers; this always went through the DS. The heads of directorates competed for access to the DG and senior policymakers. At the top, the system fostered tensions between the DG and the head of the DR. Insiders sometimes felt like the agency was integrated all but in name, pointing to a persistent gap between strategic intent and actual implementation.

Confronting the transversal threat of terrorism, the agency made an explicit effort to overcome some of these divisions and better integrate technical and human means of collection. TECHINT experts from the DT embedded within the DR, and multidirectorate teams were established within the situation center. These fixes could not overcome deeper organizational and cultural divisions. In the early 2020s DG Bernard Émié took stock of these issues and secured political support to launch the most significant reform of the DGSE in thirty years. The prominence of the terrorist threat in the first two decades of the twenty-first century had, by now, demonstrated the value of a more integrated model in which collection platforms, analysis, and action are more closely linked. A new generation of policymakers believed in and was ready to invest in intelligence, to address what they perceived to be an increasingly complex threat environment marked by transnational *and* state-based threats.

The 2022 reform has established a position of deputy director (*directeur général adjoint*), thus abandoning the chief of staff position traditionally allocated to a senior military officer.[59] The flagship—and most controversial—measure of the reform was the disbanding of the DR and its merger with the DS. The reform elevated this new entity into a

Secrétariat Général pour l'Analyse et la Stratégie (SGAS; General Secretariat for Analysis and Strategy).[60] The SGAS is now expected to take charge of analysis and serve as the main interface with DGSE's partners and consumers. The collection capabilities of the DR have moved to a new Direction de la Recherche et des Opérations (DRO; Directorate of Intelligence Collection and Operations). The reform also rebranded the DT into a Direction Technique et de l'Innovation (DTI; Technical and Innovation Directorate) and does not seem to have brought major changes to the DA. Last, but not least, to mirror the interconnected and global nature of the contemporary threat environment, the reform established a series of mission centers (*services*) orienting human and technical means. These centers focus both on thematic (counterproliferation, counterterrorism, economic security, foreign policy intelligence, collection supervision and support, and analysis and production) and geographic areas (Africa, North Africa and Middle East, etc.).[61] The latest DGSE organigram is presented in figure 2.3. The executive committee that leads the DGSE at the strategic level is now composed of all the directors and the heads of the mission centers.[62]

It is still too early to assess the reform's impact on core missions, but two signs are encouraging. First, despite the public pressure following the 2015 terrorist attacks in Paris, the reform was not rushed. Instead, it was developed behind closed doors, avoiding excessive politicization. Second, the reform signals that the agency is not trapped in stasis but is capable of self-reflection and open to new arrangements aimed at further improvement.

Resources

The DGSE's resources have grown steadily. The agency's budget is composed of two main funding lines: an ordinary budget provided through the Ministry of Armed Forces and special funds (*fonds spéciaux*) provided through the prime minister. While the ordinary budget follows a normal planning process, special funds offer added flexibility to support sensitive operations (e.g., covert actions and funding agents).[63] The agency reportedly received €283 million of funding in 1999.[64] By 2006 its budget had grown to €486 million, including €36.2 million of special funds. The budget continued to increase in the following decade to reach close to

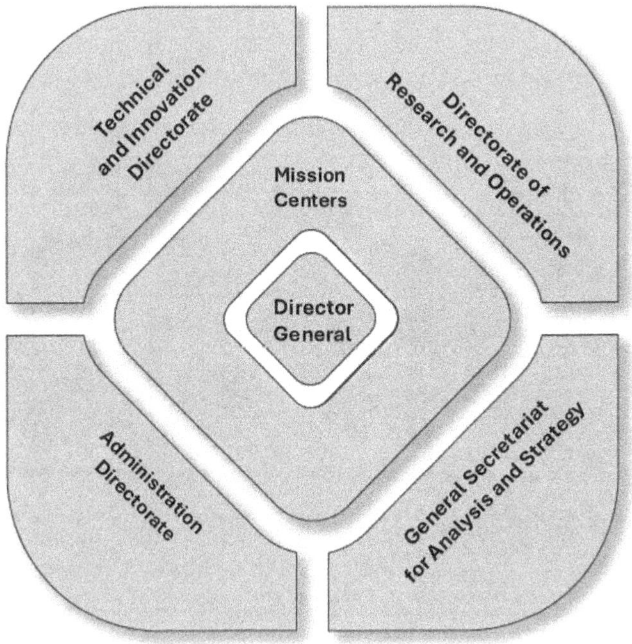

Figure 2.3: DGSE organigram, 2025

€750 million in 2014.[65] Much of this growth can be explained by significant investments in technical capacities to keep up with the information and communication technology revolution. From 2008 to 2019 French authorities invested close to €1.3 billion in upgrading SIGINT capacities.[66] In 2022 the agency's budget passed the €1 billion mark for the first time, an increase that is largely explained by a much-anticipated move from Boulevard Mortier (see figure 2.4 below) to new headquarters east of Paris at Fort Neuf de Vincennes and further investment in technical capacities.[67] This costly move has become necessary to accommodate growing energy needs while maintaining resilience and security.[68] The new headquarters will host six thousand workstations. Its supporters hope the facility will encourage the adoption of new working methods to break down persisting stovepipes and advance the path toward mutualization.[69] It was scheduled to open in 2028, but initial reports have already identified significant delays and cost hikes, pushing the move to 2030.[70]

The DGSE workforce has grown significantly over the past decades. The agency employed around 3,200 personnel in 1982. By 2003 this

Figure 2.4: DGSE headquarters, Boulevard Mortier, Paris, 2014. *Wikimedia Commons, Tangopaso*

number had risen to 4,613, including 3,244 civilians and 1,369 military personnel (excluding several hundred SA personnel). Military personnel are primarily from the army (over 1,200 in 2003) and attached to a support corps—the 44th Infantry Regiment—except for those from the agency's paramilitary branch, the SA.[71] The proportion of military personnel has remained stable at around 25 percent for well over a decade.[72] While some observers think of the DGSE as a militarized agency, the majority of its personnel have been civilian for several decades.[73] Military personnel dress in civilian clothes at the DGSE, donning their uniform only for ceremonies. The agency's workforce has continued to grow in the past two decades, gaining 1,700 employees from 2008 to 2018.[74] Personnel were expected to grow to 7,800 (and close to 6,000 full-time equivalent) by 2025.[75] By comparison the British GCHQ employed 7,107 personnel in 2020, and the SIS 4,107 (11,214 personnel if we combine them). The British government does not disclose the top budget line of these agencies, but the single intelligence account (the main budget for the British intelligence community) stood above £3 billion in 2020.[76] By that standard, the DGSE and the French intelligence community continue to lag behind their neighbor across the Channel.

Two further data points about the agency's human resources are worth mentioning. First, women constituted 25 percent of its workforce in 2003 and 2013.[77] Efforts to increase their number have had a marginal effect; women made up 28 percent of the agency's workforce in 2023.[78] This compares poorly to the 62.3 percent of women in the French civil service (2018).[79] Former DG Émié acknowledged the lack of women within the DGSE, while also noting that "it is above the average of the Ministry of Armed Forces."[80] To this day, no woman has ever led the agency or one of its directorates. In 2016–17, 38.9 percent of the employees of the British SIS were women, and 35.2 percent of the GCHQ.[81] Women currently lead the GCHQ and SIS. To remediate the lack of "professional equality between women and men" and other personnel issues in the DGSE, the agency has recently drawn up a three-year action plan.[82]

Second, civil servants, who need to pass a *concours* (competitive examination) to join the DGSE on a permanent contract, represent 39 percent of the agency workforce.[83] The agency also hires independent contractors for fixed terms; they accounted for 31.2 percent of its personnel in 2018 (compared to 24.5 percent in 2014).[84] This rise can be explained by the agency's search for more diverse profiles to fill linguistic, scientific, and technical needs.[85] For the most part, these contractors are treated like any other employee, receive the same initial training, and are issued the same badges as civil servants.

Since 2012 the agency has adopted a corpus of values to guide its employees: loyalty, exigency, discretion, and adaptability (or LEDA—the French administration, like many others, has a penchant for acronyms).[86] The choice of these four principles is the result of a consultation with the agency's staff. The service has been keen to develop its identity both for internal purposes to support self-reflection and workforce management and externally to improve its image. It has also reformed the status of its employees to align it more closely to that of civil servants in the rest of the French administration and offer them better legal protection.[87] This is a key adaptation that addresses long-standing issues explored in greater detail in chapter 4.

Interagency Coordination

Interagency relations within the French intelligence community and with the rest of the administration have not always been harmonious. One explanation assigns responsibility to senior decision-makers. President Jacques Chirac's (1995–2007) chief of military staff claims that the head of state "wanted to keep the services divided, to better control them."[88] Organizational priorities and incentives provide a more convincing explanation for coordination problems. Recurring tensions between France's domestic and foreign intelligence agencies highlight familiar cultural and organizational divides, often observed in liberal democracies. The DGSI is a security service with a domestic remit, so its officers are bound by the rule of law and legally mandated to cooperate with the judiciary. The DGSE, by contrast, is a foreign intelligence service. French law provides a legal basis for its activities, but some of its officers are likely to violate the laws of the countries they operate in. These differences have fostered the emergence of distinct organizational cultures and professional communities. Among many other examples, the director of the domestic DST from 1982 to 1985 remembers it was easier to cooperate with the British services to get foreign intelligence than with the DGSE.[89] Following the attacks committed by Mohamed Merah in Toulouse and Montauban in 2012, officials criticized the DGSE for not sharing with the domestic intelligence service information about his travels to Israel, Pakistan, and Egypt.[90] Conversely, DGSE officials complained that the DGSI bypassed their agency's role as the primary authority on SIGINT by liaising with foreign partners such as the US National Security Agency (NSA) through the Federal Bureau of Investigation (FBI).[91]

Many contemporary threats, particularly terrorism, blur the lines between domestic and foreign affairs. Structures for coordinating national counterterrorism efforts across this divide have been in place for a long time.[92] Major terrorist attacks in France over the past decade, along with increased political interest in intelligence and the emergence of the CNRLT, have brought France's domestic and foreign agencies and their leaders closer than ever before.[93] The mobility of senior officers between key agencies and the establishment of fusion cells have facilitated mutual understanding.[94] Since March 2014 the DGSI has hosted a joint cell to monitor terrorism cases in real time together with DGSE officers.[95] The following year, France's domestic intelligence agency established the Allat cell (named after a pre-Islamic Arabian goddess) to bring together the six services of the first circle together with the territorial intelligence service and the intelligence directorate of the Paris Police Prefecture. This counterterrorism cell works 24/7 to facilitate deconfliction and prioritization, focusing mostly on the targeting and corroboration of various streams of information on high-level individuals.[96] The DGs of the DGSI and the DGSE have praised its positive impact on the fluidity of exchanges between France's intelligence agencies.[97] In a joint interview with the French daily *Le Figaro*, the two leaders spoke of their "sacred union" and confessed "we do not keep secrets from each other."[98] In late 2023 President Emmanuel Macron appointed Nicolas Lerner, the head of the DGSI, to lead the DGSE.[99] These signals point to a clear rapprochement, but the extent to which strategic alignment and coordination efforts translate into sustained operational integration remains difficult for outsiders to evaluate.

The DGSE has long had an interest in military intelligence, though its remit has always been more broadly focused on foreign affairs. After the Gulf War exposed some gaps in intelligence coverage, France's foreign intelligence agency helped to create the DRM in 1992.[100] The DRM's first director (Gen. Jean Heinrich) served as director of operations at the DGSE. In its early years, the DRM reportedly engaged in covert operations, which prompted DGSE Director Jacques Dewatre (1993–2000) to step in. Since June 1994 a protocol has defined clearer boundaries between the two agencies. The DGSE handles covert actions and focuses on purely military matters when the DRM or the military asks for or can benefit from it.[101] The DRM's core mission is to support the French joint chiefs of staff, and its culture is a military one. It has operational responsibility for France's imagery satellites and acts as senior IMINT. As such, the DRM coordinates IMINT across the community and shares intercepts—and sometimes products—with the DGSE.[102] The DGSE similarly shares its SIGINT capabilities with the DRM and has long mutualized some of its collection platforms with the military intelligence agency.[103] The two agencies have established deconfliction mechanisms to make sure they do not handle the same human sources and are not being intoxicated by adversaries.[104] In one recent case, DGSE intelligence helped direct DRM drones toward Wagner Group activities in Mali. The

Wagner Group, a Russian private military company operating at the behest of the Kremlin, has been active across several conflict zones in Africa and beyond. The French Ministry of Armed Forces later released a video showing Wagner troops covering several cadavers, which aimed to counter a Russian disinformation operation alleging French armed forces' responsibility.[105]

The fight against terrorism has also reinforced coordination between the military and civilian intelligence communities. Fusion cells brought together the DGSE, DRM, and DRSD to support French engagements in Afghanistan and the Sahel.[106] For example, the Ministry of Armed Forces established a cell called Hermès that brought together the DRM, DGSE, DGSI, DNRED, DRSD, TRACFIN, and Commandement des Opérations Spéciales (COS; Special Operations Command). From October 2014 onward, Hermès pooled intelligence to plan and conduct operations in the Levant, focusing specifically on the threat posed by the Islamic State and other insurgent groups.[107]

The emphasis toward greater coordination has not totally eclipsed historical tensions. Some (often retired) senior military officers dispute the DGSE's control over France's covert capabilities. Retired general André Ranson, who led DRM operations, lamented that the DGSE did not share its access to the Northern Alliance in the early 2000s.[108] The COS, DRM, and DGSE do combine their resources—for example, to target jihadists in Mali during Operation Serval in 2013.[109] Yet each failure of the DGSE's SA provides an opportunity for the COS to argue it would do a job better. Christophe Gomart, who led the COS from 2011 to 2013 and then the DRM from 2013 to 2017, is the latest former general officer to cast doubt on the relevance and competence of the SA.[110] These critiques agree that France needs to maintain its capability to conduct actions that are not politically acknowledgeable, but they believe that France should follow the British model and use its special forces to conduct covert paramilitary actions. This view has never gained significant support at the highest level of the state. If anything, it reflects personal ambitions and bureaucratic rivalries.

Legal Basis and Oversight

For most of its history, the DGSE operated in a legal gray zone under the broad umbrella of *raison d'état*. This ambiguity strained France's commitment to liberal democratic norms and exposed officers to legal risks. The emergence of a public policy on intelligence has been accompanied by the maturation of a democratic accountability regime organized around three main pillars: administrative control, parliamentary oversight, and judicial review.[111] The French political system is based on a strong executive and the role of its parliament is more limited than in other liberal democracies.[112] This explains why the democratization of French intelligence started late, with the establishment in 2007 of a Délégation Parlementaire au Renseignement (DPR; Parliamentary Delegation to Intelligence).[113] This group of senators and deputies initially held very limited prerogatives that allowed them to follow some intelligence activities through hearings and to visit agencies. Their authority to access information and evaluate intelligence policies was reinforced in 2013, opening the door for more meaningful oversight of the government's intelligence policy and leading to more informative (and lengthier) annual reports.[114] In 2014 the Commission de Vérification des Fonds Spéciaux (CVFS; Special Funds Audit Commission), initially established in 2001, was folded into the DPR. As a result, part of the delegation conducts a posteriori control over the DGSE's use of "special funds."[115] Despite these changes, the DPR's oversight mandate remains limited. It can call directors to testify and receives key documents such as the national intelligence strategy, elements of the PNOR, and annual reports on intelligence budgets and the activities of the services, as well as observations from the Commission Nationale de Contrôle des Techniques de Renseignement (CNCTR; National Commission for the Control of Intelligence Techniques), another oversight body. However, the delegation lacks authority to oversee ongoing operations.[116] The prevailing assumption is that such oversight could compromise security and that politicization might undermine operational effectiveness.

The CNCTR is an independent administrative authority that controls the use of intelligence techniques. The commission brings together four parliamentarians (two deputies and two senators), four judicial officers, and a technical expert. This administrative body was first established in 1991 to advise the prime minister about the legality of extrajudicial wiretap requests.[117] In 2015 Parliament passed important intelligence reforms that established a more comprehensive legal basis for core intelligence activities, including interceptions.[118] This reform has been well received by the DGSE because it recognizes and protects some of its more controversial activities.[119] In counterpart, French law now offers more guarantees to

French citizens. Intelligence agencies are authorized to use "intelligence techniques"—mostly SIGINT interception—to pursue a limited list of "fundamental interests." The execution of these techniques is traceable, and the data that is acquired can be retained only for specific periods of time. Citizens can now refer their case to the CNCTR to verify the correct implementation of these techniques.[120] The evolution of the CNCTR marks an important step toward stronger democratic accountability, which is essential for maintaining public trust and institutional legitimacy.

In 2019 the main rationales used by the DGSE to implement these techniques focused on the protection of major economic, industrial, and scientific interests of the nation (60 percent) and the protection of major foreign policy interests (25 percent).[121] The CNCTR exercises oversight of these techniques by issuing prior opinions to the Prime Minister or their delegates to ensure their legality, proportionality, and subsidiarity (use of least intrusive means), and subsequently verifying their implementation.[122] The same year, the commission conducted thirty-three controls within the DGSE.[123] Bernard Émié, who led the DGSE at the time, found this control "pregnant and demanding."[124]

Reforms of the oversight regime for the intelligence community have also led to the establishment in 2014 of an inspectorate for intelligence services (Inspections des Services de Renseignement), placed under the authority of the prime minister.[125] This inspectorate contributes to the administrative control of the services through audits, studies, evaluation, and advice. The office can audit following instructions from the prime minister or propositions from a relevant minister or the CNRLT.[126] The expansion and combination of multiple forms of control (parliamentary, administrative, etc.) is a vital adaptation for French democracy. This shift has led agencies to dedicate more resources to oversight, with some DGSE officers spending up to 10 percent of their time addressing requests from overseers.[127] While some insiders may believe their time could be better utilized elsewhere, it is important to keep the broader perspective in mind: This is a small price to pay for aligning intelligence activities with liberal democratic standards.

Conclusion

Over the past two decades, the DGSE and the broader French intelligence community have undergone significant organizational change.

Political interest has reframed intelligence as a public policy, prompting new laws that expanded and legitimized the services' roles.[128] This evolution has helped normalize the agency's place within the machinery of government, aligning it more closely with democratic norms. Amid rising terrorist threats and rapid digital transformation, the DGSE received unprecedented investment, fueling its growth and deepening its integration into the state apparatus. The 2022 reorganization and the planned move to new headquarters by 2030 reflect an effort to adapt both structure and mission to a more complex security environment.

Yet this process is, by nature, incomplete. Normalization and accountability should not be considered as endpoints but instead ongoing imperatives. As the DGSE continues to grow, sustaining its integration, legitimacy, and responsiveness will require continued political attention and institutional vigilance.

Notes

1. Premier Ministre, *Décret no. 2014-474.*
2. Bernard Émié in Christophe Cornevin, "Le patron de la DGSE au Figaro: 'Aujourd'hui comme hier, nos agents sont en première ligne,'" *Le Figaro*, June 23, 2022.
3. Commission Nationale de Contrôle des Techniques de Renseignement, "Le cadre légal du renseignement."
4. Holeindre and Oudet, *Intelligence Studies in France*, 2.
5. Laurent, "L'analyse," 61.
6. Présidence de la République, *Défense et sécurité nationale*, 65.
7. Bernard Bajolet in Guisnel and Korn-Brzoza, *Au service secret de la France*, 514–15.
8. Président de la République, *Décret no. 2009-1657.*
9. Assemblée Nationale (hereafter AN), *Loi no. 2015-912 relative au renseignement.* See also Chopin and Oudet, *Renseignement et sécurité*, 31–32.
10. Président de la République, *Décret no. 2017-1095.*
11. AN, Commission de la Défense Nationale et des Forces Armées, *Hearing of Laurent Nuñez*, 3.
12. Académie du Renseignement, *La communauté française*, 7–8.
13. AN, *Rapport relatif à l'activité de la délégation parlementaire au renseignement pour l'année 2012*, 15; AN, Mission d'Information sur les Moyens de Daech, *Rapport d'information*, vol. 2, 268.
14. AN, Mission d'Information de la Conférence des Présidents sur la Résilience Nationale, *Hearing of Laurent Nuñez*, 7.
15. AN, *Hearing of Erard Corbin de Mangoux*, 4; AN, *Hearing of Jean-François Ferlet*, 3; Président de la République, *Décret no. 2022-983.*
16. Coordination Nationale du Renseignement et de la Lutte contre le Terrorisme, *La stratégie nationale du renseignement*, 2–8.

17. AN, Commission de la Défense Nationale et des Forces Armées, *Hearing of Laurent Nuñez*, 3.
18. Bajolet in Guisnel and Korn-Brzoza, *Au service secret de la France*, 517.
19. AN, Commission de la Défense Nationale et des Forces Armées, *Hearing of Laurent Nuñez*, 3.
20. Corbin de Mangoux, "Les mutations du renseignement."
21. Chopin and Oudet, *Renseignement et sécurité*, 88.
22. Since then this decree has been revised twice, in 2015 and 2022.
23. Previous decrees had confirmed the status of SDECE employees and enacted its move to the Ministry of Armed Forces.
24. See, e.g., Porch, *French Secret Services*, 480.
25. Silberzahn, *Au coeur du secret*, 103–4. See also Toreau, "Le renseignement français dans la lutte contre l'islamisme armé," 808.
26. Président de la République, *Décret no. 82-306*, article 2, 1035.
27. For an example of a recipients list, see Archives Nationales, Pierrefite-sur-Seine, box 20210031/10: Direction Générale de la Sécurité Extérieure, "Note de renseignement. Rwanda–Libye."
28. AN, Commission d'Enquête Relative aux Moyens Mis en Oeuvre par l'État, 857.
29. André Ranson in Bauer and Dupuis-Danon, *Les guetteurs*, 155.
30. Code de la Défense, article D. 3126-3 (emphasis added).
31. "L'art du renseignement," 39.
32. Ministre des Armées, *Arrêté portant organisation*, December 4, 2002, article 2.
33. AN, Commission d'Enquête Chargée de Faire la Lumière, 4, 11.
34. AN, Commission d'Enquête Chargée de Faire la Lumière, 75.
35. AN, *Rapport relatif à l'activité de la délégation parlementaire au renseignement pour l'année 2019–2020*, 142.
36. AN, *Rapport relatif à l'activité de la délégation parlementaire au renseignement pour l'année 2014*, 70.
37. Anonymous officer cited in Notin, *Les guerriers de l'ombre*, 72.
38. Ministre de la Défense, *Arrêté portant organisation*, December 21, 2012, article 5.
39. "L'art du renseignement," 40.
40. AN, *Renseignement et prospective de défense*, 3.
41. AN, *Avis sur le projet de loi de finances pour 2017*, vol. 4, 28.
42. "Interceptions invisibles," 48–49.
43. Ministre de la Défense, *Arrêté portant organisation*, December 21, 2012, article 7.
44. Ministre de la Défense, *Arrêté portant organisation*, March 10, 2015, article 4.
45. Hofnung, "Au coeur de la DGSE."
46. AN, *Rapport relatif à l'activité de la délégation parlementaire au renseignement pour l'année 2018*, 101.
47. Chopin and Oudet, *Renseignement et sécurité*, 148.
48. "Force de l'ombre," 50–51.
49. AN, *Le renforcement des forces spéciales françaises*.
50. Direction des Ressources Humaines de l'Armée de Terre, *Instruction No. 731/DEF/RH-AT/BPMF/DS*.
51. Archives Nationales, Pierrefite-sur-Seine, box 20210031/10: Direction des

Opérations, Service Missions, "Mission effectuée en mai 1992 auprès du FPR." See also Notin, *Les guerriers de l'ombre*, 14, 69, 73, 234.

52. Notin, *Les guerriers de l'ombre*, 144–45.
53. Notin, *Les guerriers de l'ombre*, 14.
54. "L'art du renseignement," 43.
55. Ministre de la Défense, *Arrêté portant organisation*, December 21, 2012, article 6.
56. AN, *Avis sur le projet de loi de finances pour 2007*, 12.
57. Ministre de la Défense, Arrêté portant organisation, March 10, 2015, article 3; Ministre des Armées, *Arrêté portant organisation*, July 13, 2022.
58. Bernard Émié in Notin, *DGSE*, 11.
59. Jacques Follorou, "Révolution culturelle au sein des services secrets français," *Le Monde*, January 31, 2023.
60. In French administrative jargon, a general secretariat carries more weight than a directorate. Ministre des Armées, *Arrêté portant organisation*, July 13, 2022.
61. "Centres de missions," Annuaire Service Public, August 9, 2023, https://lannuaire.service-public.fr/gouvernement/ecd1cc64-cad8-4484-851f-98ac010e082d; "DGSE Reform: The DR Is Dead, Long Live the DR!"
62. Notin, *DGSE*, 84.
63. "Des héros très discrets," 37; Jacques Isnard, "En France, forces spéciales et services de renseignement recrutent," *Le Monde*, November 22, 2001; Tibère, "Fonds spéciaux," 396–98.
64. "Le chef de la DGSE est remercié après les échecs de son service en Yougoslavie," *Le Monde*, December 19, 1999.
65. Bajolet, "La DGSE, outil de réduction," 29.
66. Armor, "La DGSE," 23.
67. Ministère de l'Économie, *Projet de Loi de Finances 2022*.
68. AN, *Rapport relatif à l'activité de la délégation parlementaire au renseignement pour l'année 2018*, 110; Ministère des Armées, "Réponse à une question parlementaire," 6645.
69. Sénat, *Rapport sur le projet de loi de finances pour 2023*, 21.
70. AN, *Avis sur le projet de loi de finances pour 2022*, vol. 2, 14; AN, *Avis sur le projet de loi de finances pour 2024*, 11–13; Notin, *DGSE*, 25.
71. "Des héros très discrets," 37. This number remained stable for several years. See AN, Commission des Finances, *Compte rendu 8*, 2–3 (3,224.5 full-time-equivalent civilian and 1,397 military personnel for a total of 4,621.5 full-time-equivalent employees in 2007); AN, Commission de la Défense Nationale et des Forces Armées, *Compte rendu 13*, 3 (4,620 full-time-equivalent employees in 2009).
72. AN, *Rapport relatif à l'activité de la délégation parlementaire au renseignement pour l'année 2018*, 101 (25.5 percent in 2014 and 23.1 percent in 2018).
73. Laurent, "La gouvernance supérieure du renseignement," 477; Académie du Renseignement, *La communauté française*, 13.
74. AN, *Rapport sur le projet de loi de finances pour 2018*, annex 13, 63; AN, *Avis sur le projet de loi de finances pour 2021*, vol. 4, 16.
75. AN, Commission d'Enquête Chargée de Faire la Lumière, 74; AN, *Rapport d'information sur l'environnement et la prospective*, 8.
76. UK Parliament, Intelligence and Security Committee, *Annual Report 2019–2021*, 29.

77. “Des héros très discrets,” 37; AN, *Hearing of Corbin de Mangoux*, 3.
78. DGSE director of human resources cited in Baudoin Eschapasse, “Cyberespions: Le ‘Piscine’ recrute,” *Le Point*, special issue no. 11, July/August 2023, 40.
79. Institut National de la Statistique et des Études Économiques, *Répartition des effectifs*.
80. Émié in Notin, *DGSE*, 16.
81. UK Parliament, Intelligence and Security Committee, *Diversity and Inclusion in the UK Intelligence Community*, 14.
82. Premier Ministre, *Décret no. 2023-1039 modifiant les dispositions générales applicables aux fonctionnaires et aux agents contractuels de la direction générale de la sécurité extérieure*, November 15, 2023, article 11.
83. DGSE director of human resources cited in Eschapasse, “Cyberespions,” 40.
84. French law requires authorities to turn temporary contractor positions into permanent civil servant positions after six years of service. AN, *Rapport relatif à l’activité de la délégation parlementaire au renseignement pour l’année 2018*, 101.
85. AN, *Rapport relatif à l’activité de la délégation parlementaire au renseignement pour l’année 2015*, 49.
86. Christophe Cornevin, “Le patron de la DGSE au *Figaro*: ‘Aujourd’hui comme hier, nos agents sont en première ligne,’” *Le Figaro*, June 23, 2022.
87. AN, *Rapport relatif à l’activité de la délégation parlementaire au renseignement pour l’année 2014*, 92–95. The reform of DGSE officers’ status culminated with a decree: Ministre de la Défense, *Décret no. 2015-386*.
88. Bernard Norlain in Guisnel and Korn-Brzoza, *Au service secret de la France*, 434.
89. Yves Bonnet in Guisnel and Korn-Brzoza, *Au service secret de la France*, 177. For a detailed overview of these tensions, see Toreau, “Le renseignement français dans la lutte contre l’islamisme armé,” part 2.
90. See, e.g., Jean-Marc Bailleul in AN, Commission d’Enquête sur le Fonctionnement des Services de Renseignement Français, 146.
91. “Pris dans leurs rivalités, les services français ont privilégié leurs liens avec la NSA et le GCHQ,” *Le Monde*, December 10, 2016. See also Silberzahn, *Au coeur du secret*, 39–40.
92. The Unité de Coordination de la Lutte Anti-Terroriste (UCLAT; Counterterrorism Coordination Unit) of the National Police was established in 1984. In 2004 the DST and DGSE established a common operational section. See Ministère de la Défense, “Réponse à une question parlementaire de M. Rivière Jérôme,” 9204.
93. AN, Commission de la Défense Nationale et des Forces Armées, *Hearing of Laurent Nuñez*, 4.
94. AN, Commission d’Enquête Chargée de Faire la Lumière, *Compte rendu* 26, 3; AN, Mission d’Information sur les Moyens de Daech, *Rapport d’information*, vol. 2, 271.
95. AN, Commission d’Enquête Relative aux Moyens Mis en Oeuvre par l’État, 817.
96. AN, Commission d’Enquête Chargée de Faire la Lumière, *Compte rendu 11*, 14.
97. AN, Commission d’Enquête Relative aux Moyens Mis en Oeuvre par l’État, 824; AN, *Hearing of Bernard Bajolet*, 861.
98. Christophe Cornevin, “Terrorisme: DGSE-DGSI, l’interview exclusive des chefs du renseignement,” *Le Figaro*, November 13, 2020.
99. Président de la République, *Décret no. 2023-295*.

100. Président de la République, *Décret no. 92-523*.
101. Dewatre cited in Toreau, "Le renseignement français dans la lutte contre l'islamisme armé," 290; Cousseran and Hayez, *Leçons sur le renseignement*, 41; AN, Commission de la Défense Nationale et des Forces Armées, *Compte rendu 49*, 13.
102. AN, Commission des Finances, *Rapport sur le renseignement par l'image*, 4, 53. See also Hofnung, "Au coeur de la DGSE."
103. AN, Commission de la Défense Nationale, *Projet de loi de finances pour 2009*, vol. 1, 18; AN, *Hearing of Corbin de Mangoux*, 2.
104. AN, Commission d'Enquête Chargée de Faire la Lumière, *Compte rendu 31*, 5.
105. Émié in Notin, *DGSE*, 20; Cyril Bensimon and Morgane Le Cam, "Mali: Dans la guerre de l'information, l'armée française réplique et accuse le Groupe Wagner," *Le Monde*, April 23, 2022.
106. AN, Commission de la Défense et des Forces Armées, *Compte rendu 47*, 9.
107. AN, Commission d'Enquête Relative aux Moyens Mis en Oeuvre par l'État, 894–95. The Bureau Central du Renseignement Pénitentiaire (Central Bureau of Prison Intelligence), Service Central du Renseignement Territorial (Central Territorial Intelligence Service), Direction du Renseignement de la Préfecture de Police (Intelligence Directorate of the Paris Police Prefectorate), and Sous-Direction de l'Anticipation Opérationnelle de la Direction des Opérations et de l'Emploi de la Gendarmerie Nationale (Sub-Directorate for Operational Foresight of the Directorate for Operations and Employment of the Gendarmerie) are also represented. See AN, *Rapport relatif à l'activité de la délégation parlementaire au renseignement pour l'année 2018*, 45.
108. Ranson in Bauer and Dupuis-Danon, *Les guetteurs*, 156.
109. Lawmakers make a similar argument in AN, *Le renforcement des forces spéciales françaises*. On Serval, see Cousseran and Hayez, *Leçons sur le renseignement*, 247–48.
110. Gomart, *Soldat de l'ombre*, 256–27; Follorou, "Renseignement." For an earlier verison of this claim by former Chief of Defense Staff Adm. Jacques Laxande (who helped to establish the COS in 1991), see Silberzahn, *Au coeur du secret*, 189–90; Faligot, Guisnel, and Kauffer, *Histoire politique*, 466.
111. Vadillo, "Les modalités du contrôle," 40–42.
112. Pannier and Schmitt, *French Defence Policy*, 16.
113. AN, *Loi no. 2007-1443*. For a detailed history of parliamentary oversight of intelligence in France, see Laurent, "Le contrôle parlementaire," 372–96.
114. AN, *Loi relative à la programmation militaire pour les années 2014 à 2019*; Laurent, "Le contrôle parlementaire," 393.
115. Conseil Constitutionnel, *Décision no. 2001-456 DC*. The commission cannot exert budgetary control over ongoing operations.
116. Conseil Constitutionnel, *Décision no. 2001-456 DC*. For overviews, see Chopin and Oudet, *Renseignement et sécurité*, 214; Laurent, "Le contrôle parlementaire," 393–95.
117. AN, *Loi 91-646*.
118. AN, Commission des Lois Constitutionnelles, *Rapport relatif à la prévention d'actes de terrorisme et au renseignement*, 124.
119. Bernard Émié in AN, *Rapport relatif à l'activité de la délégation parlementaire au renseignement pour l'année 2018*, vol. 2, 23.

120. Fundamental interests of the nation include national security, major foreign policy interests, major economic and scientific interests, preventing terrorism, organized crime, and collective violence. AN, *Loi no. 2015-912* (oversight regime for domestic intercepts); AN, *Loi no. 2015-1556* (regime for international intercepts). Prior to that, see AN, *Loi no. 91-646*.
121. These percentages are for 2019. AN, *Rapport relatif à l'activité de la délégation parlementaire au renseignement pour l'année 2019–2020*, 68–69.
122. Commission Nationale de Contrôle des Techniques de Renseignement, *Le contrôle exercé par la CNCTR*. In 2018 the commission issued negative opinions in only 7 percent of the cases it reviewed. See AN, *Rapport relatif à l'activité de la délégation parlementaire au renseignement pour l'année 2019–2020*, 52.
123. AN, *Rapport relatif à l'activité de la délégation parlementaire au renseignement pour l'année 2019–2020*, 98.
124. Jacques Follorou, "Renseignement: Le contrôle 'prégnant et exigeant' de la CNCTR," *Le Monde*, May 18, 2018.
125. Président de la République, *Décret no. 2014-833*.
126. Président de la République, *Décret no. 2014-833*, article 2.
127. Bernard Émié in AN, *Rapport relatif à l'activité de la délégation parlementaire au renseignement pour l'année 2018*, vol. 2, 25.
128. Oudet, "Une politique publique du renseignement."

3

Leadership

This chapter examines the leadership of the DGSE through the individuals who served as director general and their capacity to steer institutional adaptation. It explores their vision for the agency, the reforms they pursued, and the political context that shaped their impact. Leadership offers a crucial vantage point on change, revealing how adaptation unfolded not only through formal restructuring but also shifts in discourse, values, and assumptions.

The chapter begins by identifying key dimensions of intelligence leadership, then traces the DG's evolving relationship with France's senior political leaders. It maps trends in leadership before analyzing the backgrounds and reform strategies of successive directors. Though DGs wielded formal authority, their capacity to enact change depended on political support, institutional positioning, and their ability to align internal culture and practices with strategic goals. Over time, the cumulative efforts of these leaders and increased political support have improved the agency's position within the French state, modernized its structure and processes, and enhanced its image.

Framing Leadership

The analysis developed below adopts a leader-centric approach to examine how successive DGs managed to mobilize and transform France's foreign intelligence agency and perceptions of its role and performance both within and outside the agency. Spy chiefs are first and foremost organizational leaders who derive their authority from their position, but their influence depends on more than formal power.[1] Their mission is to make sure that their agency is adapted to its missions and that it fulfills these missions.[2] The challenges they and their agency confront are both exogenous and endogenous. They emerge from the threat environment, relations with policymakers, and broader society. They also originate within the agency, its structure, processes, and workforce.

Studying leadership involves examining how leaders have sought to implement changes to address these challenges. As this chapter shows, leaders can drive changes to organizational structures, processes, and capacities as well as more intangible aspects such as values, attitudes, and identity.[3] Increasingly in the contemporary era, spy chiefs need to construct and promote a positive image of their agency to muster support from intelligence officers, political overseers, and the nation.[4]

A variety of factors affect leaders' ability to implement their vision for change. These factors can be represented as a series of concentric circles, with the leader's qualities, attributes, and vision at the center; the organization, its structure, culture, processes, and capacities in the middle; and the broader administrative and political environment as the outermost circle.[5] A leader cannot implement change if their subordinates, peers, and political masters are not receptive to their vision for change.[6] Where available, the analysis also considers how leadership was perceived from below, acknowledging that authority within large bureaucracies often rests on more than rank.

Assessing the role and impact of leaders on organizations is notoriously difficult.[7] Isolating the impact of a single leader is methodologically challenging, particularly in a large organization like the DGSE that employs thousands of personnel. Memoirs, interviews, scholarly analyses, and media coverage provide a basis to paint impressionist portraits and trace how DGs envisioned and pursued change and how their efforts intersected with broader forces of adaptation and inertia. Some of these sources are problematic. Memoirs and interviews often read more like attempts to justify past decisions and enhance reputations rather than genuine assessments of performance. They tell us how DGs project their own leadership and how they see and want us to see their role as agents of change. While several leaders sought publicity, others have been much more discreet, and little information is available on their directorship.

Ultimately leaders serve an organization, and this frame provides a measure of their success. Did they manage to mobilize others to follow their vision? Did they improve the performance and perceptions of the DGSE?[8] The analysis that follows thus presents DGs' attributes and qualities, their vision for the agency and the strategy they followed, and the results they achieved. The following sections provide a general characterization of the relationship between DGSE leaders and top-level policymakers, before moving on to a chronological examination of successive DGs and the change they tried to produce.

For the President's Eyes Only?

The French Constitution assigns the president a central role in driving foreign and security policy. Within the administration, DGs are appointed by the president on the advice of the prime minister and the minister of armed forces, formally granting them significant executive authority. In practice, however, France's most senior policymakers have long preferred to keep their foreign intelligence agency and its directors at arm's length, delegating control to the small Bureau Réservé (Restricted Office).[9] This distance reflected the poor reputation of the SDECE and the DGSE, both for operational missteps and limited analytical value.[10]

With limited access to the president and poor integration into the broader French administration, early DGs lacked the political capital and network to overcome turf wars and administrative inertia. While the agency strived to produce relevant intelligence and covert options, its leaders often struggled to secure the means to implement the changes they had envisaged and capture policymakers' attention for the right reasons.

Over time, successive efforts gradually realigned the DGSE with shifts in the political and security environments—ranging from postcolonial crises to the rise of terrorism—and embedded it more firmly within the French state apparatus. The agency played a secondary, but not negligible, role in French foreign and security policy from 1982 to the end of the twentieth century. As terrorism rose on the political agenda in the twenty-first century, DGs began to carve out a greater role for the agency. Rising political support became particularly apparent following President

Nicolas Sarkozy's election (2007) and continued during the presidencies of François Hollande (2012–17) and Emmanuel Macron (2017–today), providing leaders with leverage to secure reforms and resources.

Presidents' preferences and their receptivity to and support for intelligence are crucial enablers of reform. DGSE leaders are political appointees who need political guidance and support to drive change. Presidents tend to nominate personalities they feel they can trust, not only to ensure loyalty but also to maintain indirect control over a secretive and sometimes volatile domain of statecraft. This does not mean that the DGs systematically receive instructions from the head of state. The French political system scatters political power, particularly given the dyarchy of a president (who makes the big decisions) and a prime minister (who is responsible for their implementation).

Several observers believe this institutional divide at the top of the French executive explains historical weaknesses in the intelligence-policy nexus. Another argument highlights shortcomings in "intelligence culture" among French political elites, who have struggled to grasp the utility and limitations of intelligence as an instrument of power.[11] For decades, DGs did not receive consolidated directives from political leaders, leading the service to largely self-direct. This ambiguity increased the risks of misalignment between intelligence efforts and policy needs.[12] The establishment of a coordinator for intelligence, explained in chapter 2, marked a turning point that significantly improved the intelligence-policy nexus over the past decade.

Figure 3.1. places France's successive presidents and the thirteen DGs they appointed in a timeline ranging from the start of François Mitterrand's presidency (1981) to today. The timing of the appointments confirms the political nature of the process. Since 1982 most electoral swings have been followed by the nomination of a new director. President Mitterrand served two mandates of seven years, during which he appointed six directors. He clearly struggled to find the right fit, nominating a new DG on average every two years. This instability can also be explained by periods of "cohabitation," when prime ministers led Center-Right governments (Jacques Chirac from 1986 to 1988 and Édouard Balladur from 1993 to 1995) under a Center-Left or Socialist presidency, and vice versa with Socialist PM Lionel Jospin (from 1997 to 2002) serving

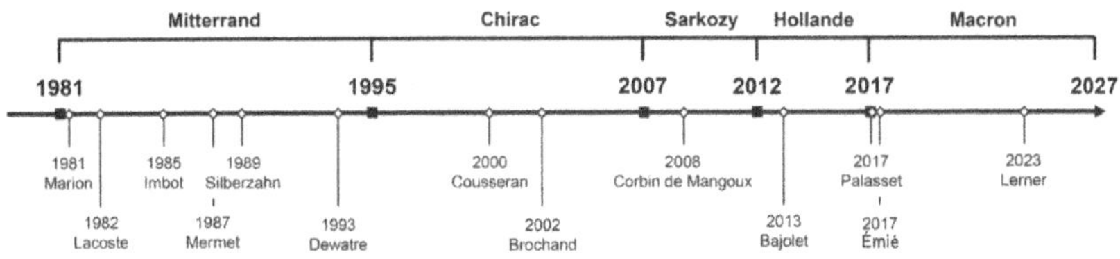

Figure 3.1: Presidents and directors general of External Security, 1981–2025[13]

under Center-Right President Jacques Chirac (1995–2007). This situation, which results from the dyarchy of heads of state and government in the French political system, creates political tensions at the top of the executive and often leads to new appointments requiring approval from both.[14] Since the last period of cohabitation in 2002, Presidents Sarkozy (Center-Right) and Hollande (Center-Left) have both kept their predecessor's DG in their post for a year following their election; President Macron did not keep DG Bernard Bajolet in his post following his election. The DGSE was initially led by an interim DG (Gen. Jean-Pierre Palasset, who was Bajolet's chief of staff) for just over a month before the appointments of Bernard Émié and more recently of Nicolas Lerner.

The Directors General

When François Mitterrand began his first term as president, he appointed Pierre Marion as the head of the SDECE. A senior executive from the private sector, Marion had no military background beyond conscription. He was followed by three general officers—from the navy, army, and air force—a sequence that suggests President Mitterrand was keen to maintain a balance between the three branches of the French military. Since 1989 all the DGs (apart from Acting Director Palasset's brief tenure) have been civilians, with experience as a prefect (top-ranking public servant) or an ambassador. This shift reflects the increasing civilianization of the agency's senior personnel and its gradual integration into the elite networks of the French administration (see chapter 2).

A closer look at the profiles of DGSE leaders reveals some interesting trends. The DGs are men aged between forty-five and sixty years old when taking their position. With an average age of fifty-six on the day of their nomination, all but one of them (Lerner) were in the closing stage of their careers. DGSE leaders are primarily selected for political reasons and not for their backgrounds in intelligence. Three out of twelve DGs (Jacques Dewatre, Jean-Claude Cousseran, and Palasset) served in the SDECE or DGSE before their appointment. No DG was a career intelligence officer. This approach contrasts with the British SIS, where most directors since World War II have had experience in intelligence. This difference can be explained by the character of the two agencies. The integrated nature of the DGSE requires generalists, while the SIS's narrower focus on HUMINT underlines the importance of professional experience in leading intelligence operations. At the DGSE, subordinate (i.e., deputy) directors tend to provide the professional background and expertise the DG often lacks. The director of strategy had always been a diplomat until the 2022 reform and the appointment of a civil servant as secretary-general for analysis and strategy. The director of operations (now director of research and operations) is always a two-star general, and the technical director an engineer with a specialization in telecommunications. The DR was led by generals (1980s), senior police officers (1990s and 2000s), a diplomat, and a career DGSE officer before it was dissolved by the 2022 reform. Finally, prefects with experience in the Ministry of the Interior tend to lead the DA. At this secondary level of leadership, the directors have also always been men that are well advanced in their career.[15]

Figure 3.2 represents the length of each DG's tenure. The average term of a general directorship is 3.5 years (excluding the current DG, Lerner), with a range from one month for Acting Director Palasset to over six years (eighty months) for DG Dewatre. Paradoxically, a lot of information is available on Pierre Marion, who served the shortest tenure of all the DGs, and very little information is available on Dewatre, who led the agency for the longest time. The remainder of the chapter provides an overview of DGs' profiles, their initial diagnostic and vision for the agency, and the change they oversaw. Four subsections emphasize their backgrounds, following a loosely chronological order. The DGSE was first led by an outsider from the private sector (1982), followed by three general officers (1982–89), three prefects (1989–99, 2008–13), and four diplomats (1999–2008, 2013–23).

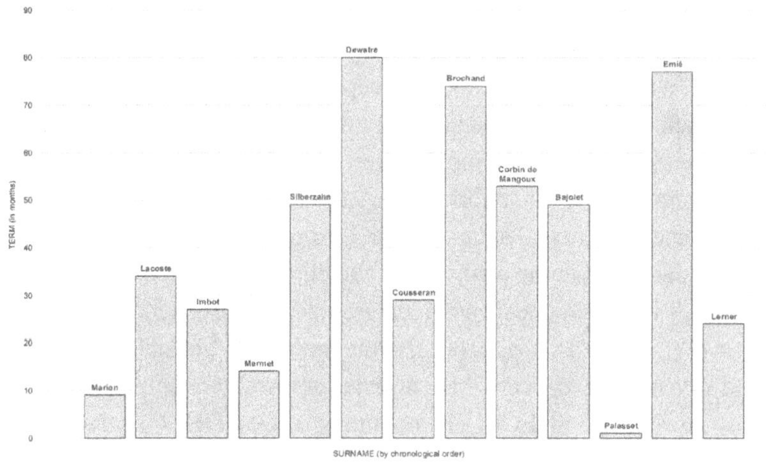

Figure 3.2: Longevity of the directors general, 1982–2025.

The CEO

François Mitterrand's election marked a turning point in French political and intelligence history. In the late 1970s, the Socialist Party considered dismantling the foreign intelligence service due to concerns about its lack of legal basis, perceived militarization, and hostility toward the Left. The party eventually opted for reform.[16] Mitterrand's accession to the presidency and the nomination of Communist Party members as ministers in his government alarmed both Western allies and French securocrats in the context of the (new) Cold War.[17] Alexandre de Marenches, an aristocrat who led the SDECE from 1970 to 1981, was a fervent anticommunist who resigned and refused to support the transition to his successor. A wave of officers who placed political loyalty over their duty to the republic similarly preferred to leave the agency.

On June 17, 1981, President Mitterrand nominated Pierre Marion—a senior executive in the air and space industry—as director of the SDECE. By his own reckoning, Marion had no real experience in intelligence and a limited understanding of security issues.[18] His career in the industry equipped him with managerial and negotiation skills, and he had international experience in the United States and East Asia. Marion was a man of networks who owed his nomination to his friendship with then–Defense Minister Charles Hernu, with whom he shared political views and membership in a Masonic lodge. Hernu had put forward a friend on whom he felt both he and the president could rely.[19]

Marion was, by all accounts, a disruptive figure.[20] His two memoirs reveal a lack of discretion and tact that do not align with what one would expect from a spy chief. Marion does not spare criticisms of the SDECE, French administrative and political elites, and international partners.[21] His reminiscences also reveal a lucid understanding of the diminished role of France in the world in the postwar era and elites' illusions of grandeur.[22]

Marion's initial diagnosis painted a troubled picture: a factional, technologically outdated service, poorly integrated into the state and led by second-rate military officers.[23] He initiated a series of reforms that would durably reorient the SDECE. The renaming of the SDECE as the DGSE followed an internal reorganization and was accompanied by an effort to formalize recruitment and formation and further civilianize the agency's cadres.[24] This was an important decision that enabled the DGSE to professionalize and diversify its workforce. Marion's background in aerospace made him particularly aware of the need to develop the agency's technical capabilities. He established a science, technology, and economic intelligence unit and sought to bring the DGSE closer to the French defense industry.[25] He also sought to develop the production of the agency—for example, by establishing a division for foresight, planning, and evaluation that developed a weekly evaluation of international events.[26] However, poor access to policymakers—who held the agency in low esteem—hindered these initiatives.[27]

An impatient leader, Marion grew frustrated. As an outsider he had a limited understanding of French bureaucratic and political idiosyncrasies and lacked networks in the public sector and the military. Soon key relationships turned sour. The DG felt he did not receive sufficient guidance and support from President Mitterrand (whom he met once a month on average).[28] Both Mitterrand and his defense minister preferred to delegate the matter to their advisers.[29] Marion's authoritarian leadership style and bad temper affected his relationship with DGSE personnel.[30] Following a series of public controversies and terrorist attacks, President Mitterrand grew concerned with Marion's leadership.[31] Marion himself had lost respect for the president, whom he describes as "my principal problem,"[32] adding that "his main strength resides in his gigantic egocentrism that is not tempered by any moral sense."[33] His directorship had become unsustainable, and he submitted his resignation.[34] No outsider from the private sector has led the DGSE since.

In eighteen months at the helm—the shortest director's tenure since 1946—Marion's disruptive leadership succeeded in identifying big directions and providing an initial impulse that set France's foreign intelligence agency on a reform trajectory. Nevertheless, his abrasive personality, difficult relationship with the president, and the gulf that continued to separate the DGSE from the rest of the French state significantly hampered his ability to bring about change.

The General Officers

Marion's successor, Vice Adm. Pierre Lacoste, was a much less controversial figure, but his tenure (1982–85) is remembered for the worst fiasco in the DGSE's history: the sinking of Greenpeace's flagship, the *Rainbow Warrior*. Lacoste was eighteen years old when he escaped France's unoccupied zone in 1942 to join the French Navy in North Africa. He pursued his entire career in the navy, rising to the rank of vice admiral before President Mitterrand followed the advice of Defense Minister Hernu and nominated him to lead the DGSE.[35] The French daily *Le Monde* presents him as a "classic" military officer, a "prudent and courteous" figure.[36] His leadership style reportedly fostered loyalty on the part of his subordinates.[37]

His nomination came as a surprise to him. Lacoste reports he had some concern about serving a Socialist president known for his political maneuvers. However, he concluded that as Mitterrand served as president, the man's personal ambition would align with the national interest. Duty to his country prevailed.[38] Lacoste was the first naval officer to lead France's foreign intelligence agency.[39] His career equipped him with technical knowledge and an understanding of strategy, defense planning, and leadership. As a former military adviser to the defense minister and the prime minister, he was familiar with the French administration and had contributed to intelligence coordination meetings.[40] This background placed him in a good position to pursue the reforms launched by Marion.[41]

Lacoste's diagnosis echoed Marion's: The service was fragmented and poorly linked to the rest of the French administration. Some regions of the world—including important targets such as the Soviet Union—were not well covered, while others such as Africa were more prominent, but the agency's production there was undermined by the subsistence of parallel networks of influence. Morale was low.[42] The admiral identified three urgent priorities: Reform the status of personnel and further civilianize the workforce to improve recruitment, upgrade infrastructure and equipment, and modernize core processes.[43] Lacoste continued investing in technical capabilities and elevated technical intelligence into a new directorate.[44] He was aware of the need to improve the DGSE production but recognized this would require efforts across the entire intelligence cycle.[45] He was keen for the DGSE to develop better relations with the Ministry of Foreign Affairs and pushed heads of geographic sections to hold periodic meetings with their counterparts at the Quai d'Orsay.[46] Despite his good intentions, Lacoste lacked authority and political capital to improve relationships with his domestic counterpart, the DST.[47]

Admiral Lacoste's relationship with Mitterrand was cordial but distant. He would disturb the president only for big and particularly sensitive decisions and met with him around fifteen times over a three-year period (every two to three months on average). His primary interlocutor at the Elysée, the chief of the military staff of the president (*chef de l'état-major particulier*), seemed to have limited interest in the DGSE. Lacoste coordinated more frequently with the chief of staff of the prime minister on interceptions and counterterrorism issues and found more receptive consumers in the defense minister's cabinet.[48]

Lacoste's tenure was marked by a series of incidents. On October 23, 1983, the Beirut barracks bombing killed 241 US and 58 French military personnel. The DGSE pinned responsibility on Iran and attempted a punitive operation again the Iranian embassy in Lebanon, which protected the terrorists. Service Action operators failed to detonate a car they had loaded with explosives and placed in front of the embassy. Lacoste thinks friction (the gap between plans and reality) and bad luck explain this failure. Policymakers more readily linked it to incompetence, and Lacoste was forced to fire the commanding officer of the SA.[49] Operational successes, such as tracking the infamous Nazi war criminal Klaus Barbie with the help of Bolivian authorities who arrested him in February 1983, were overshadowed by the fiasco that followed.[50]

On the evening of July 10, 1985, DGSE frogmen sank the *Rainbow Warrior*, the flagship of the environmental organization Greenpeace, which was moored off New Zealand. The sabotage inadvertently killed a photographer, leading to the arrest of two DGSE officers who were under nonofficial cover. French political authorities refused to acknowledge responsibility for the operation despite mounting public evidence of their involvement, and the failure escalated into a fiasco.[51] Eventually, Defense Minister Hernu was forced to resign—a tacit recognition of his responsibility—and Admiral Lacoste followed him. More than a decade later, Lacoste confirmed he had received a green light from the president to conduct an operation. What this authorization allowed was and remains up to interpretation. Lacoste acknowledges that the operational scenario he had validated "was not defensible," too complicated, and risky. Besides operational errors, the fiasco epitomized the gulf that continued to separate intelligence and policy in France. Vague political directives left too much room for interpretation, and operators oversold their capabilities to act covertly and failed to mitigate the full range of risks. In his own words, Lacoste would leave a poisonous legacy for his successors.[52] In addition to the human consequences, the reputation of the DGSE was durably affected.

Following the *Rainbow Warrior* controversy, political authorities were keen to restore authority and order. President Mitterrand nominated another general officer with a stellar record and a reputation for loyalty and discipline.[53] Gen. René Imbot was a resistant during World War II who then served in the Foreign Legion for twenty years. In 1983 he became chief of staff of the army, liaising closely with the defense minister to lead an important reform.[54] Shortly after his appointment in 1985, the new DG appeared on national television in uniform to announce that he had "cut off the rotten branches" and "locked up" the service. Taking stock of the *Rainbow Warrior* debacle, he disbanded the SA and moved its frogmen from Aspretto in Corsica to the colder waters of Quélern in Brittany.[55]

Though Imbot's career equipped him with an understanding of intelligence, he was neither a diplomat with a fine understanding of international affairs nor a connoisseur of the French administration. His background and the weight of political expectations for him to restore order limited his ability to reform the agency. Imbot pursued efforts to modernize the agency's information technology infrastructure and sought to update the status of agency personnel to align it to the status of other civil servants.[56] The DGSE continued to struggle with recruitment and retention of specialized personnel and the quality of its production.[57] Imbot left the DGSE in 1987, having reached retirement age.

Following Lacoste (navy) and Imbot's (army) tenures, President Mitterrand nominated Gen. François Mermet (air force) to lead the DGSE (1987–89). These nominations underline the persisting military character of the DGSE hierarchy.[58] Mermet's nomination followed the end of a period of cohabitation. His experience working with senior policymakers—liaising with Defense Minister Giraud to reform the French nuclear experiments center and serving as a military adviser at the Elysée—explains why he was picked.[59]

In Mermet's first meeting with the president, Mitterrand repeated a familiar critique of the DGSE: poor coordination with domestic services, flawed operations, and subpar production. It lacked the capabilities and clout to shape foreign and security policy.[60]

The beginning of Mermet's tenure was marked by terrorist attacks, the death of a DGSE officer, and a hostage situation in Lebanon. This was a period when Islamist terrorism spilled over from the Soviet-Afghan War and rose on the political agenda. The agency started to focus more of its sensors and work on the terrorist threat from North Africa, the Middle East, and South Asia. Mermet's initial diagnosis identified three problems. First, the DGSE staff was too small to cope with its range of missions. Second, the agency continued to have a recruitment problem. Promising military officers did not want to sacrifice their career by joining an agency in disrepute, and civilian recruitment was hampered by the lack of visibility of the service. Third, technical means remained insufficient to support cryptography and data processing and dissemination. With access to only one satellite, the agency faced difficult decisions on whether to prioritize the focus of the Ministry of Foreign Affairs on the Iran-Iraq War or the Ministry of Defense's focus on Chad.[61] Mermet decided to invest in data-processing capabilities and managed to expand DGSE access to satellite platforms.[62]

The air force general reports excellent relations with the Ministry of Foreign Affairs.[63] However, the DGSE continued to be embroiled in turf battles with the DST and the military establishment. The agency's paramilitary branch ran into problems during his tenure, losing two of its members in the assault of the Ouvéa cave in the French territory of New Caledonia. This unfortunate event followed the rise of the independentist movement in the French Pacific islands. Among other reforms, Mermet emphasizes his efforts to impose new methods on the SA, including closer political and hierarchical control of its operations and more systematic contingency planning. Mermet also pursued his predecessors' efforts to build the economic intelligence capabilities of the service. He remembers the agency used HUMINT assets to support the French position in European negotiations for a common agricultural policy and to develop a better understanding of US trade policy toward France.[64] Mermet also made a controlled effort to "open" the service to selected outsiders—briefing parliamentarians and some journalists—with the authorization of the defense minister.

Mermet was forced to leave his post when the Socialists won the legislative elections, thus ending a period of cohabitation. Both Mitterrand and new Socialist Prime Minister Michel Rocard reportedly wanted another director at the helm to demonstrate political control over the agency.[65] Rocard's interest in intelligence and his support for the DGSE—whose headquarters he visited in December 1988—would provide the agency with some of the political support it had long been lacking.[66]

The Prefects

Claude Silberzahn's tenure (1989–93) durably changed the agency's structure and brought it closer to the rest of the French administration. His directorship was a turning point, marked by the end of the Cold War and by a rapprochement between the DGSE and senior policymakers—a shift that enabled significant reform and put the DGSE on a path toward normalization.

When Mitterrand nominated him, Silberzahn was an experienced prefect, with a lifelong interest in the French overseas territories. This background meant he had an intimate understanding of the French administration and a first-rate professional network. Though he was not formally affiliated with the Socialist Party, his experience—working as an adviser for Socialist Prime Minister Laurent Fabius (1984–86)—and reputation placed him on the center-left of the political spectrum. When Mitterrand asked him what he wanted for his career at the start of his second mandate in 1989, Silberzahn expressed his desire to lead the DGSE.[67] The *Rainbow Warrior* crisis had convinced him the agency's distance from the state apparatus had made it unmanageable. Mitterrand's decision to appoint a prefect rather than a general reflected a desire to further demilitarize DGSE leadership. This likely stemmed from frustration with military figures and doubts about their loyalty, especially after forty-five retired general officers publicly urged voters to support Center-Right candidate Jacques Chirac.

Silberzahn's good relations with the president, the prime minister, and the defense minister provided him with significant political capital. At the Elysée, his main interlocutor was the president's chief of staff, also a prefect. Following his nomination, Prime Minister Rocard discussed the DGSE's poor integration and production with the president, who gave him the green light to reform the service.[68] Silberzahn's nuanced understanding of the French administrative apparatus, coupled with the necessary political support, placed him in a powerful position to implement his vision for change.[69] His initial assessment was not fundamentally different than his predecessors'. The agency's TECHINT and HUMINT capabilities were outdated. Its culture remained predominantly military. The organization was heavily divided, and morale was low. Silberzahn set himself two main objectives: to build stronger foundations through clear missions, structures, and methods and to give the agency its due place within the institutions of the republic.[70]

With the prime minister's approval, Silberzahn established two new directorates (focusing on strategy and operations) and elevated all the agency's directorates into "central administration directorates," thus making them more powerful.[71] The Conseil des Ministres (Council of Ministers, the highest executive decision-making body in the French government) would now appoint the agency's (deputy) directors by decree, a move that ostensibly linked these leaders to political authorities. The Directorate of Strategy—presented in chapter 2—became the more visible face of the agency, seeking to align outputs with the needs of foreign and security policymakers. Silberzahn appointed a seasoned diplomat, who would take the pulse of French foreign policy, to lead this directorate. The Directorate of Operations became the only directorate led by a military officer. Gen. Jean Heinrich, who led the directorate at the time, remembers that Silberzahn's reform was well received, made sense, and rebalanced capabilities away from Directorate of Intelligence, which had become too important.[72] A senior police officer would now lead the DR, and an experienced civil administrator the DA.[73] The DT was left largely untouched but benefited from further investment to develop its data-processing and SIGINT capabilities.[74] These changes brought the DGSE closer to the standards of the French administration and improved coordination across ministries. To further oil the cogs of the state machinery, Silberzahn made a deliberate effort to socialize with his peers in other agencies and ministries. For instance, he used his affiliation with the prefectorial corps—a senior civil service body responsible for ensuring the enforcement of national laws and policies at the regional and departmental level—to smooth tensions and improve coordination with the DST.[75]

When he took the reins of the agency, two-third of its workforce was civilian, but military officers continued to hold 90 percent of the senior executive positions within the agency. Rank trumped competence. Silberzahn wanted all personnel to benefit from a similar status, whether they were military, civilian, or contractors, but he lacked time to complete this reform.[76] He did, however, pursue the civilianization of the agency personnel, establishing a civil service examination to recruit more senior and educated civil servants.[77] He also facilitated mobility; personnel could now spend a few years at the Ministry of Foreign Affairs, for example.[78]

For some intelligence leaders, the public's ignorance about France's intelligence activities was seen as proof of a professionalism based on secrecy. However, Silberzahn recognized that this approach created a perception of inactivity and widened the gap between decision-makers and the agency.[79] He reinforced the controlled effort to communicate more publicly about the DGSE's role and capabilities, giving two interviews to *Le Monde*.[80] The DS would pursue this effort behind closed doors.

Silberzahn's mandate ended when a period of cohabitation began in 1993. A new, Center-Right prime minister—Édouard Balladur—required his departure.[81] Silberzahn is rightly remembered as a transformative leader, whose structural reforms lasted three decades. Following his passing, the DGSE offered a rare public comment, writing that "he left a strong memory among the personnel and a real mark on the service, notably in terms of governance, diversity of recruitment, and the principle of collegiality in decision-making."[82] His director of strategy, who would go on to serve as DG a few years later, remembers Silberzahn set a new atmosphere, new norms, and a simple structure for the agency.[83] Yet, looking back at his time at the helm, Silberzahn could not help but express continuing concern about the poor integration of the DGSE into national decision-making.[84]

His successor, Jacques Dewatre, was also a prefect, whose nomination garnered support from both Mitterrand and Balladur.[85] Dewatre had served in the military for sixteen years, including a period of time in the shock troops used by the SA of the SDECE, before he moved on to the civil service at the end of the Algerian War of Independence.[86] Dewatre had significant experience as a civil servant, leading the cabinet of the minister of cooperation in the early 1980s before being appointed prefect in 1985. His directorship (1993–2000) was the longest of any DG (excluding the last director of the SDECE, Alexandre de Marenches). He was able to navigate changing political waters, serving a Socialist president cohabiting with a Center-Right government and then a Center-Right president—Jacques Chirac—who had distrusted intelligence services since his time as a conscript during the Algerian war.[87]

Despite his seven years at the helm, very little information is available on Dewatre's directorship. At least two key issues rose onto the agency's agenda during his tenure: counterterrorism and the wars in Bosnia and Kosovo. Dewatre claims around three hundred officers were assigned to counterterrorism during his tenure.[88] For *Le Monde*, Dewatre kept too low a profile when the conflicts in the former Yugoslavia emerged.[89] His distant leadership and poor communication reportedly created a divide between senior officers and the rank-and-file.[90] DGSE officers were allegedly frustrated with his decision to sideline a reform of their status—a recurring issue—as well as the project to move the agency's headquarters to a bigger and more appropriate infrastructure.[91]

The Diplomats

Jean-Claude Cousseran (1999–2002) was the first diplomat to lead the DGSE. Cousseran spent most of his career in the Middle East, holding posts in Beirut, Baghdad, and Tehran and then serving as an ambassador to Syria and Turkey. He also served in the cabinet of the minister of defense and helped to establish and lead the DS at the DGSE.[92]

Cousseran is the first DG who reports making a positive diagnosis upon taking office. He remembers that "the structure was simple and the responsibilities were clearly defined between directorates, personnel were better recruited and formed, more diverse and younger, the budget was healthy and growing."[93] Yet problems persisted. Compartmentalization between directorates hampered coordination, and tensions with the DST and the DRM endured. Cousseran reports that his relationship with political authorities lacked structure and regrets the absence of political guidance to develop a more coherent strategy for the service. Like his predecessors, he met with the president only occasionally, and his relationship with the prime minister and his office was largely procedural, except in matters of counterterrorism and coordination. His most structured and systematic relationship was with the Ministry of Defense, under whose authority the DGSE is administratively placed.[94]

Under his directorship, the agency pursued its reorientation away from the Cold War to focus on the terrorist threat, which reached the top of the political agenda following the September 11 attacks. Writing about the attacks, Cousseran remembers the DGSE, like its American counterparts, had identified several signals but did not sufficiently connect them and anticipate the full range of possible implications.[95] This failure underlined the difficulty of discerning changes in terrorist movements' intentions, capabilities, and strategies. While France and its services had confronted terrorism throughout the 1980s and 1990s,[96] the attacks proved a political turning point, prompting two decades of investments in intelligence personnel and technical capabilities. With the start of the War in Afghanistan (2001–21), the DGSE revived its historical contacts with the Northern Alliance and grew increasingly concerned about the influence of terrorist movements in the Sahel region of Africa.[97]

Internally, Cousseran reinforced the means available to the DG. He oversaw the creation of the agency's situation center and established a position of legal counsel and an office of the inspector general to better control the agency. He reorganized the directorate of intelligence into two services, one focusing on security (terrorism, proliferation, organized crime, and economic subversion) and another on political intelligence across a series of geographic areas. By the time he took office, the modernization of the Technical Directorate had already significantly increased the agency's ability to collect and process intercepts. The main challenge was to reform the legal basis to use these techniques and to rethink the pooling of responsibilities and resources with other services.[98]

Cousseran's departure followed the end of another period of

cohabitation. It was reportedly precipitated by President Chirac's concern about an investigation the DGSE had been asked to conduct on Japanese financial influence. A rumor had emerged that the president had become a person of interest in the agency's investigation.[99] Looking back on his tenure, Cousseran points out the persistent distance between political authorities and the DGSE and shares two main regrets. First, he did not manage to elevate the role of analysis within the DGSE. Second, he did not sufficiently reinforce the agency's capacities to understand sociopolitical developments in the Sahel, the Mediterranean region, and the Middle East.[100] Nonetheless, his reform of the means available to the DG outlasted his tenure. He led the agency at a historical turning point, after which senior policymakers started to pay much more attention to France's foreign intelligence capabilities.[101]

Cousseran's successor, Pierre Brochand (2002–8), was also a diplomat and the first graduate of the prestigious École Nationale d'Administration (ENA; National School of Administration) to lead the DGSE. The centrality of this school in the production of French administrative and political elite is hard to overstate. The accession of an ENA graduate at the head of the DGSE is another sign that the agency was progressively completing its integration into the core executive. After graduating from the ENA, Brochand led a successful career as a diplomat, serving as an ambassador to Hungary, Israel, and Portugal. He was close to Jacques Chirac and his foreign minister, Dominique de Villepin.[102]

Brochand's tenure cemented the rapprochement between the DGSE and France's most senior policymakers. Under his leadership, the agency piloted important hostage negotiations in Afghanistan, Iraq, and off the Somalian coast.[103] These missions demonstrated the DGSE's operational capacity and political relevance. Ahead of the US-led war in Iraq in 2003, the DGSE produced thorough reports to independently evaluate American and British assertions that Saddam Hussein was pursuing a weapons of mass destruction program. While it is unclear how extensively policymakers read or relied on these reports, they ultimately opposed the war. The DGSE production likely underscored its value to French political leaders—always eager to showcase France's role in counterbalancing the dominance of the Anglo-American special relationship on the global stage.[104]

During Brochand's tenure, the agency continued the expansion of its SIGINT capabilities, most notably through investments in cryptanalysis and decryption.[105] The DG also pursued the limited opening of the agency, supporting the publication of a special issue on the DGSE in a French Army magazine and inviting selected journalists to visit the DGSE.[106] In an interview, he explained the agency could not escape increasing mediatization and needed to shape its public image to counter stereotypes while preserving secrecy.[107]

Brochand's tenure was marked by broader intelligence reforms. The French defense and national security doctrine elevated "knowledge and anticipation" as a core strategic function and emphasized the role of intelligence in dealing with an increasingly complex array of threats. Soon afterward, the president established the CNR, and Parliament set up a delegation focusing on intelligence oversight. The end of Brochand's directorship followed the appointment of the first national coordinator for intelligence—another diplomat, Bernard Bajolet.

His successor, Erard Corbin de Mangoux, was not a diplomat but rather a former naval commissioner and senior civil servant who had worked with Nicolas Sarkozy when he was minister of the interior. From 2007 to 2008 he served as a domestic affairs adviser to President Sarkozy at the Elysée, a role in which he also monitored intelligence issues.[108] Sarkozy elevated him to the rank of prefect and nominated him as DG in 2008. His tenure (2008–13) saw growing political attention and investment, helping the DGSE to catch up with the British and German services.[109] The nomination of a DG with a more domestic profile and the establishment of a national coordinator for intelligence was expected to bring the DGSE and the DGSI closer at a time when counterterrorism continued to dominate the agenda.[110]

Corbin de Mangoux led an important internal reform of the status of senior civil servants at the DGSE, establishing a position of DGSE administrator comparable to the civil administrators found elsewhere in the French administration. This reform eased senior executives' mobility and pursued the integration of the agency into the fabric of the French state.[111] The DG initiated an internal survey to identify the agency's core values: loyalty, exigency, discretion, adaptability.[112] He also pursued the controlled public communication effort of the agency, giving a rare interview to a French academic journal on international affairs to explain the role of the DGSE.

When Socialist candidate François Hollande became president, he retained Corbin de Mangoux in his position for several months before parting ways with a director that—he felt—did not communicate enough information on some of its operations.[113] Hollande nominated the former national coordinator for intelligence and then ambassador to Afghanistan Bernard Bajolet to the helm of the DGSE in April 2013. Bajolet had graduated from the ENA before pursuing a successful career as a diplomat. A fluent Arabic speaker, he held a series of posts in North Africa and the Middle East before serving as an ambassador in Jordan, Bosnia-Herzegovina, Iraq, Algeria, and Afghanistan. In these "hot" countries, he witnessed firsthand the rise of terrorism and political violence.[114] As an ambassador he gained experience as a consumer of intelligence and managed difficult hostage negotiations together with the DGSE.[115] In his memoir, Bajolet presents himself as a "not so diplomatic ambassador" who does not hesitate to speak his mind,[116] and he comes across as a curious and passionate diplomat. Bajolet knew President Hollande personally. In the late 1970s he supervised and befriended Hollande, then an ENA student completing an internship at the French embassy in Algiers. In Bajolet's words, Hollande wanted a DG he had complete trust in.[117] His direct access to the president reportedly caused frictions with the Ministry of Defense, whose leaders were not systematically kept in the loop.[118]

Bajolet's tenure (2013–17) was marked by a series of terrorist attacks, starting in 2013 and culminating with the coordinated attacks in Paris on November 13, 2015 (see box below). President Hollande's response was firm and involved a series of reprisals against perpetrators linked with the Islamic State. Bajolet thus oversaw the rise of aggressive covert action against terrorist networks. He relied on his experience as a diplomat to supervise several hostage crises together with the Ministry of Foreign Affairs and the Office of the President, six of which were resolved before his departure. Several hostages did not survive, including DGSE officer Denis Allex, who was executed by al-Shabaab during a failed rescue attempt by an SA commando team (see chapter 4).[119]

Success and Failure

The 2015 attacks in Paris were the deadliest France experienced since the end of World War II. The attacks were planned outside France and organized in Belgium. From this perspective, they constitute a significant intelligence failure for the DGSE as well as for the DGSI—since they took place on the national territory.

The DGSE was aware of the intentions and threat posed by Abdelhamid Abaaoud, the coordinator of the attacks.[120] The agency had been monitoring his network since January 2015, following a terrorist plot by the "Verviers group," which the DGSE helped Belgian authorities thwart.[121] The DGSI was also aware of Abaaoud but did not consider him a priority. The attackers used covert methods, minimal communication, and a compartmentalized cell structure, which limited opportunities for detection. Despite deploying technical and human means, and relying on international cooperation to anticipate and disrupt terrorist threats, the French services and their European partners failed to locate Abaaoud before the attacks. They knew he had visited Syria but not that he had returned to France, which became clear only after the November 13 attacks.[122]

While this was a clear failure to prevent a known threat, the DGSE reportedly found no major error on its part. If accurate, this suggests that the pieces of the puzzle at the time were simply not sufficient to anticipate the full picture. One valid criticism would then remain that the agency's sensors and analysis were not sufficiently aligned to anticipate this specific threat. For Bajolet, who led the agency at the time, the DGSE lacked neither the means nor the resources; it simply could not prevent every attack. Yves Trotignon, a former DGSE officer who left the agency several years earlier, prefers to emphasize a broader range of structural issues, including the methods and operational practices of the agency, its training, and leadership.[123]

While he recognized the 2015 failure, Bajolet was also keen to counterbalance this narrative:

> Since January 2013, my service has contributed to the conception, planning, and conduct of sixty-nine operations that disrupted terrorist threats: Twelve have allowed us to prevent attacks against French interests abroad, six were projects of attacks likely to target Western interests, . . . and fifty-one operations have sought to reduce the terrorist threat through arrests, uncovering of plots, and disrupting terrorists.

continued on next page

continued

> [The DG later explains this means to neutralize through arrests and other means.] These operations have taken place in the following regions, by descending order: sub-Saharan Africa, the Afghan-Pakistani zone, the Horn of Africa, Syria, Europe, Libya, and Egypt. . . . Our role has been to transmit intelligence to our partners to enable them to prevent terrorist attacks in twenty-nine cases, and in forty operations we have directly contributed to these operations. Sometimes the sources were solely human sources, but more often the information came from human and technical [means].[124]

Steady investments and reforms culminating in 2015 (see chapter 2) strengthened the DGSE. The agency's expanding role in counterterrorism, along with the warning signaled by public outrage following the 2013 global surveillance disclosures by former NSA contractor Edward Snowden in the United States, underlined the need "to show the role of intelligence in securing France and French people."[125] Bajolet was a very public director who wrote articles that presented the DGSE as a "tool to reduce uncertainty" and underlined "the democratic character" of the agency and its missions.[126] Under his directorship, the DS structured its outreach efforts to enroll experts that could support strategic analysis.[127]

After two extensions of his directorship, Bajolet retired in 2017 after Macron's election. According to *Le Monde*, Bajolet's style, his desire to maintain a direct link with the president, his activism and visibility, and his disputes with the chief of the defense staff—especially over defending the capabilities of the SA against those of the Special Operations Command—had left him politically isolated.

Macron decided to nominate a more moderate diplomat, Bernard Émié.[128] Émié had also developed significant expertise on North Africa and the Middle East throughout his career. A seasoned diplomat, both Presidents Sarkozy and Hollande entrusted him with major ambassadorships in Lebanon, Turkey, and the United Kingdom.[129] These positions brought him into direct contact with DGSE directors to manage hostage situations and kidnappings.[130] Bipartisan support made him an ideal candidate in the eyes of Macron, whose party sought to disrupt French politics through the rise of a centrist political group. Macron himself is said to be "an intelligence buff" and has already visited the DGSE headquarters at least twice.[131]

Two main points have emerged from Émié's directorship (2017–23). First, he directed the most significant reform of the DGSE since DG Silberzahn's tenure at the end of the Cold War. This overhaul, covered in chapter 2, reorganized the internal structure of the agency and formalized changes to the status of its employees.[132] After nearly two decades of investments and growth, DG Émié also managed to secure a costly move to a new headquarters. These are significant achievements that testify to the level of political support he was able to secure. He also pursued the agency's public communication efforts. Under his leadership the agency's communication strategy emphasized its bonds with Free France,[133] presumably to build a stronger sense of belonging and loyalty to the service. Other communication efforts have emphasized the DGSE's cooperation with the DGSI as well as coordination with the French armed forces to warn of possible terrorist attacks in Europe and "neutralize" senior jihadists in the Sahel.[134] Émié remains the only director to use a Twitter (now X) account. He joined the platform before his nomination as DG and primarily used it to promote the memory of the Resistance.

Bernard Émié was on course to become the longest-serving DG when President Macron decided to replace him with Nicolas Lerner. French journalists cite the accumulation of setbacks during the final years of Émié's tenure—most notably the failure to anticipate Russia's invasion of Ukraine in 2022 and a wave of coups in the Sahel—as key factors behind his departure.[135]

Nicolas Lerner led France's domestic intelligence agency before he took the helm of the DGSE in January 2024. At forty-five years of age, he is the agency's youngest director. A graduate of the ENA from the same class as Macron, Lerner built most of his career at the Ministry of the Interior, gaining extensive experience in security matters. Known for his attentive leadership, he has already begun reshaping the agency, including a revamp of the agency's internal security structure.[136]

Conclusion

There is a striking continuity in how successive DGs diagnosed the DGSE's core problems and envisioned its reform. Across decades, leaders identified the same recurring challenges: weak integration into the French state, poor alignment with intelligence consumers, and persistent personnel issues. These were not fixed overnight. Gradual change required not just internal resolve but also external political support. The directors behind the most ambitious and visible reforms—Silberzahn in the early 1990s and, more recently, Émié—combined access to top political figures with a deep understanding of the French administration. That blend enabled them to translate reform plans into lasting institutional change.

Three core factors combined to empower leaders to reform the DGSE. First, political support from the head of state and government was essential. Second, changes in the international environment, including the rise of the terrorist threat and the digital revolution, created both pressure and opportunity for adjustment. Third, DGs who understood the workings of the French administration were better able to adopt the right methods to reconfigure the agency. These factors mirror the broader framework of institutional adaptation highlighted in the introduction: Political change and external shocks provided opportunities for reform, but change also depended on leaders' ability to institutionalize new practices, align internal networks, and shift values.

The evolving profiles of DGSE leaders reflect the agency's shifting focus and progressive integration within the French state. Until 2024 its recent leaders were all diplomats, many with expertise in North Africa and the Middle East. This pattern aligns with a recent reform that dissolved the French diplomatic corps' special status, integrating diplomats into a broader pool of generalist administrators who can move between ministries.[137] It also reflects the DGSE's tighter connection with French foreign policy as well as France's enduring interests in neighboring regions where France maintains substantial economic and political interests.[138] These leadership changes signal a gradual shift in underlying assumptions about the DGSE's identity and role at the core of the executive.

Today foreign intelligence commands more attention and higher expectations at the top of the French state than ever before. This visibility brings opportunities but also constraints. Despite its growing budget, the DGSE must be clear: It cannot be omnipresent. Compared to global intelligence powers such as the United States and China, France operates with more modest resources. Even in those countries, intelligence can inform and support policy, but it cannot dictate it. As the DGSE continues to evolve, its leaders will need to manage ambition with realism and visibility with discretion. Their ability to align structural reforms with political expectations, while managing the agency's internal culture and practices, will remain the core challenge of adaptation.

Notes

1. Maddrell, "Introduction," 3.
2. Silberzahn, *Au coeur du secret*, 110.
3. Walsh, *Intelligence Leadership*, 4.
4. Moran, Iordannou, and Stout, *Spy Chiefs*, 10, 302–3; Maddrell, "Conclusion," 249.
5. Jean-Claude Cousseran in Bauer and Depuis-Danon, *Les guetteurs*, 143; Maddrell, "Introduction," xi; Walsh, *Intelligence Leadership*, 7–8, 29–30.
6. Walsh, *Intelligence Leadership*, 18, 26–29; Moran, Iordannou, and Stout, *Spy Chiefs*, 4–5, 10, 302–5.
7. Walsh, *Intelligence Leadership*, 29.
8. Maddrell, "What Is Intelligence Leadership," 8; Walsh, *Intelligence Leadership*, 7–8, 29–30.
9. Laurent, "La gouvernance supérieure du renseignement," 474; Laurent, "Politisations et politiques du renseignement," 299–302; Porch, *French Secret Services*, 404–21; Arboit, *Des service secrets*, 373–74.
10. See, e.g., Faure, *Aux services de la république*, 474.
11. Laurent, "La gouvernance supérieure du renseignement," 491.
12. Silberzahn, *Au coeur du secret*, 109, 314–15.
13. The year of nomination is used as starting year for each DG.
14. See, e.g., Faure, *Aux services de la république*, 539–80.
15. The names of these (deputy) directors can be found in the *Journal officiel de la république française* and parliamentary reports.
16. Vadillo, "L'administration à l'épreuve du politique," 5; Vadillo, "Personnalisation et pratiques," 3.
17. Dominique Fonvielle in Guisnel and Korn-Brzoza, *Au service secret de la France*, 192.
18. Marion, *Mémoires de l'ombre*, 51–69.
19. Marion, *La mission impossible*, 33.
20. See, e.g., the view of his successor, Adm. Pierre Lacoste, in Laurent, *Les espions français parlent*, 561–62.
21. See, e.g., Marion, *Mémoires de l'ombre*, 176.
22. Marion, *Mémoires de l'ombre*, 40–41.
23. Marion, *Mémoires de l'ombre*, 163–78, 190; Marion, *La mission impossible*, 49–64.
24. Marion, *La mission impossible*, 26–27.
25. Marion, *Mémoires de l'ombre*, 168–69, 178, 200. See also Jacques Isnard, "La création d'un état-major de direction au SDECE entraîne des départs chez les officiers du renseignement," *Le Monde*, January 27, 1982; Jacques Isnard, "Les

services secrets sont invités par le gouvernement à franciser leur informatique de renseignement," *Le Monde*, November 8, 1982.

26. Marion, *La mission impossible*, 26, 122, 128. See also Fonvielle in Guisnel and Korn-Brzoza, *Au service secret de la France*, 193, and Jacques Isnard, "Renforcement des postes extérieurs du contre-espionnage: Création d'une cellule d'analyse politique et économique," *Le Monde*, November 18, 1981.
27. Fonvielle in Guisnel and Korn-Brzoza, *Au service secret de la France*, 198.
28. Marion, *La mission impossible*, 34, 129, 223.
29. Marion, *La mission impossible*, 33. See also Vadillo, "Personnalisation et pratiques," 4.
30. Fonvielle in Guisnel and Korn-Brzoza, *Au service secret de la France*, 193; Alain Chouet in Guisnel and Korn-Brzoza, *Au service secret de la France*, 311; Lacoste in Laurent, *Les espions français parlent*, 550–51. Marion himself recognizes he has a "strong character" in Marion, *Mémoires de l'ombre*, 158.
31. Vadillo, "Personnalisation et pratiques," 5.
32. Marion, *Mémoires de l'ombre*, 179.
33. Marion, *Mémoires de l'ombre*, 228.
34. "M. Pierre Marion est remplacé à la D.G.S.E. par le vice-amiral d'escadre Pierre Lacoste," *Le Monde*, November 11, 1982.
35. Dufourcq, "In memoriam," 13–16; Vadillo, "L'administration à l'épreuve du politique," 590.
36. Jacques Isnard, "Remue-ménage chez les agents secrets," *Le Monde*, August 28, 1985.
37. Fonvielle describes him as a "fine" and "cultivated" man in Gusinel and Korn-Brzoza, *Au service secret de la France*, 194.
38. Lacoste, *Un amiral au secret*, 20–22; Lacoste in Laurent, *Les espions français parlent*, 548–49; Lacoste in Bauer and Dupuis-Danon, *Les guetteurs*, 39.
39. "M. Pierre Marion est remplacé à la D.G.S.E."
40. Lacoste, *Un amiral au secret*, 48–50.
41. Xavier Guilhou in Guisnel and Korn-Brzoza, *Au service secret de la France*, 384.
42. Lacoste, *Un amiral au secret*, 23–25; Lacoste in Laurent, *Les espions français parlent*, 553; Lacoste in Guisnel and Korn-Brzoza, *Au service secret de la France*, 238–42.
43. Lacoste, *Un amiral au secret*, 125.
44. Lacoste in Laurent, *Les espions français parlent*, 552, 555–56; Lacoste in Bauer and Dupuis-Danon, *Les guetteurs*, 40.
45. Lacoste, *Un amiral au secret*, 131–35.
46. Lacoste in Laurent, *Les espions français parlent*, 559; Lacoste, *Un amiral au secret*, 136.
47. Lacoste, *Un amiral au secret*, 138.
48. Lacoste, *Un amiral au secret*, 138; Lacoste in Laurent, *Les espions français parlent*, 558–59.
49. Lacoste in Laurent, *Les espions français parlent*, 564.
50. Lacoste in Guisnel and Korn-Brzoza, *Au service secret de la France*, 243; Silberzahn, *Au coeur du secret*, 297–98.
51. Lacoste, *Un amiral au secret*, 11; Lacoste in Laurent, *Les espions français parlent*, 570–71; Lacoste in Guisnel and Korn-Brzoza, *Au service secret de la France*, 245–46.

52. Lacoste, *Un amiral au secret*, 126, 147–49.
53. Paul Quillès in Guisnel and Korn-Brzoza, *Au service secret de la France*, 277.
54. "Le général Maurice Schmitt lui succède à la tête de l'état-major de l'armée de terre," *Le Monde*, September 26, 1985.
55. Jacques Isnard, "Cherchons véritables clandestins à la DGSE (bérets rouges s'abstenir) . . . ," *Le Monde*, November 22, 1985.
56. "Pour ressouder des services secrets démoralisés: Un projet de statut commun aux 3,500 agents civils et militaires de la DGSE," *Le Monde*, August 4, 1990. For a more comprehensive discussion of this workforce issue, see Arboit, *Des services secrets*, 377–79.
57. Laurent Zecchini, "René Imbot, ancien patron de la DGSE," *Le Monde*, February 23, 2007.
58. Vadillo, "L'administration à l'épreuve du politique," 590.
59. "Le général Mermet est nommé conseiller du gouvernement," *Le Monde*, March 24, 1989.
60. François Mermet in Bauer and Dupuis-Danon, *Les guetteurs*, 67.
61. François Mermet in Bauer and Dupuis-Danon, *Les guetteurs*, 77–79.
62. François Mermet in Bauer and Dupuis-Danon, *Les guetteurs*, 88–89.
63. François Mermet in Bauer and Dupuis-Danon, *Les guetteurs*, 84.
64. François Mermet in Bauer and Dupuis-Danon, *Les guetteurs*, 91.
65. François Mermet in Bauer and Dupuis-Danon, *Les guetteurs*, 93.
66. François Mermet in Bauer and Dupuis-Danon, *Les guetteurs*, 75–76.
67. Silberzahn, *Au coeur du secret*, 16–24.
68. Michel Rocard in Guisnel and Korn-Brzoza, *Au service secret de la France*, 460.
69. Silberzahn, "Les mutations de la DGSE," 15; Gilles Ménage (Mitterrand's chief of staff from 1989 to 1992) in Guisnel and Korn-Brzoza, *Au service secret de la France*, 272; Silberzahn, *Au coeur du secret*, 20–25; Silberzahn in Guisnel and Korn-Brzoza, *Au service secret de la France*, 480–81.
70. Silberzahn, *Au coeur du secret*, 10, 26–27.
71. Claude Silberzahn in Laurent, *Les espions français parlent*, 588.
72. Jean Heinrich in Guisnel and Korn-Brzoza, *Au service secret de la France*, 421.
73. Silberzahn, *Au coeur du secret*, 37–43; Silberzahn in Guisnel and Korn-Brzoza, *Au service secret de la France*, 472.
74. Silberzahn, *Au coeur du secret*, 142–45.
75. Silberzahn, *Au coeur du secret*, 74–80.
76. Silberzahn, *Au coeur du secret*, 63.
77. Silberzahn, *Au coeur du secret*, 46–47; Silberzahn in Guisnel and Korn-Brzoza, *Au service secret de la France*, 469.
78. Silberzahn, *Au coeur du secret*, 129.
79. Silberzahn, *Au coeur du secret*, 88–89.
80. "Un entretien avec le patron des services secrets M. Claude Silberzahn propose un plan de renforcement de la DGSE," *Le Monde*, January 31, 1990; Jacques Isnard, "L'Europe du renseignement se construit plus vite que l'Europe politique," *Le Monde*, March 31, 1993; Silberzahn, *Au coeur du secret*, 100–101; Silberzahn, "Les mutations de la DGSE," 16.
81. Silberzahn, "Les mutations de la DGSE," 17.
82. Jacques Follorou, "La mort de Claude Silberzahn, ancien patron de la DGSE," *Le Monde*, April 23, 2020.

83. Cousseran in Bauer and Dupuis-Danon, *Les guetteurs*, 131.
84. Silberzahn, *Au coeur du secret*, 314.
85. Vadillo, "L'administration à l'épreuve du politique," 591.
86. "Le retour en force du pouvoir militaire," *Le Monde*, June 18, 1993; Jacques Isnard, "Le chef de la DGSE est remercié après les échecs de son service en Yougoslavie," *Le Monde*, December 19, 1999.
87. Toreau, "Le renseignement français dans la lutte contre l'islamisme armé," 34n122.
88. Dewatre cited in Toreau, "Le renseignement français dans la lutte contre l'islamisme armé," 256.
89. Isnard, "Le chef de la DGSE est remercié."
90. Lewis, "French DGSE Adapts to New World Order," 13.
91. Jacques Isnard, "Des changements en perspective dans les services de renseignement," *Le Monde*, January 22, 1998.
92. "Défense," *Le Monde*, February 11, 2000.
93. Cousseran in Bauer and Dupuis-Danon, *Les guetteurs*, 131.
94. Cousseran in Bauer and Dupuis-Danon, *Les guetteurs*, 133–34.
95. For extracts of DGSE reports on the threat posed by al-Qaeda in the lead-up to 9/11, see Guillaume Dasquié, "11 septembre 2001: Les Français en savaient long," *Le Monde*, December 27, 2007.
96. Alain Chouet (chief of counterterrorism at DGSE in 2001) in Guisnel and Korn-Brzoza, *Au service secret de la France*, 323.
97. Cousseran in Bauer and Dupuis-Danon, *Les guetteurs*, 129–31, 137, 140–42.
98. Cousseran in Bauer and Dupuis-Danon, *Les guetteurs*, 142–45.
99. Chouet in Guisnel and Korn-Brzoza, *Au service secret de la France*, 324–25; "Plusieurs clans s'affrontent au sommet de l'État pour faire nommer un nouveau directeur de la DGSE," *Le Monde*, December 2, 2003.
100. Cousseran in Bauer and Dupuis-Danon, *Les guetteurs*, 146–47.
101. Bajolet, "La DGSE, modèle français d'intégration," 6.
102. "Jeu de chaises musicales dans l'administration," *Le Monde*, August 9, 2002.
103. Gérard Davet and Laurent Zecchini, "Nicolas Sarkozy place un fidèle à la tête de la DGSE," *Le Monde*, October 7, 2008; "Pierre Brochand va quitter la direction de la DGSE," *Le Monde*, October 6, 2008.
104. See chapter 4 for further details and references.
105. AN, Commission de la Défense Nationale et des Forces Armées, *Avis sur le projet de loi de finances pour 2006*. See also Jean-Dominique Merchet, "Ce que l'on sait du Pôle national de cryptanalyse et de décryptement," *L'Opinion*, April 20, 2015.
106. Faligot, Guisnel, and Kauffer, *Histoire politique*, 579.
107. Bastide, "Pierre Brochand," 10–11.
108. Davet and Zecchini, "Nicolas Sarkozy place un fidèle."
109. Corbin de Mangoux, "Les mutations du renseignement."
110. Cousseran and Hayez, *Leçons sur le renseignement*, 194.
111. Bajolet, "La DGSE, modèle français d'intégration," 7.
112. Guisnel, *Histoire secrète de la DGSE*, 288–89.
113. François Hollande cited in Davet and Lhomme, *Un président ne devrait pas dire ça*, 481.
114. Bajolet, *Le soleil ne se lève plus à l'est*.

115. Bernard Bajolet in Guisnel and Korn-Brzoza, *Au service secret de la France*, 512; Bajolet, *Le soleil ne se lève plus à l'est*, 413–32.
116. Bajolet, *Le soleil ne se lève plus à l'est*, 17.
117. Bajolet, *Le soleil ne se lève plus à l'est*, 15, 30–36.
118. Coudurier, *Jean-Yves Le Drian*, 104–5.
119. Bajolet, *Le soleil ne se lève plus à l'est*, 432–35.
120. See reference to the following reports in Suc, *Les espions de la terreur*, 374: Direction Générale de la Sécurité Extérieure, "Abdelhamid Abaaoud, acteur clé de la menace projetée vers l'Europe," September 9, 2015; Direction Générale de la Sécurité Extérieure, "Menaces liées au dossier Abderlhamid Abaaoud," November 3, 2015.
121. Suc, *Les espions de la terreur*, 163–66, 178–79.
122. AN, Commission d'Enquête Relative aux Moyens Mis en Oeuvre par l'État, 857–59.
123. Trotignon, "Les failles du renseignement français."
124. AN, Commission d'Enquête Relative aux Moyens Mis en Oeuvre par l'État, *Hearing of Bernard Bajolet*, 860.
125. Bajolet in Guisnel and Korn-Brzoza, *Au service secret de la France*, 516.
126. Bajolet, "La DGSE, outil de réduction," 30–31.
127. Hofnung, "Au coeur de la DGSE."
128. Jacques Follorou, "Renseignement: Une nouvelle ère s'ouvre à la DGSE," *Le Monde*, June 22, 2017.
129. Julia Pascual, Luc Leroux, Soren Seelow, Marc Semo, and Elise Vincent, "Trois nouveaux hommes-clés à la tête des services de renseignement," *Le Monde*, June 8, 2017.
130. Émié in Notin, *DGSE*, 14.
131. Vincent Nouzille, "Comment Macron mène ses guerres secretes," *Le Figaro*, September 25, 2020.
132. Premier Ministre, *Décret no. 2023-1039 modifiant les dispositions générales applicables aux fonctionnaires et aux agents contractuels de la direction générale de la sécurité extérieure*, November 15, 2023.
133. Musée de l'Ordre de la Libération, "Les agents secrets du général."
134. Elise Vincent, "Au Mali, les djihadistes 'réfléchissent à des attaques en Europe,' selon le patron de la DGSE," *Le Monde*, February 3, 2021; "Death of Sahrawi a 'Blow' for Islamic State"; Émié cited in Cyril Bensimon and Morgane Le Cam, "Au Sahel, l'État islamique, affaibli par la mort de son fondateur, reste actif," *Le Monde*, September 21, 2021.
135. Elise Vincent, "DGSE: Nicolas Lerner va remplacer Bernard Émié à la tête du renseignement extérieur," *Le Monde*, December 20, 2023; Jean-Dominique Merchet, "Services secrets: Bernard Émié remplacé, à la tête de la DGSE, par le patron de la DGSI," *L'Opinion*, December 19, 2023.
136. Izambard and Renaud, "La sécurité interne de la DGSE fait sa révolution."
137. AN, *Rapport d'information sur la réforme du corps diplomatique*.
138. Émié in Le Fur and Wasjman, "Les ambitions du renseignement."

4

Activities

The DGSE's remit spans countering a wide range of foreign threats to national security, including the proliferation of weapons of mass destruction, terrorism, international crime, and the defense of French economic interests.[1] Geographically, the agency concentrates on an "arc of crisis" that stretches from Mauritania to Central Asia. Within this arc, French historical access to assets and networks in sub-Saharan and francophone Africa provide distinct advantages over many Western partners.[2]

To fulfill its missions, the agency collects, analyzes, and disseminates intelligence to support government decision-making. It also conducts covert action aimed at disrupting threats to French interests—a role that leads French practitioners to present the DGSE as a "special service." This chapter examines four core activities: intelligence collection, analysis, covert action, and security. The discussion emphasizes the agency's enduring operational culture. DGSE officers are expected to develop field experience to climb up the professional ladders, and the agency has no dedicated career path for analysts. This professional norm reflects an underlying assumption about intelligence work that privileges operations over analysis and shapes career trajectories, internal status, and the agency's self-image.

Yet the DGSE's activities extend well beyond operations. As the threat environment has evolved, the agency has demonstrated a broader versatility often overlooked in popular accounts. Some of this adaptation is visible in the emergence of new missions and structures to develop analytic capabilities and evolving practices—for instance, in the domain of hostage rescue. The discussion underlines both the persistence of assumptions about the agency's operational role and its capacity for adaptation, revealing an intelligence service more capable and complex than its public image suggests. This juxtaposition points to an institution where formal structures and practices have shifted in response to external demands, even as deeper assumptions continue to shape hierarchies and professional identity.

Collection

French practitioners tend to conceive of intelligence as a form of protected information that the services seek to gather. From this perspective, the main raison d'être of the DGSE is its capacity to collect secret intelligence. Much of the structure and organization of the DGSE reflects the central role its sensors play in the production of intelligence. The agency engages in the collection of human and technical intelligence (mostly signals intelligence). A third discipline, operational research, leverages human and technical means to directly collect documents and observations from the field.[3] For instance, DGSE operators were able to recover sarin gas grenades to corroborate the Bashar al-Assad regime's chemical attack during the Syrian Civil War.[4] Sometimes international cooperation is also considered a form of intelligence collection, but this will be discussed separately in chapter 5. Intelligence gathered from these different sources generally leads to two types of reports: recording the conditions (when, where, how) in which intelligence was gathered and assessing the reliability of the source and the credibility of the information they convey.[5]

Case officers collect HUMINT in the field, where they receive guidance from analysts and research officers. In theory, analysts are expected to identify the structure that the OTs have to infiltrate. In practice, they often indicate more general intelligence requirements to officers, who then need to identify and gain access to relevant sources. In areas where the DGSE has greater expertise, OTs can be expected to access sources unavailable through other (diplomatic, military, or open-source) means. Terrorist networks in the Middle East and North Africa are a good example. In the early 1980s some of the agency's HUMINT efforts focused on

Lebanon, an unstable country where the growing influence of the Palestinian Liberation Organization and Hezbollah threatened French interests. Agency officers collected intelligence to uncover terrorist plots and disrupt their networks.[6] By the early 1990s Algeria became a key preoccupation. In 1993 the Groupe Islamique Armé (GIA; Armed Islamic Group) assassinated several French citizens living there. The following year a GIA commando unit hijacked an Air France flight in Algiers, planning to crash it into the Eiffel Tower. The plot was foiled but alerted political and security elites. Yet the GIA was able to stage successful attacks in the Paris Métro in July 1995 and December 1996.[7] The DGSE then redoubled its efforts to surveil and penetrate Salafist networks linked to the Soviet-Afghan War (1979–89) and the breakup of Yugoslavia (1991–2001), which were expanding into Western Europe.[8] A former Service Action officer reports he was sent to London in the mid-1990s to covertly gather intelligence on Islamist networks.[9] A decade later the DGSE anticipated growing instability and a terrorist presence in the Sahel region of West Africa and refocused some of its technical and human means toward this region, in parallel with more openly military operations such as Barkhane (2014–22), a French intervention aimed at combating Islamist insurgent groups and stabilizing the Sahel.[10]

The DGSE's Technical Directorate is France's lead SIGINT hub. French overseas territories provide the agency with a global network of stations covering the Americas (e.g., French Guiana and Saint Barthélemy), the Pacific Ocean (French Polynesia and New Caledonia), the Indian Ocean (Mayotte), and East Africa (Djibouti), to name just a few locations.[11] France's geography places the DGSE in a good position to tap submarine cables that carry modern communications.[12] The agency also relies on a range of mobile platforms operated by the military, including the naval vessel *Dupuy de Lôme*, as well as airplanes and communication intelligence (COMINT) satellites.[13] In the words of a generous observer, France's SIGINT coverage is "second only to the Five Eyes," the alliance that brings together Australia, Canada, the United Kingdom, the United States, and New Zealand.[14] More accurately, French SIGINT capabilities are significant but limited. The DGSE needs to be more restrictive than great intelligence powers such as the United States and its partners and China in its selection of targets.[15]

These SIGINT capabilities support a range of missions to further economic, political, and military interests. In the 1980s the media revealed that France used SIGINT to spy on the communications of major American corporations and HUMINT assets to give French companies an edge in particularly important sectors such as information technology and defense contracts.[16] In 1994 a French station in the Central African Republic intercepted the communications of Tutsi leader Paul Kagame and continued to provide intelligence on the conflict and genocide that devastated Rwanda.[17] In 1987 a French Navy maritime patrol aircraft served as a communication and electronic interception platform to monitor Libyan forces operating in Chad.[18] More recently, Bernard Barbier—who led the agency's Technical Directorate from 2006 to 2014—explained that DGSE capabilities were deployed alongside French troops to block adversary communications, presumably to prevent the detonation of improvised explosive devices in Afghanistan and other theaters of operation.[19]

SIGINT is also crucial for tracking terrorists. With the emergence of the Syrian Civil War, the DGSE started to focus more intensely on the threat posed by the Islamic State (also known as ISIS, the Islamic State in Iraq and Syria, or Daesh, its Arabic acronym). By the mid-2010s the French services were busy tracking several hundred French citizens who had left for Syria as well as a larger group of francophone fighters who did the same.[20] According to Barbier, the agency tapped the communications of French jihadists in Syria when they called their relatives.[21] The focus on terrorism throughout the 2000s prompted adaptations toward a more target-centric approach, which progressively spilled over to other disciplines and missions.[22]

Significant investments over the past two decades have expanded the DGSE's SIGINT capabilities to better align them with the requirement of the digital revolution.[23] At the same time, the growing concern among the French and wider European public about big data and surveillance has placed greater scrutiny on these developments.[24] In July 2015 French law provided a democratic basis and set constraints for the agency to conduct bulk metadata collection.[25] This capability can be used for a variety of purposes but was largely justified by France's efforts to counter terrorism as well as cyberattacks. In this context, the DGSE also has the capability to detect, characterize, and attribute cyberattacks targeting French interests and assess their damage.[26] Combining the agency's technical, human, and operational means is particularly helpful in this domain.[27]

The agency reportedly engages in offensive cyber operations as well. According to an entry from the US intelligence wiki platform Intellipedia, a source with indirect access claimed that in 2002 the DGSE "delivered computers and fax equipment to Senegal's security services and by 2004 could access all the information processed by these systems."[28] In 2014 the French daily *Le Monde* revealed a cyber operation identified in a presentation by Canada's SIGINT agency Communications Security Establishment (CSE) that had been leaked by NSA contractor Edward Snowden.[29] The CSE had discovered a vulnerability that provided computer network exploitation access to a third party and was used to record keystrokes and collect emails, audio conversations, and other communications from targeted accounts.[30] The capability targeted Iranian science and technology accounts, including the Atomic Energy Organization of Iran, as well as European organizations, former French colonies, and French-language media organizations. Digital forensics uncovered several French-language artifacts embedded in the malware code—such as the name "Babar" (a reference to the French cartoon elephant), "titi" (a common French diminutive), and file-size indicators using "ko" (short for *kilo-octet*, French for kilobyte). Combined with the targeted victim set, these linguistic and technical clues led the Canadian techies to assess with moderate certainty that this was a state-sponsored effort put forth by a French intelligence agency.[31] Several years later, the technical director of the DGSE admitted responsibility in a talk he delivered to students (one of whom was recording him) at his alma mater. By then cybersecurity researchers had linked the Babar malware to a broader family of cyber capabilities that profiled, mapped, and targeted persons of interest for further monitoring.[32]

Processing More than Analysis

France has produced many celebrated thinkers. Yet its foreign intelligence culture places limited emphasis on "the thinking part of the intelligence process": analysis.[33] The DGSE prioritizes *exploitation* over analysis. *Exploitation* encompasses the processing of data emanating from multiple sensors and sources (HUMINT, GEOINT, SIGINT, open-source intelligence [OSINT], etc.) into information that is appropriately contextualized. This is a key step during which the reliability of the sources is evaluated and leads to the production of internal notes. From this view, it is processing, not analysis, that differentiates raw information from finished intelligence.[34]

The DGSE does not have a dedicated career track for analysts. Officers typically start their career as analysts before they move on to roles closer to the field or higher up in the management chain.[35] Proponents of this approach believe it contributes to a sense of integration that bridges the divide between collection and analysis, the field and headquarters. The recruitment committee that evaluates budding officers puts it very clearly:

> The analyst function represents only a minority of the career path of a category A civil servant within the DGSE. Fieldwork and management are generally the two dominant aspects that await young *attachés* [officers] after a first part of their career in analytic functions. . . . It is difficult to offer a fulfilling career in the DGSE to people who are unwilling or unable to evolve toward intelligence-gathering functions after the first few years of analysis. . . . The jury has rejected candidates expecting a job that is above all strategic, even cerebral, and focused solely on writing syntheses. In reality, the exploitation of intelligence is based on investigation and the ability to combine all the means of collection, with a view to proposing actions and seeking impact.[36]

The agency's culture thus privileges operations, both by design and by default. Gathering intelligence and influencing world outcomes are considered the "noble" parts of the job.[37] DG Émié points out that the DGSE is an "operational secret service, where one takes risks."[38] Despite a growing budget, senior DGSE officials consider they do not have the resources to maintain a large cadre of career analysts specializing in the vast array of countries, political movements, and emerging threats around the world. From this standpoint, researchers in academia and think tanks—who work in less restricted environments than intelligence officers—are better placed to develop deep expertise on specific countries or political movements and write on grand strategic issues. Within the DGSE, employees who develop substantive expertise on a particular region or threat and have a taste for analysis face limited options to pursue a long career beyond operational roles and managerial positions. This contrasts with other "integrated" agencies such as the Central Intelligence Agency (CIA), where analysts can pursue an entire career focusing on a region, with the most successful advancing to the senior analytic service.[39]

Notwithstanding this predilection for the field, analysts make up about a quarter of the agency's workforce.[40] The DGSE produces and disseminates several thousand reports each year. Their primary audience is a select group of senior decision-makers often referred to as "the big five"—the president, the prime minister, the minister of armed forces, the foreign affairs minister, and the interior minister—plus the chief of the defense staff and the minister of the economy and finance.[41] DGSE products reach hundreds of recipients working for these decision-makers. The agency's two flagship products are intelligence reports (*notes de renseignement*; see the box below for an example) and evaluations. The former tend to be concise and factual reports that present and contextualize pieces of human, technical, or operational intelligence; the latter develop a broader interpretation of a situation and identify implications.[42] When deemed sufficiently important, reports are validated and turned into *notes jaunes* (yellow notes), which are disseminated to key consumers in government and sometimes beyond—for example, to national companies.[43] Unlike some other services such as the Office of the Director of National Intelligence in the United States and the General Intelligence and Security Services of the Netherlands, the DGSE does not produce reports for public consumption. DG Bajolet explains, "Our mission is to produce intelligence for the government, not the public. [Public] communication—through the publication of foresight analysis for instance—requires resources that are not aligned to our current priorities."[44]

Extract of a Note de Renseignement on the Islamic State

THE DECISION CHAIN FOR PROJECTING THE THREAT FROM THE ISLAMIC STATE

Lessons learned from the recent attacks outside the Levant by the Islamic State have validated the existence of a structured decision-making chain responsible for the terrorist organization's external operations.

The commonalities between the latest external operations provide insights into the decision-making chain of these attacks:

- sponsorship link involving the organization's high command of the organization
- the existence of operational supervision levels
- centralization of the planning of operations

The proliferation and professionalization of the Islamic State's operational projects result from the progressive consolidation of the backbone of the organization's middle management of the organization.[45]

DGSE products are primarily focused on tactical matters. High expectations from policymakers, coupled with limited resources, have led the agency to concentrate on what it considers its core mission: gathering intelligence from sources that diplomats, commercial providers, and open-source investigators cannot easily access. This prioritization reflects internal culture as much as external demands. DGSE reports tend to be descriptive, with analysis typically limited to short- to medium-term projections included in a comment section at the end of the report. DG Cousseran (1999–2002) remembers the service's products focused on evaluating sources, specifying targets, and contextualizing raw intelligence, leaving broader geopolitical analyses to the diplomats.[46] Nevertheless, the DGSE did establish a unit specializing in foresight and alternative analysis during DG Bajolet's tenure (2013–17).[47] For instance, nearly a year before the 2016 US presidential election, this unit produced a note that sought to anticipate the consequences of a Donald Trump victory.[48] Its focus was on the short to medium term and not on the strategic horizon (beyond five years).

Unlike in the United States where thousands of CIA and National Intelligence Council products are publicly available, very few DGSE reports are. This lack of openness is understandable but offers outsiders little basis for assessing the agency's analytic practices and performance. In the absence of such evidence, major failures tend to attract outsiders' attention to perceived analytic shortcomings. Cases of success are more difficult to identify and document. In his memoirs, former DG Silberzahn remembers that the agency anticipated the crisis between Iraq and Kuwait in the early 1990s, though it did not predict Iraq's invasion of Kuwait, which triggered the Gulf War. Partial access to the agency's detailed postmortem on the war—made possible by a waiver of the standard fifty-year classification period, authorized by DG Lerner—largely confirms Silberzahn's recollection. The DGSE's assessment of Iraqi intentions and capabilities consistently highlighted the likelihood of a war, but neither the agency nor its close partners could pinpoint the exact date of the Iraqi invasion of Kuwait.[49] The DGSE also reportedly foresaw that Yugoslavia would implode and called for an early reflection on the new geography of the region and its population. In both cases, Silberzahn argues that more precise predictions would have been unlikely to change the position of senior policymakers—who did not pay much attention to DGSE products at the time.[50]

Officials have pointed out that DGSE reporting empowered French decision-makers to take a stance against the US-led war in Iraq. Cousseran, who led the agency at the time, remembers that reporting expressed skepticism about the value and reliability of the sources the US community used to establish the existence of an Iraqi program of nuclear and bacteriological weapons.[51] Alain Chouet, whose responsibilities at the DGSE included counterproliferation issues until 2002—after which he left the agency—remembers "numerous research operations had led us to the conclusion that there were no more weapons [of mass destruction] in this country. . . . We gave the French core executive sufficient arguments so that [Foreign Minister] Dominique de Villepin could argue that one cannot act based on a lie in front of the UN."[52]

Officers directly involved in the case have made more cautious public statements. A counterproliferation officer who has worked at the DGSE since the late 1990s explains, "We did not have sufficiently conclusive and reliable intelligence to say that Saddam Hussein is restarting a chemical or biological program."[53] This judgment was based on a range of sources, including interceptions, satellite imagery, HUMINT, and international partners, as well as open sources including Iraq's own declarations. Another DGSE officer working on counterproliferation at the time explains the agency could rely on its own network of (human) sources and that imagery of suspicious sites in Iraq returned indeterminate results, not necessarily because nothing was there but because French capabilities (the SPOT satellite) did not offer sufficiently high resolution.[54] French networks also provided a platform for the DGSE to discount allegations that Iraq had purchased yellowcake in Niger.[55] It is likely the service also cast doubt on the assertion of Iraqi defector Rafid Ahmed Alwan al-Janab (a source commonly known as "Curveball" following the code name the US Defense Intelligence Agency assigned to him) that Iraq had developed mobile biological weapon laboratories.

Documentary evidence made available for this research reveals how the DGSE relied on its own expertise to independently evaluate evidence and assessments presented by the United States as well as International Atomic Energy Agency inspectors.[56] Classified reports produced by the agency counterproliferation unit in early 2003 reflect the initial ambiguity surrounding Iraq's procurement of anodized aluminum tubes, which, as one "yellow note" mentioned, "could correspond to a nuclear usage."[57]

The limited documentary base supports the claim that the French intelligence community's assessments provided a basis for policymakers to oppose the US-led war in Iraq.[58] However, as is so often the case, intelligence reporting could reduce uncertainty only marginally.

Key policymakers, such as President Chirac and then-Minister of Foreign Affairs de Villepin, do not refer directly to any intelligence in their memoirs. Chirac merely notes that he "did not, at that time, have any proof of the existence of such weapons in Iraq."[59] Bruno Le Maire, a diplomat who served as an adviser in de Villepin's cabinet at the time, recognizes the detailed—and at times contradictory—reporting provided by the DGSE, DST, and DRM. He also underscores the inherent limitations of intelligence in reducing uncertainty.[60] Regardless of the extent to which intelligence influenced French opposition to the war, some insiders now view this episode as a turning point that demonstrated the significance of foreign intelligence to French leaders.

The Full Spectrum of Covert Action

The DGSE has a monopoly on French covert actions abroad. The agency is formally entrusted with a mission to "detect and disrupt, outside of the national territory, espionage activities directed against French interest in order to prevent their consequences." As such, it carries out "within the framework of its attributions, *any action* that is entrusted by the government."[61] The 2015 intelligence reform expanded this basis, noting that intelligence services contribute to "disrupting" risks and threats likely to affect the life of the nation. The interpretation of the term "disruption" (*entrave*, which can also be translated as "obstruction") is broad. A former DG writes that it refers to any means necessary to prevent an undesirable event.[62] The 2019 national intelligence strategy defines *entrave* as "the ability to prevent a threat from materializing and to stop it" and points out that "it can take several forms: judicial, military, political, diplomatic, or administrative."[63] This mission is integral to intelligence because it is implemented by the service and relies on intelligence produced by the service.

The French do not use the term "covert action"; they talk about *actions* or *opérations clandestines*. Just like in the United States, covert action is different from special operations, which are conducted by uniformed military personnel.[64] Despite the semantic difference, the French approach is comparable to the American doctrine of plausible deniability. Covert operations are supposed to be nonattributable (*non imputable* in French) because they are carried out beyond legal boundaries abroad. This provides added room for maneuver to decision-makers, a so-called third option between war and peace.[65] French authorities have the option to acknowledge them when or if they become public.[66] Their link to the president cannot be formally established, but several senior officials confirm that the DGSE requires political authorization from the highest sphere of the executive branch. Gen. Jean Heinrich, who led the Directorate of Operations, explains that the president "draws an outline, then the director of the service ensures we work within these boundaries and in coherence with the political option the president has defined."[67]

French *opérations clandestines* encompass a range of activities similar to anglophone covert actions, from information operations to political and paramilitary actions. The French conception of these operations readily merges covert action and covert intelligence collection. Action feeds collection, and vice versa. Both types of operation engage similar means to ensure a degree of covertness and occasionally rely on the same units and individuals. Covert operators can act as sensors conducting operational research (observation) or planting bugs to identify targets in conflict zones, for example.[68] François Mermet, who led the DGSE in 1988 and 1989, remembers a successful covert operation that collected a sample of the coating of a Soviet submarine.[69] The current director for research and operations is adamant that these operations are systematically authorized by the DG and stresses their political character.[70] The sections below survey DGSE covert actions, ordered along a spectrum ranging from influence operations to assassination.

Political Influence

DGSE covert operations have a softer side that is often overlooked. Considering political action, France's foreign intelligence agency maintained networks of influence in its African sphere of interest long before and after the independence of its former colonies in the 1960s. Successive DGs have all recognized the strategic value of these networks and the political capital they provide to the service. For better or worse, the African continent is durably linked to the image of the DGSE and is part of its mythology.[71] This rich and controversial history invites deeper analysis of the DGSE's political influence.

The transition from the SDECE to the DGSE did not fundamentally alter the role and actions of France's foreign intelligence agency in Africa. Following the fall of the self-styled emperor Jean-Bédel Bokassa in 1979, the Central African Republic became a key platform for the French military and foreign intelligence services to operate in the region, specifically in neighboring Chad. This strategic position meant that French authorities were particularly keen to protect the regime of the successive presidents David Dacko (1979–81) and André Kolingba (1981–93) and overlook their repressive and kleptocratic natures.[72] France's foreign intelligence service dispatched one of its officers, Col. Jean-Claude Mantion, to be a security adviser to the president. The post was distinct and more visible than that of the chief of station (*chef de poste*). Mantion reformed the presidential guard, disrupted opposition plots, and oversaw efforts to secure the country's territory from Libyan encroachments. By the early 1990s, assignments like his seemed increasingly outdated. The Cold War had ended, and public opinion demanded more democratic or less visible means of influence to avoid neocolonial accusations.[73] The service had many other ways to exert influence abroad.

On April 22, 1989, groups of Dakar residents attacked dozens of shops owned by Mauritanians, resulting in the deaths of many. Shortly afterward, Mauritanians launched a series of retaliatory attacks against Senegalese residents in Nouakchott. The violence escalated, triggering a mass exodus of tens of thousands of citizens from both countries.[74] With the approval of President Mitterrand, DG Silberzahn used his personal connections and the Directorate of Strategy to establish and facilitate secret negotiations to facilitate a dialogue between Presidents Maaouya Ould Sidi Ahmed Taya of Mauritania and Abdou Diouf of Senegal on contentious issues such as borders and fishing zones.[75] The two countries eventually signed a peace agreement in 1992, making no mention of the role the DGSE had played.[76] Reflecting on this episode, Silberzahn later argued that the negotiation's secrecy was key to its success. A more overt intervention could have been taxed of neocolonialism, making negotiations more difficult. From the French perspective, political support from the president and the government empowered the DG and the agency to intervene and covertly de-escalate the emerging conflict.

The DGSE's involvement in covert diplomacy can create tensions with the Ministry of Foreign Affairs. The agency often operates against the prevailing diplomatic approach to hedge France's bets, enabling authorities to establish or maintain ties with a variety of potential future leaders. When France was officially close to the Serbs at the start of the Bosnian War, the DGSE developed ties with the Croats. While France supported Hissène Habré in Chad, the DGSE maintained ties with his rival, Idriss Déby. The DGSE's value lies in its access to places and people that diplomats cannot or will not engage, so that France can adapt when the situation and authorities call for it.[77] This often requires a blend of covert collection and action.

Support to Insurgents

Moving up the ladder of violence, France's interests in Central Africa prompted it to maintain a strong overt and covert presence in Chad, where French troops were deployed from 1969 onward.[78] The country's strategic position would support French influence in the Sahel, a region where France competed with Libya and Sudan, the Soviet Union, and the United States.[79] Under Adm. Pierre Lacoste's directorship (1982–85), the agency expanded its footprint in the region, establishing a cell in Bangui, the capital of the neighboring Central African Republic, to support its men in Chad. The DGSE helped to establish Chad's intelligence service, the Direction de la Documentation et de la Sécurité (DDS; Documentation and Security Directorate) in the early 1980s and trained its officers for several years.[80] Following a request from Habré and support from senior French policymakers, the DGSE enrolled a few dozen mercenaries to launch a "bridging operation" preparing for a larger military operation named Manta. The mercenaries landed in N'Djamena in July 1983 to train the Armed Forces of the North (FAN), the rebel group initially led by Habré during the First Chadian Civil War (1965–79). A handful of SA officers deployed to train the mercenaries in radio transmission and the use of advanced weapon systems, particularly the MILAN antitank missile. The operation also intercepted SIGINT beyond Chad's borders, extending into Libya against the backdrop of the Chadian-Libyan War (1978–87).[81] This effort bought time for the deployment of conventional forces and the start of Operation Manta on August 9, 1983.[82] DGSE paramilitary officers would continue to support Habré until the end of the 1980s, providing him with advisers, operational research, and HUMINT and SIGINT capabilities to target Libyan forces in the following years.[83] But in 1990 French authorities decided to side with Déby, and Habré was pushed away from power.

Thousands of miles away from Chad, France's foreign intelligence agency was also covertly involved in the Soviet-Afghan War (1979–89). The SA provided military advice; trained combat leaders in urban guerrilla warfare, communications, and sabotage; and supplied weapons to specific mujahideen groups in Afghanistan.[84] Multiple memoirs and interviews detail how the agency supported the guerrilla campaign of Ahmad Shah Masoud's Northern Alliance against the Soviet occupation.[85] France's covert presence in Afghanistan leveraged its liaison partnership with the agency Inter-Services Intelligence in neighboring Pakistan, not unlike the CIA did. The DGSE maintained a presence in Afghanistan throughout the 1990s, which enabled France to acquire intelligence directly from the field in the lead-up to and the aftermath of the 9/11 attacks.[86] DGSE paramilitary officers embedded with the Northern Alliance as early as November 2001 to gather intelligence and facilitate the subsequent arrival of French forces.[87]

Hostage Rescue

In the two decades since the 9/11 attacks, most of the information that has surfaced about French covert action reflects the prominent place of counterterrorism on the political and intelligence agenda. Among other types of operations, the role of the DGSE in hostage-rescue missions has attracted a lot of attention, not least because of the high visibility of these missions and the political capital they can generate. Successful rescues can also provide a valuable source of intelligence on terrorist networks.[88] General Heinrich, who led the SA and then the Operations Directorate at the turn of the 1980s, remembers a range of successful hostage-rescue operations in South Sudan, South America, Congo, and Angola.[89] More recently, the service rescued hostages in Afghanistan and Iraq and on the yacht *Le Ponant* in 2008. Confronted with a growing number of French hostages (close to sixty from 2001 to 2014), the DGSE asserted its role as a negotiator with terrorists, combining its capacity to operate in difficult environments and to take more forceful action if necessary.[90]

Hostage-rescue missions demand diverse capabilities: in-depth knowledge of local networks and terrain and the ability to establish contact with interlocutors and negotiate with intermediaries and kidnappers discreetly.[91] This requires collection, analytic, and liaison capabilities and diplomatic skills that are likely to involve the DG as well as diplomats. These operations are intensive and have consumed a significant portion of agency resources over the past two decades.[92]

Not all the agency's rescue operations have been successful. One particularly dreadful failure was the effort to rescue Denis Allex, an SA officer who was kidnapped while on a mission to train government forces in Somalia in the summer of 2009. Following his kidnapping, Allex was transferred to the Islamist group al-Shabaab and remained in captivity for over three years. The DGSE eventually located him and launched a rescue operation on January 11, 2013. Approximately forty operators from the SA were dispatched ten kilometers south of the town of Bulo Marer where the al-Shabaab security service kept Allex. Their progression alerted a guard, resulting in Allex's execution and the death of two additional DGSE officers.[93] The failure reinvigorated the debate about the respective roles and relationship between the SA and the French special operations command.[94]

Sabotage

The sabotage of the *Rainbow Warrior* has long skewed public perception of the DGSE. The DGSE has presumably engaged in dozens of more successful sabotage operations, though few of them are publicly known. DG Pierre Marion (1981–82) recalls that after a British warship was sunk by a French-made Exocet missile during the Falklands War (April–June 1982), the agency located and sabotaged additional shipments en route to Argentina, thereby supporting the British.[95] Insiders sometimes feel frustrated by the amount of attention given to the sinking of the *Rainbow Warrior*. However, this event is too significant to omit from a book about the DGSE because the extensive media coverage has profoundly shaped the public's perception of the agency. It has also provided a wealth of information that is often missing when examining specific operations. More important, the episode highlights the DGSE's troubled relationship with its political masters at the time.

Following a series of American nuclear tests in Alaska (1969, 1971), antinuclear protest movements gained momentum and played a key role in the formation of Greenpeace. Building on this energy, the group soon turned its attention to disrupting French nuclear tests in the Pacific. The ecologists' flagship vessel had sailed to Auckland to prepare a protest against French atomic tests on the atoll of Mururoa. Ensuring the test's security was paramount for the French authorities. Minister of Defense Charles Hernu tasked the DGSE with mounting a covert action that would deny Greenpeace access to the French waters where the test was planned. DGSE planning considered multiple approaches—contaminating the *Rainbow Warrior*'s fuel, temporarily incapacitating the crew—but a lack of time, political pressure, and poor judgment meant a more dangerous sabotage operation prevailed.

In May 1985 the agency infiltrated one of its officers into Greenpeace to gather information on its plans and activities. Two other DGSE officers, posing as a couple ("the Turenges") on holidays, were dispatched to New Zealand to provide technical support for the operation. On the evening of July 10, 1985, two DGSE frogmen positioned a limpet mine on the hull of the *Rainbow Warrior* at its mooring. Its explosion provided a warning meant to force the crew to leave the vessel. But Dutch photographer Fernando Pereira returned to the ship to get his material and was killed following the explosion minutes later of a second mine positioned to sink the vessel. From New Zealand's perspective, this was the first terrorist operation ever on its national territory.[96] The local police launched an investigation that quickly revealed several flaws in the operation, leading to the arrest of the Turenges, the resignation of Defense Minister Hernu, and the firing of DG Lacoste.

Admiral Lacoste later admitted he "misestimated the weaknesses of the plan and the difficulty of the execution."[97] The DGSE had lacked time for more meticulous reconnaissance, preparation, and validation. The director had nevertheless accepted a dangerous operation, possibly to build trust with his political masters. Several operational errors pin some of the responsibility for the fiasco on the SA. The use of short timers on the limpet mines was supposed to mitigate some risks but also meant that all the officers could not be exfiltrated before the sinking. The rubber boat used by the divers was sunk but easily recovered by the New Zealand police. The Turenges panicked when the operation did not go to plan and called their controller back in Paris. The New Zealand authorities could not access the conversations, but, with the support of the French police, they were able to link the number the Turenges called to the French Ministry of Defense.[98] The fake spouses were arrested a few days after the operation on charges relating to their passports. New Zealand investigators identified several irregularities that further raised their suspicions. The Turenges' passports "should have had consecutive numbers, no attempt had been made to backstop them in the event of inquiries being made. There was similar carelessness about their French driving licenses." The operatives asked for a refund of their car rental fees when they decided to leave earlier than planned, while they could simply have left the vehicle and the country the morning following the operation. The officer posing as the wife also appeared shaken by the killing of Pereira. Her behavior while under arrest "gave the impression she was facing a situation she had not contemplated. She immediately [sought] directions from Paris."[99] On August 27 the interim assessment of the New Zealand security service concluded that the DGSE had mounted the operation. It assumed the operation had political clearance "at least at Minister of Defence level."[100]

Operational failures were followed by political ones. This was no rogue operation. President Mitterrand had authorized the operation—even if indirectly—and his chief of defense staff had authorized its special budget.[101] When New Zealand authorities and media disclosures ramped up the pressure on Paris, ministers denied the obvious for too long and prevented DG Lacoste from negotiating a quiet resolution with New Zealand through back channels.[102]

The fiasco had grave consequences. It damaged the DGSE's reputation both internationally and at home, where it widened the distance between the agency and the core executive. The Turenges' real identities were revealed to the public. They were convicted, sentenced to ten years' imprisonment, and eventually transferred to France. The affair raised questions about the DGSE's governance model, capabilities, and professionalism. French authorities eventually acknowledged responsibility and decided with New Zealand to request that the UN secretary-general mediate and propose a solution that both parties had agreed in advance to accept. The secretary-general's ruling required France to apologize for the actions of its officers and pay a compensation of $7 million to New Zealand. As a part of the settlement, New Zealand also contained assurances from France that it would compensate Greenpeace and the family of the deceased.[103] Greenpeace used this compensation to acquire a deep-sea-fishing vessel and refit it as the *Rainbow Warrior II*. The environmental advocacy group resumed its fight against the French nuclear tests in Polynesia until they were completely stopped.[104]

Overall, the affair illustrates the position of the DGSE at the time. The agency lacked political direction and control and suffered from its poor relations with the rest of the administration, not least with the Ministry of the Interior.

Assassination

At the more extreme end of the spectrum of violence, the DGSE has been involved in assassinating terrorists. In 1983 the SA reportedly killed the militiamen who had assassinated the French ambassador to Lebanon, Louis Delamare, in Beirut two years earlier.[105] In his memoirs, DG Silberzahn implicitly suggests that the agency executes terrorists but specifies "in reality very few" of them.[106] He argues that in these situations, the DGSE operates within its mandate, stepping beyond legal boundaries to engage terrorists on their own terms when necessary. Publicly discussing these actions can serve as a deterrent against terrorism, but politicians cannot be publicly tied to such operations, as this would jeopardize them.[107] Silberzahn explains that if a director is convinced that such an operation will succeed, remain covert, and have no significant diplomatic repercussions, then the agency can fly solo. Otherwise, obtaining some form of presidential approval becomes necessary.

With the evolution of counterterrorism in the context of the wars in Afghanistan and Syria and the French intervention in the Sahel, the DGSE has been engaged in multiple eliminations. Depending on the circumstances, the agency can play a leading or more secondary role, supporting operators from its own SA or the French special forces or engaging allied airstrikes.[108] For example, the former technical director of the DGSE explains:

> I managed to convince the Service Action to work with my technical directorate during a first joint operation in July 2010 on a team that wanted to blow up the French embassy in Nouakchott, Mauritania. We showed to the military that, thanks to satellites, we could make a 3D model of their place of intervention [a jihadist camp] in the middle of dunes and thus enable them to virtually choose their path. They eliminated them as they were waking up.[109]

In 2021 DG Bernard Émié appeared on television with Chief of Defense Staff Gen. Thierry Burkhard and Defense Minister Florence Parly to announce the "neutralization" by drone strike of the leader of the Islamic State in the Sahel, Adnan Abu Walid al-Sahrawi.[110] According to Émié, this decapitation followed a series of other operations targeting the high command of the Islamic State in the Sahel, contributing to an "in-depth destruction of the group which will struggle to replace its cadre."[111] When asked about the DGSE's involvement in eliminations in the Sahel, the former DG neither confirms nor denies and explains that the DGSE has "a long memory. . . . Attacking French interests is something that, indeed, does not go without consequences. There is a price for everything."[112]

Counterintelligence and Security

Very little information is available on counterintelligence and security at the DGSE. Perhaps this should not come as a surprise as this function is all about controlling information. Historically, these capabilities included counterterrorism because of a perception that the Soviet Union was manipulating terrorist-nationalist movements in Lebanon, Ireland, Libya, and beyond. The prioritization of the terrorist threat in the 1990s and 2000s led to a clearer delineation between the two functions.[113]

Focusing on counterespionage more specifically, one of the most prominent and only cases to have made the headlines concerns a Chinese penetration. In December 2017 the DGSE referred two former officers to a public prosecutor on charges of treason, providing information to a foreign power, and incitement to such a crime.[114] The case concerned retired colonel Henri M., born in 1946, and Pierre-Marie H., born in 1952. Henri M. pursued his career in counterintelligence and served as chief of the DGSE station in China. He had an affair with a Chinese interpreter working for the French ambassador and believed to be affiliated with the Chinese services. When the DGSE was informed of this affair in 1998, it decided to pull Henri M. and some of its officers out of China. Henri M. subsequently left the service and created a private consultancy specializing in China, before returning there to marry his lover in 2004.[115] He then recruited his stepson, Pierre-Marie H., who was still working for the DGSE.[116]

The decision to go public and prosecute these officers stands out from a long tradition of silence surrounding security breaches at the DGSE. Two main factors seem to explain the decision to go public. First, the decision was made under the directorship of Bernard Bajolet, whose track record shows he favored a measured opening of the agency, most likely to convey messages. Second, this case emerged at a time when China was becoming a growing concern on the agenda of Western powers. The case thus communicated to DGSE staff, China, and other adversaries that the agency was ready to publicly assign responsibility for security breaches—in this case a penetration—to specific actors when red lines were crossed.

Conclusion

This chapter offered an overview of core DGSE activities, including intelligence collection, analysis, action, and security. While the threat environment and the agency's capabilities have evolved, the core missions and functions of the DGSE have remained remarkably stable. Three key themes emerge from this fragmentary picture.

First, the public record indicates that the DGSE culture continues to prioritize "the field" over analysis. Efforts to elevate the place of analysis, most recently with the establishment of a new General Secretariat for Analysis and Strategy, illustrate attempts at deliberate reform, which will inevitably confront deeper institutional assumptions about the operational character of foreign intelligence.

Second, within the spectrum of covert actions, evidence suggests the DGSE continues to emphasize its paramilitary capabilities, whether for intelligence collection, influencing foreign affairs, or eliminating threat actors. The agency's logo, featuring an eagle with a prominent claw, symbolizes its self-perception as a hunter with sharp eyesight and powerful talon capable of capturing, subduing, and killing its prey. This visual artifact encapsulates the DGSE's institutional identity, reinforcing a deep-rooted emphasis on coercive action. While such operations demonstrate tactical agility and responsiveness to external threats—especially terrorism—they also reveal the persistence of older values about what constitutes intelligence. This focus on paramilitary action aligns well with the demands of countering terrorism abroad, but it is less useful in the battle for hearts and minds, which has become a growing priority in today's information environment. Further adaptation is likely in the coming decade as the agency seeks to expand its capabilities in influence operations, strategic communication, and digital intelligence.

Third, the DGSE's activities span a wide geographic range, from Europe to Africa and from the Middle East to Asia, showcasing its capability and versatility. This broad reach reflects France's enduring ambition as a great power but requires strict prioritization due to the agency's limited resources. This is a long-standing challenge that is unlikely to disappear. Efforts to adapt by reallocating capabilities and reorganizing the agency showcase how strategic learning and environmental pressures can drive incremental change. Yet the recurring need to manage overreach also points to a gap between strategic goals and institutional capacity. One key strategy to compensate for limited resources is to strengthen cooperation with international partners.

Notes

1. Bernard Bajolet in Assemblée Nationale, Commission de la Défense Nationale et des Forces Armées, *Avis sur le projet de loi relatif au renseignement*, 78.
2. Silberzahn, *Au coeur du secret*, 250–51; Faure, *Aux services de la république*, 562. For a more contemporary explanation of the prioritization process, see Assemblée Nationale, Commission des Finances, de l'Économie Générale et du Plan, *Rapport d'information en conclusion des travaux*, 208.
3. "L'art du renseignement," 39; Cousseran and Hayez, *Leçons sur le renseignement*, 162.
4. Author's observation, DGSE exhibition, Paris, 2023; Government of France, "Synthèse nationale de renseignement déclassifié."
5. Anonymous DGSE officer in Allard and Kreplak, "La méfiance au quotidien," 71–93.
6. Marion, *La mission impossible*, 139–40.
7. Silberzahn, *Au coeur du secret*, 241, 295.

8. Chouet, *Au coeur des services spéciaux*, 209; Gregory, "France and the War on Terrorism," 130–33.
9. Martinet, *DGSE*, 209–16, 249–69. See also Nasiri, *Inside the Global Jihad*.
10. Alexandre in Notin, *DGSE*, 86, 93; Jean in Notin, *DGSE*, 94–100. (To guard their anonymity, the interviewees in *DGSE* were identified only by their first names.) On recent military operations in the region, see Goya, *Le temps des guépards*, 243–80.
11. Assemblée Nationale, Commission de la Défense Nationale et des Forces Armées, *Projet de loi de finances pour 2008*, vol. 2, 43; Assemblée Nationale, Commission de la Défense Nationale et des Forces Armées, *Projet de loi de finances pour 2010*, vol. 2, 17. See also Lewis, "French Intelligence Adapts," 13; Manach, "Frenchelon"; Aid, "French SIGINT."
12. Jauvert, "Comment la France écoute (aussi) le monde."
13. Assemblée Commission de la Défense Nationale et des Forces Armées, *Projet de loi de finances pour 2009*, vol. 1, 15. On early naval platforms, see Faligot, "France, SIGINT," 202–3; Jean-Yves Le Drian (French minister of armed forces, 2012–17; minister for Europe and Foreign Affairs, 2017–22) in Assemblée Nationale, *Loi relative à la programmation militaire*, 12169.
14. "A Look at the Latest French Laws on Intelligence Collection," Electrospaces, February 26, 2016, https://www.electrospaces.net/2016/02/a-look-at-latest-french-laws-on.
15. Bajolet in Hofnung, "Au coeur de la DGSE."
16. Jean Lesieur, "Le scandale des espions français," *L'Express*, May 18, 1990, 58–59; Jean Lesieur, "Vrai-faux démentis: La DGSE a bel et bien espionné l'informtique américaine," *L'Express*, May 25–31, 1990, 46; Schweizer, "Growth of Economic Espionage," 12–14; Interagency OPSEC Support Staff, *IOSS Intelligence Threat Handbook*, 36–38.
17. Faligot, "France, SIGINT," 203; Commission de Recherche sur les Archives Françaises Relatives au Rwanda et au Génocide des Tutsi, *La France*, 621.
18. Faligot, "France, SIGINT," 197.
19. Bernard Barbier in Assemblée Nationale, Office Parlementaire d'Évaluation des Choix Scientifiques et Technologiques, *Rapport sur le brouillage*, 35.
20. Bernard Bajolet in Assemblée Nationale, Commission d'Enquête Relative aux Moyens Mis en Oeuvre par l'État pour Lutter contre le Terrorisme depuis le 7 Janvier 2015, *Tome 2*, 865; Bernard Bajolet in Assemblée Nationale, Mission d'Information sur les Moyens de Daech, *Rapport d'information*, 270.
21. Bernard Barbier in Jacques Follorou, "Les confessions d'un maître de l'espionnage français," *Le Monde*, September 3, 2016.
22. Alexandre in Notin, *DGSE*, 92; Damien Van Puyvelde, "Le renseignement face à la menace terroriste," *Annuaire francais de relations internationales*, no. 22 (2021): 127–37.
23. Didier Le Bret (national coordinator for intelligence) in Assemblée Nationale, Commission d'Enquête relative aux Moyens Mis en Oeuvre par l'État pour Lutter contre le Terrorisme depuis le 7 Janvier 2015, *Tome 2*, July 5, 2016, 737.
24. See, e.g., Félix Tréguer, "Feu vert à la surveillance de masse," *Le Monde diplomatique*, June 2015, 1, 4–5; European Parliament, "LIBE Committee Inquiry."

25. "A Look at the Latest French Laws on Intelligence Collection."
26. Ministère des Armées, Instruction No. 101000/ARM/CAB; Louis Gautier (secretary-general for defense and national security) in Assemblée Nationale, Commission de la défense et des Forces Armées, *Compte rendu 36*, 7; Ulysse, in Notin, *DGSE*, 174.
27. Assemblée Nationale, Délégation Parlementaire au Renseignement, *Rapport relatif à l'activité de la délégation parlementaire au renseignement pour l'année 2019–2020*, 273; Assemblée Nationale, Commission de la Défense Nationale et des Forces Armées, *Rapport d'information en conclusion d'une mission d'information sur la cyberdéfense*, 49–50.
28. "Airgapped Network Threats."
29. Jacques Follorou and Martin Untersinger, "Quand les Canadiens partent en chasse de 'Babar,'" *Le Monde*, March 21, 2014.
30. "Babar: Espionage Software."
31. Communications Security Establishment Canada, "SNOWGLOBE."
32. Singh, "Morgan Marquis-Boire on Babar and Casper Malware"; Paganini, "Animal Farm APT."
33. Hayez, "Renseignement," 476. The expression "thinking part" comes from Bruce and George, "Intelligence Analysis," 1.
34. In contrast with the United States, where analysis is the key step. See Davies, "Ideas of Intelligence," 63.
35. "L'art du renseignement," 42–43; Lionel in Notin, *DGSE*, 28.
36. Direction Générale de la Sécurité Extérieure, *Rapport du jury sur le concours externe*, 3–5.
37. "Des héros très discrets," 38; anonymous officer cited in "L'art du renseignement," 42.
38. Émié, in Notin, *DGSE*, 13.
39. Central Intelligence Agency, "Intelligence Events Timeline."
40. Cousseran and Hayez, *Renseigner les démocraties*, 97.
41. Erard Corbin de Mangoux in Commission de la Défense Nationale et des Forces Armées, *Compte rendu 56*, 3; Bajolet, "La DGSE," 28–29. On consumers, see also Silberzahn, *Au coeur du secret*, 105.
42. Bajolet, "La DGSE," 28–29. See, e.g., Archives Nationales, Pierrefite-sur-Seine: Direction Générale de la Sécurité Extérieure, "Note de renseignement No.4420/T."
43. Cécile (analyst) in Notin, *DGSE*, 79–80.
44. Bajolet in Moinet, "Communiquer pour expliquer," 112.
45. Direction Générale de la Sécurité Extérieure, "La chaîne décisionelle" (author's translation).
46. Jean-Claude Cousseran in Bauer and Dupuis-Danon, *Les guetteurs*, 146.
47. Assemblée Nationale, Commission des Affaires Étrangères, *Avis sur le projet de loi de finances pour 2021*, vol. 4, 42.
48. Bajolet in Jacques Follorou, "Dès la fin 2015, la DGSE envisageait une victoire de Trump," *Le Monde*, January 14, 2017.
49. Direction Générale de la Sécurité Extérieure, *Propos sur la guerre du Golfe*, sections 1 and 2.
50. Silberzahn, *Au coeur du secret*, 285–86, 306.
51. Cousseran in Bauer and Dupuis-Danon, *Les guetteurs*, 140.

52. Chouet in Guisnel and Korn-Brzoza, *Au service secret de la France*, 326. See also Notin, *Les guerriers de l'ombre*, 162; Siramy, *25 ans dans les services secrets*, 150. See also Bernard Bajolet in Hofnung, "Au coeur de la DGSE" (Bajolet had not yet become ambassador to Iraq at the time).
53. Alexis in Notin, *DGSE*, 54.
54. Anne, in Notin, *DGSE*, 49–50.
55. Chouet quoted in Tom Hamburger, Wallsten, Peter, and Bob Drogin, "French Told CIA of Bogus Intelligence," *Los Angeles Times*, December 11, 2005.
56. National Intelligence Council, *Iraq's Continuing Programs*, 6; ElBaradei, "Status of Nuclear Inspections in Iraq."
57. Direction Générale de la Sécurité Extérieure, "Iraq."
58. Dominique de Villepin, address on Iraq, United Nations Security Council, New York, February 14, 2003.
59. Chirac, *My Life in Politics*, 267; de Villepin, *Mémoire de paix pour temps de guerre*.
60. Le Maire, *Le ministre*, 40–44.
61. Ministre de la Défense, *Arrêté n° 82-306 portant création et fixant les attributions de la direction générale* (emphasis added).
62. Cousseran and Hayez, *Leçons sur le renseignement*, 192.
63. Coordination Nationale du Renseignement et de la Lutte contre le Terrorisme, *La stratégie nationale*, July 2019, 9–10.
64. Sénat, Commission des Affaires Étrangères, de la Défense et des Forces Armées, *Rapport d'information no. 525 (2013–2014)*.
65. Champtiaux, "Les opérations spéciales"; Jean-Luc, "Forces spéciales," 77.
66. Anonymous officer in "Force de l'ombre," 50–51.
67. Jean Heinrich in Guisnel and Korn-Brzoza, *Au service secret de la France*, 420–21; Claude Silberzahn in Laurent, *Les espions français parlent*, 584; Champtiaux, "Les opérations spéciales."
68. Jean-Luc, "Forces spéciales," 78–79; Champtiaux, "Les opérations spéciales"; Silberzhan in Laurent, *Au service secret de la France*, 482.
69. Mermet in Bauer and Dupuis-Danon, *Les guetteurs*, 81.
70. Bertrand in Notin, *DGSE*, 122–23.
71. Bat, "Le Secteur N (Afrique)," 43.
72. Silberzahn, *Au coeur du secret*, 202–5.
73. Bat, "Le Secteur N (Afrique)," 53–55.
74. Silberzahn, *Au coeur du secret*, 223–24.
75. Silberzahn in Laurent, *Les espions français parlent*, 583.
76. Silberzahn, *Au coeur du secret*, 223–27; Silberzahn in Laurent, *Les espions français parlent*, 583–84; Bernard Bajolet in Assemblée Nationale, Commission d'Enquête Relative aux Moyens Mis en Oeuvre par l'État pour Lutter contre le Terrorisme depuis le 7 Janvier 2015, *Tome 2*, 857.
77. Silberzahn, *Au coeur du secret*, 127–28.
78. See Powell, *France's Wars in Chad*; Silberzahn, *Au coeur du secret*, 219–20.
79. For a detailed account of the period 1969–90, see Mireval, "Armées, sécurité et rebellions."
80. Mireval, "Armées, sécurité et rebellions," 292–93, 379; François Mermet in Bauer and Dupuis-Danon, *Les guetteurs*, 80.

81. Lacoste in Bauer and Dupuis-Danon, *Les guetteurs*, 46.
82. Mireval, "Armées, sécurité et rebellions," 308–13.
83. Mireval, "Armées, sécurité et rebellions," 328–31. See also Faure, *Aux services de la république*, 583–627.
84. Marion, *La mission impossible*, 144; Rondot, "Face aux menaces diffuses."
85. Lacoste in Guisnel and Korn-Brzoza, *Au service secret de la France*, 242; Silberzahn, *Au coeur du secret*, 184; Notin, *Les guerriers de l'ombre*.
86. Jacques Dewatre in Toreau, "Le renseignement français dans la lutte contre l'islamisme armé," 159.
87. Assemblée Nationale, Commission de la Défense Nationale et des Forces Armées, *Rapport d'information en conclusion des travaux d'une mission d'information sur les conséquences*, 80; Jean-Luc, "Forces spéciales," 78. For a detailed account of DGSE operations in Afghanistan, see Notin, *La guerre de l'ombre*.
88. Chesnot and Malbrunot, *Mémoires d'otages*, 29–42; Suc, *Les espions de la terreur*.
89. Jean Heinrich in Guisnel and Korn-Brzoza, *Au service secret de la France*, 420.
90. Cousseran and Hayez, *Leçons sur le renseignement*, 185, 193; Rondot, "Face aux menaces diffuses," 34–36.
91. Assemblée Nationale, Commission des Affaires Étrangères, *Rapports sur la proposition de resolution no. 2382*, 10.
92. Pascal Teixeira (former head of the DS at the DGSE) in Cousseran and Hayez, *Leçons sur le renseignement*, 203.
93. Guisnel, *Histoire secrète de la DGSE*, 94–111.
94. Gomart, *Soldat de l'ombre*.
95. Marion, *Mémoires de l'ombre*, 209.
96. New Zealand Security Intelligence Service, "*Rainbow Warrior*," 3.
97. Lacoste in Laurent, *Les espions français parlent*, 568.
98. New Zealand Security Intelligence Service, "*Rainbow Warrior*."
99. New Zealand Security Intelligence Service, "*Rainbow Warrior*," 9.
100. New Zealand Security Intelligence Service, "*Rainbow Warrior*," 7.
101. Marion, *Mémoires de l'ombre*, 240; Attali, *Verbatim II*, 1192, 1286; Faure, *Aux services de la république*, 534–35.
102. Dominique Fonvielle (former SDECE and DGSE officer) in Guisnel and Korn-Brzoza, *Au service secret de la France*, 196.
103. United Nations Secretary-General, *Ruling on the* Rainbow Warrior. On legal implications, see Davidson, "*Rainbow Warrior* Arbitration," 446–57.
104. Assemblée Nationale, Commission de la Défense Nationale et des Forces Armées, *Rapport sur la proposition de loi visant à la prise en charge*, 18.
105. Guisnel and Violet, *Les services secrets*, 40. See also Marion, *Mémoires de l'ombre*, 202.
106. Silberzahn, *Au coeur du secret*, 111.
107. Silberzahn, *Au coeur du secret*, 244–46.
108. Nouzille, *Les tueurs*; Bolelli in Bauer and Dupuis-Danon, *Les guetteurs*, 214–15; Guisnel, *Histoire secrète de la DGSE*, 228–29.
109. Barbier, "Espionnage et cybersécurité." See also Jacques Follorou, "Les confessions d'un maître de l'espionnage français," *Le Monde*, September 3, 2016.
110. "Death of Sahrawi a 'Blow' for Islamic State in Sahel, French Minister Says," France 24, September 16, 2021; Jean Guisnel, "François Hollande a ordonné

l'exécution du chef djihadiste somalien Ahmed Godane," *Le Point*, September 12, 2014.

111. Émié cited in Cyril Bensimon and Morgane Le Cam, "Au Sahel, l'état islamique, affaibli par la mort de son fondateur, reste actif," *Le Monde*, September 21, 2021.
112. Émié in Notin, *DGSE*, 15.
113. Alexandre in Notin, *DGSE*, 88–92.
114. "Deux ex-agents secrets français présentés à un juge, soupçonnés de trahison," *Le Figaro*, May 24, 2018.
115. Guisnel, *Histoire secrète de la DGSE*, 87.
116. For a detailed account, see Izambard, *Trahison à la DGSE*, 19–104.

5

International Partners

France's history and its global ambitions provide a strong foundation for the DGSE to maintain an extensive network of international partners. The first section of this chapter explains the expansion of this network over the past decades and links it to shifts in the threat landscape and political environment. The rise of the terrorist threat has driven greater cooperation, particularly in regions where France and other Western countries have limited access, thereby increasing their reliance on local partners and accelerating operational adaptation. Additionally, the digital revolution has introduced increasingly complex technical demands, placing a significant burden on intelligence agencies, which can opt to share some of these costs and geographical coverage through collaboration. Internally, the establishment of a Directorate of Strategy (now SGAS) and the nomination of diplomats in key posts consolidated the DGSE's policy of international cooperation.

The second section highlights bilateral cooperations between the DGSE and historically prominent partners such as the United States, Germany, and the United Kingdom as well as with secondary partners such as Pakistan and Russia. The major difference between these two groups is political. Developing broad and meaningful cooperation is easier with other liberal democracies that share similar values and concerns. These shared values foster strategic alignment and trust. Yet even among close partners, frictions persist, interests diverge, and tensions emerge.

On economic issues, for example, the DGSE was accused of spying on American technology companies. In the lead-up to the war in Iraq in 2003, French analysis was more cautious, and French policymakers were keen to voice their disagreement with their American and British allies. This episode still resonates in France, where some observers use it to underline the limits of international cooperation and importance of independent intelligence capabilities.

Political factors also explain variation in multilateral cooperation, the subject of the third section. France's political ambition to drive European integration partly accounts for multilateral initiatives such as the launch of the Intelligence College in Europe (ICE). The terrorist threat also prompted European countries to enhance sharing between their services. Yet while new initiatives and rhetoric reflect common values, national attachments to sovereignty and control continue to constrain the scope of integration. The idea of a European CIA remains implausible, not just for legal or technical reasons but also because of the enduring assumption that intelligence remains a core attribute of state sovereignty.

A Broad Network

Given the DGSE's international mission, the agency is France's designated lead in establishing and maintaining liaison with cognate services throughout the world. Its network of partners has expanded tremendously since 1982. In his memoirs, DG Pierre Marion describes a network of forty or so partner countries ranging from traditional allies such as the CIA and francophone African services to (then) less common ones such as the Israeli Mossad.[1] Marion repeatedly emphasizes the importance of building personal relationships with heads of foreign services and political figures, highlighting the semidiplomatic role that the DG can play.[2] This emphasis on personal trust and ties illustrates how cooperation is embedded not only in formal structures but also in the social fabric of intelligence.

By the turn of the twenty-first century, the DGSE had a much larger network of liaisons with more than 250 partners in over one hundred countries.[3] The breadth, depth, and degree of institutionalization of these relations varies. In some domains, such as counterterrorism, the French services share as much as 95 percent of their information with their partners.[4] In other domains, such as economic intelligence, one can assume the agency—and its counterparts—adopt much more competitive behaviors. DG Erard Corbin de Mangoux distinguishes between a close circle of ten partners with whom the agency maintains particularly "dense" relations and a second circle of fifty partners with whom relations are "frequent."[5] Neighboring countries such as Germany, Spain, and the United Kingdom and historical allies such as the United States, but also Israel, all belong to this close circle.[6] The second circle probably includes services from the North Atlantic Alliance and historical partners in Africa and the Middle East. This layered structure reflects both historical ties and strategic calculations shaped by threat proximity, political alignment, and access needs.

The DGSE has formal representation in dozens of countries through a network of stations—called *postes totem* in agency jargon—that are hosted by French embassies and led by a *chef de poste* (chief of station). Within the agency, the General Secretariat for Analysis and Strategy (formerly the Strategy Directorate) is responsible for these posts, which collect intelligence through local liaisons, and steers the overall partnership policy with foreign counterparts.[7] The existence of these posts varies according to contemporary interpretations of the national interest and the political conditions in key regions, such as North Africa, the Middle East, West Africa, and Central Africa.[8] The DGSE also has formal representations in China and Russia.[9] In keeping with intelligence customs, French embassies provide official (diplomatic) cover to the officers working in these stations.

Intelligence cooperation takes multiple forms, from exchange of raw intelligence to sharing or coproduction of analysis and more specific assistance to partner services. Insiders sometimes present cooperation as a market in which information and services are exchanged.[10] For DG Claude Silberzahn, "when the DGSE provides something to a foreign service, it expects at least an equivalent return in quality or quantity."[11] This aligns with the orthodox view holding that national interests and power maximization drive cooperation. This lens explains why cooperation tends to be stronger on issues for which national services share a common interest, such as counterterrorism, and weaker on issues that are more directly driven by the pursuit of national interests, such as economic and even political intelligence. The remainder of the chapter examines bilateral cooperation with close partners and more distant partners and then multilateral cooperation. As a rule of thumb, bilateral cooperation offers greater control over information and facilitates more operational collaboration, while multilateral cooperation tends to be more restrictive.[12]

Bilateral Cooperation

It is generally easier to work with countries that share similar values and with which cooperation has been ongoing for decades. These close relationships provide a foundation for deeper bilateral engagement.

The United States

Franco-American relations have been marked by a mix of cooperation and rivalry, which is apparent in the domain of intelligence.[13] One of the primary drivers of this cooperation is the respective strengths of the two national intelligence communities: the sheer size and technical capabilities of the United States versus French access to African and Middle Eastern networks.[14] In his memoirs, DG Marion explains the DGSE and the CIA shared intelligence and analyses on regions of common interests. The American community reportedly provided the DGSE with satellite imagery to follow troop movements in Chad in 1982, for example.[15] This is a good example of how the US intelligence community's technical primacy makes it an essential partner.

The rise of the terrorist threat has driven much international intelligence cooperation over the past decades, including between France and the United States. The DGSE's presence in Afghanistan since the 1980s has provided valuable access to sources on the emergence of jihadist groups in the region. DG François Mermet reportedly warned the CIA about the risks posed by its support to Sunni extremists such as Gulbuddin Hekmatyar during the Soviet-Afghan War.[16] At the turn of the twenty-first century, the DGSE had maintained access to selected Afghan warlords and continued to exchange intelligence with international partners. In a report from January 5, 2001, the agency underlined al-Qaeda's plan to highjack a plane flying toward the United States.[17] The report was shared with the CIA chief of station in Paris and likely contributed—in a small way—to the strategic warning the US intelligence community sounded ahead of September 11.[18] The attacks then put counterterrorism firmly on top of the Western security agenda and brought the DGSE closer to its American partners. In a memo reflecting on his time in Paris, a US SIGINT liaison officer who served in the early 2000s explains:

> Within minutes of the attack, DGSE was immediately on the phone expressing their sorrow and outrage at what happened. Both the DGSE and the DST immediately went to work providing whatever SIGINT and HUMINT they had or could acquire related to the attack. Over the next few months, DGSE for the first time provided NSA with raw voice cuts and technical information whenever there was a threat to a US person or facility.
>
> This kernel of cooperation born from a horrific event has proved to be the building block of even closer, more cooperative SIGINT relations. . . . We have moved from a very formal memo-passing relationship based on faxes signed by national authorities to one where we can send an "e-mail" message from a SIGINT analyst in the SID [Signals Intelligence Directorate] Africa shop to the computer desktop of an analyst in DGSE.[19]

Several examples of cooperation corroborate the impressions of this liaison officer. In the mid-2000s the NSA supported the DGSE efforts to locate and free two French journalists who had been kidnapped in Iraq. A courier subsequently hand-delivered DG Pierre Brochand's thank-you note to Gen. Michael Hayden, then NSA director, via the US embassy in Paris. The local NSA attaché thought "DGSE could have faxed this note or sent it via the bilateral line. . . . We Americans would consider this wasting time."[20] Several years later, the DGSE Technical Directorate signed a protocol with the NSA to exchange large volumes of data focused on regions and issues of common interest.[21] In a parliamentary hearing on the Syrian Civil War, the French defense minister boasted, "We have reached a level of intelligence exchange with the Americans that is equivalent to that of the Five Eyes."[22] In reality, sharing within the Five Eyes is integrated to a level that would make most French policymakers and officers uncomfortable. The French value their autonomy and are conscious their national interests do not systematically align with those of their anglophone partners. This tension between cooperation and autonomy remains a defining feature of the relationship. France is a valuable partner, but not a member, of the Five Eyes.

Franco-American cooperation also extends to human intelligence and operations. On the HUMINT front, the CIA reportedly shared with the French intelligence elicited from senior al-Qaeda detainees.[23] US officials even allowed DGSE officers to directly interrogate French detainees in Guantanamo.[24] The DGSE also cooperated closely with its American partners to track high-value targets linked to al-Qaeda and the Islamic State. French media report a mutualization of targets and collaboration between the DGSE's paramilitary branch, American commandos, and local forces to eliminate them.[25] Reflecting on her experience at the helm, CIA Director Gina Haspel praised the DGSE as a "top 3 partner" that is not risk-averse and has developed peerless expertise on counterterrorism and Africa.[26] Such praise reflects recognition of the DGSE's niche capabilities, particularly in regions where it retains historical access and cultural fluency.

Every relationship experiences highs and lows. At least three notable rifts have opposed the two allies in the last decades. First, tensions crystallized in the late 1980s when an espionage operation by the DGSE at General Electric on behalf of French electronics company Thomson/CSF was uncovered.[27] A few years later, CIA Director William Webster made it clear to DG Mermet that American companies had complained to President George H. W. Bush about French industrial espionage.[28] These tensions persisted when media revealed further DGSE operations to penetrate companies such as IBM and Texas Instruments.[29] The scandals revealed the rise of economic intelligence on the DGSE's agenda and French decision-makers' readiness to leverage DGSE capabilities to pursue economic interests.

A second prominent rift emerged in the 2002–3 run-up to the US-led Iraq War. The US and French services did not share the same assessment on the presence of weapons of mass destruction in Iraq (see chapter 4).[30] However, political tensions did not fundamentally affect cooperation between the services.[31] The episode did, nevertheless, reinforce the impression in some officials' mind that the US intelligence community should not be followed blindly. When the French community failed to predict Russia's 2022 invasion of Ukraine, some commentators referred to the Iraqi WMDs episode to justify why officials would have discarded the US assessment that Russia was about to invade.[32] While superficially plausible, this argument is not convincing. The two countries have cooperated on hundreds of operations and assessments since 2003, indicating that ties remain strong despite past tensions. Still, the episode shows how past strategic divergences embed themselves in institutional memory and durably shape elite perceptions.

Third, the Wikileaks and Edward Snowden revelations of 2013 caused another rift in the Franco-American relation. The leaks revealed that the NSA had spied on French officials in the United States as well as on France's most senior policymakers.[33] The technical director of the DGSE at the time, Bernard Barbier, later revealed the NSA had compromised the computer network of the Elysée.[34] Insiders and senior officials would and likely did expect foreign signals intelligence agencies to spy on their communications, but the very public character of the disclosures required a response. Barbier visited the NSA to complain directly to its director, Gen. Keith Alexander, and reportedly got him to acknowledge American responsibility.[35] French policymakers pushed for an agreement not to spy on each other, but—unsurprisingly—this never materialized. Despite their public reservations, "gentlemen" still read each other's mail when they have the opportunity.[36] Intelligence remains a tool of state power, even between close allies, so trust has clear limits.

Technical Cooperation with the Bundesnachrichtendienst

France and Germany regard each other as closest and most important partners in Europe. Their national interests often align, leading to regular and intensive coordination across most political levels and areas.[37] Unsurprisingly the French and German intelligence communities have developed close ties.

Both DG Mermet and DG Silberzahn report they had good relations with their German counterpart, Hans-Georg Wieck, who led the Bundesnachrichtendienst (BND; Federal Intelligence Service) from 1985 to 1990. The two foreign intelligence agencies have long complemented each another, with the BND focusing on Eastern Europe and Russia and the DGSE on Africa and the Middle East.[38] Cooperation seems to be particularly developed in the domain of SIGINT. The partners reportedly exchange communications intelligence related to political and military issues and electronic intelligence and cooperate on cryptography.[39] For instance, they agreed to intercept traffic relayed through civilian communication satellites in orbit over the Americas.[40] The two communities also arranged to exchange French imagery and German radar intelligence.[41] Former DGSE technical director Barbier confirms that the Germans are "strong partners" with whom Technical Directorate officers work frequently, "transmitting our know-how but also providing technical means." He likely refers to cooperation on cryptologic and decryption methods as well as joint access to the German station at Bad Aibling in Bavaria, considered by the NSA to be the most powerful SIGINT center in Europe.[42] The technical director was so convinced of the value and potential of this cooperation that he called for the BND and DGSE to merge their capabilities, a call that remained unanswered.[43] The cold reality is that decision-makers in both countries prefer to maintain a degree of autonomy and, when necessary, want to be able to spy on each other.

In the late 1990s German media reported that the DGSE was spying on the negotiations between the German technology conglomerate Siemens and South Korea.[44] More recently, the Snowden leaks showed that the BND acted on behalf of the NSA and spied on France via the telecommunications group Deutsche Telekom.[45] A senior BND officer confirmed as much to the Bundestag, specifying that targets included French personalities as well as the defense company EADS.[46] Even with strong technical ties and aligned political values, both sides continue to see value in monitoring their closest partners.

The United Kingdom

The Franco-British relationship is equally close but marked by more palpable political tensions. The two countries have long had strong rationales for, and a history of, cooperation in defense and security. They are neighbors that confront similar threats, have global responsibilities at the United Nations Security Council, and spend significant public money on security and defense.[47] They also compete for attention on the global stage and strive to maintain their status there. This paradoxical relationship is also apparent in the realm of intelligence, dating back at least to World War II. Charles de Gaulle's intelligence service relied heavily on British expertise and resources while simultaneously striving to maintain its independence. That early dynamic of cooperation conditioned by strategic autonomy set a familiar pattern that continues today.

In recent decades the two communities have continued to cooperate closely on a range of issues. For example, they worked together to resolve hostage crises in Lebanon during the directorship of François Mermet in the late 1980s.[48] In the field of counterterrorism, they reportedly shared HUMINT sources. Omar Nasiri, a DGSE asset who infiltrated al-Qaeda, reveals in his memoir that the agency lent his services to the British Security Service (MI5) and SIS.[49] Cooperation also extends to SIGINT. The DGSE signed a cooperation agreement with GCHQ as a secret annex to the Lancaster House Defense Treaty of 2010, signaling a willingness to further institutionalize their relationship.[50]

Just like with the United States and Germany, close cooperation has not prevented the partners from spying on each other. Media reports claim that the French have intercepted communications from British defense firms, petroleum companies, and other relevant commercial targets.[51] Even in the counterterrorism field, France sometimes prefers to play solo. In one operation, the agency sent undercover officers to keep an eye on Islamist preacher Abu Walid in Wembley, apparently without informing its British counterparts. This inference is supported by the fact that the French officers, operating under nonofficial cover, had to leave the UK after two British police officers checked their cover identities while they were sitting in the car they used for surveillance.[52] These operations reflect enduring assumptions that while cooperation is necessary, it should never compromise national freedom of action.

Cooperation between the two countries can also be marked by prejudices. For instance, former senior DGSE officer Alain Chouet expresses concern about the British proximity to Washington.[53] Such statements point perhaps less to mistrust than to a deeply rooted belief in the need to safeguard French independence. Intelligence ties with the United Kingdom remain strong, but as with other close partnerships they are filtered through a lens of autonomy and strategic self-reliance.

Second and Third Circle Partners

The DGSE collaborates with a broader range of partners beyond major Western powers. Cooperation with this second and third circle of partners, to reuse DG Corbin de Mangoux's expression, is equally important. France's historical presence on the African continent has long facilitated

DGSE's access to heads of state, core executives, and security apparatuses in francophone countries. For decades DGSE officers held senior advisory positions there on defense and security issues, supporting heads of state to ensure friendly regimes' stability.[54] Recently a series of coups d'état in Mali (2020), Guinea (2021), Burkina Faso (2022), Gabon (2023), and Niger (2023) has undermined France's historical position in West Africa, raising questions about the DGSE's ability to anticipate threats and decision-makers' willingness to protect friendly regimes.[55] At a more operational level, however, cooperation on shared security concerns likely persist, with several countries in the region continuing to work with the DGSE to track terrorists, rebels, and foreign influence operations.[56] Strategic interests and institutional ties can outlast political alignment, even as trust erodes.

The DGSE has also developed liaison relationships with various partners beyond France's traditional sphere of influence. This reflects its global ambition and the diffuse nature of contemporary threats. For instance, its relationship with Pakistan's agency Inter-Services Intelligence (ISI) dates back to French support for selected mujahideen groups during the Soviet-Afghan War. DG Marion recalls negotiating with the Pakistanis to intercept Soviet communications and access their analyses of the Soviet Union.[57] Cooperation between the two services continued even after the war in Afghanistan, particularly to monitor jihadist networks.[58] Not unlike the Americans, French officers have expressed frustration about the ambiguity and duplicity of their Pakistani counterparts.[59] This might explain why, in the early 2000s, the DGSE preferred to cooperate with the Intelligence Bureau—Pakistan's security service—to infiltrate combatant networks in the region rather than the ISI.[60] Concerns about ISI's reliability reflect a fundamental principle of liaison: It is always contingent on the alignment of interests and bound by perceptions of reliability.

Finally, the DGSE also cooperates with countries that would—today—be considered as adversaries. For example, the agency worked with Russia's Federal'naya Sluzhba Bezopasnosti (FSB; Federal Security Service) in the lead-up to the 2014 Olympic Games in Sochi.[61] Such cooperation illustrates the pragmatic logic that often governs intelligence work. Despite political tensions, services collaborate when security imperatives align. This pragmatism highlights how operational needs can temporarily override political differences, revealing intelligence agencies as institutions driven more by function and self-preservation than by diplomacy and rhetoric.

Multilateral Cooperation

The DGSE participates in various multilateral cooperation initiatives. Similar to bilateral cooperation, the transnational nature of many threats to international security, along with the comparative advantages of different national agencies, often justify pooling resources to achieve shared goals. This has led to the development of a range of multilateral efforts, from ad hoc meetings to more institutionalized structures.

Building on its historical relationship with regimes in North Africa and the Sahel, the DGSE established the Médi Club in 1982 to bring together the Spanish intelligence service (Centro Superior de Información de la Defensa) and the Italian military intelligence and security service (Servizio per le Informazioni e la Sicurezza Militare) as well as the Tunisian and Moroccan services.[62] More recently, the DGSE organized a meeting between the heads of intelligence of Nigeria, Cameroon, Niger, Chad, and Benin in parallel to a 2014 summit on security in Nigeria following the rise of Boko Haram.[63] These initiatives demonstrate how regional ties and legacy networks shape France's multilateral posture, especially in areas where it maintains historical access and influence.

In the aftermath of 9/11, the CIA pushed for several Western services (from Australia, Canada, France, Germany, the United Kingdom, and the United States) to establish an operational cooperation platform to fight against al-Qaeda. The result—Alliance Base—was located in Paris, primarily funded by the CIA, and led by a French general attached to the DGSE. The organization aimed to facilitate intelligence sharing and joint operations to identify and locate terrorists. For investigative journalist Dana Priest, who broke the story about the existence of Alliance Base, two main factors explain its location: France's permissive legal environment and the DGSE networks in the Middle East and North Africa.[64] Looking back, the then–CIA chief of station in Paris considers the organization worked very well.[65] For one thing, the cooperation platform reportedly facilitated French authorities' arrest of Christian Ganczarski, a German convert to Islam suspected of links to a 2002 suicide attack against a synagogue in Djerba, Tunisia.

French perspectives, however, have been more skeptical. A French counterterrorism police chief disputes the claim that Alliance Base enabled Ganczarski's arrest, and several French intelligence officials have questioned its value. From this viewpoint, the establishment of Alliance Base and its public disclosure—amid international criticism of the CIA's black sites scandal—offered political benefits but little operational utility. Eventually, the Barack Obama administration decided to disband the organization in 2009.[66] The episode illustrates how multilateral cooperation can become entangled in the high politics of foreign policy, even when its justification lies in the low politics of operational need.[67]

The best-established and most well-known multilateral cooperation platform is by far the Five Eyes alliance between the SIGINT services of Australia, Canada, New Zealand, the United Kingdom, and the United States. Several third parties, including France's DGSE, cooperate formally with the Five Eyes. The Nine Eyes alliance includes the Five Eyes plus Denmark, France, the Netherlands, and Norway. This group was reportedly set up to exchange military signals intelligence related to operations in Afghanistan. The Fourteen Eyes alliance adds Belgium, Germany, Italy, Spain, and Sweden to the group. This initiative, formally called the SIGINT Senior Europe (SSEUR), started in 1982 to monitor the Soviet Union. SSEUR meetings are attended by the head of the signals intelligence agencies of all fourteen countries, which coordinate data sharing through a dedicated system.[68] Of course, taking part in these initiatives does not mean all participants operate on equal footing. France is a top-tier intelligence power and a leader in Europe, but its reach and capabilities remain limited compared to the Five Eyes.

European Cooperation

The DGSE also contributes to a variety of multilateral initiatives at the European level. Geographic proximity provides a firm basis for repeated and durable exchanges. In 1976 Denmark initiated Maximator, a signals intelligence cooperation with Sweden and Germany. (Maximator is the only intelligence cooperation platform in the world named after a [German] beer.) The alliance grew over the next few years to include the Netherlands in 1978 and France in 1985. Research has identified two main rationales for its establishment. First, its members have sought to share the burden of investment in technical interception following the maturation of satellite technology. In this context, they continue to coordinate the interception of diplomatic communications and share some of the encrypted messages they collect. Second, the partners also share cryptanalytic tools and algorithms.[69] This example illustrates how technical innovation drives interdependence, with cooperation enabling small and medium-sized powers to remain competitive on the global stage.

Cooperation with European allies and with NATO has expanded significantly in the past two decades. A French Parliament report notes that the "DGSE has reached an unprecedented level of trust with its NATO and European partners in the field of counterterrorism, where cooperation is unrestricted." The report continues, somewhat optimistically, "The objective is to create a European intelligence core alongside the Five Eyes network."[70] The ambition signals a push for greater European autonomy, but there remains a clear gap between aspiration and actual capacity.

Despite occasional calls to create a European CIA, political will among member states remains limited. The Treaty on the European Union clearly holds that national security remains the responsibility of member states.[71] The main hub for (civilian) intelligence sharing within the European institutions is the European Union Intelligence and Situation Centre (INTCEN), a part of the European External Action Service, which reports directly to the European Union (EU) high representative for foreign affairs and security policy. The DGSE, like other member state agencies, contributes staff and information to this center. INTCEN lacks independent collection capabilities and depends on the goodwill of member states to access intelligence. This limits its autonomy but not necessarily its utility. France and others have a strong interest in having well-informed senior EU decision-makers.[72] In one notable instance, INTCEN, together with the EU Military Staff Intelligence Directorate, produced a report that anticipated the Arab Spring.[73] This suggests that EU-level intelligence, which always relies on sources from multiple member states as well as open sources, can be well placed to produce strategic assessments. Yet the extent to which European—let alone national—decision-makers pay attention to these warnings is debated.[74]

Moving beyond the strict boundaries of EU institutions, a group of twenty-three European countries have recently (2019) set up the ICE. France, and by extension the DGSE, have played a key role in developing this project.[75] This intergovernmental initiative—which is independent from the European Union—seeks to offer "a platform for reflection, sharing and outreach" to socialize European intelligence officials, national and European decision-makers, and academics. The main objective is not to facilitate operational cooperation—other channels are already in place for this—but to develop a common European intelligence culture.[76] This cultural turn mirrors a broader shift in the literature, moving beyond realist assumptions of self-interest to highlight how socialization and shared norms shape cooperation over the medium to long term.[77]

Conclusion

France's foreign intelligence agency maintains a global network of partners spanning North America, Africa, Asia, Europe, and the Middle East. This broad network bolsters its status as a major intelligence power. However, recent coups in West Africa, along with Chinese and Russian influence on the continent, are challenging France's standing in its historical sphere of interest. These developments raise questions not only about access and trust but also about the DGSE's ability to anticipate political shifts and adapt its partnerships accordingly.

In recent decades, international cooperation has been largely driven by the threat of terrorism. Its prominence on the political agenda has brought intelligence cooperation into the realm of high politics. The DGSE has used this shift to deepen its integration within the French administration and strengthen its ties with the nation's administrative and political elite. Counterterrorism has thus served both as an operational priority and as a catalyst for international cooperation and institutional consolidation.

The growing importance of digital technologies has also spurred further technical cooperation, particularly to share (some of) the burden of collecting, storing, and processing SIGINT with other major intelligence powers such as the United States. Despite this, French policymakers remain firmly committed to national sovereignty and expect the DGSE to maintain a high degree of autonomy. They view France as a driver of European integration and hope that fostering socialization among European elites will enhance cooperation over time. However, they agree with professionals that intelligence should not be fully integrated at the European level. The prevailing view is that intelligence remains fundamentally linked to national power, strategic autonomy, and state identity. Even as Russia's threat to Europe grows, few in France dare to question this assumption.

Notes

1. Marion, *Mémoires de l'ombre*, 172–77.
2. Marion, *La mission impossible*, 88–91.
3. Hofnung, "Au coeur de la DGSE."
4. DGSE official cited in Oudet, "Interconnected in Practice," 86.
5. Corbin de Mangoux, "Les mutations du renseignement."
6. Nicolas (chief of station), in Notin, *DGSE*, 42.
7. Ministre des Armées, *Arrêté portant organisation*, July 13, 2022, article 3.
8. Assemblée Nationale, Délégation Parlementaire au Renseignement, *Rapport relatif à l'activité de la délégation parlementaire au renseignement pour l'année 2015*, 49.
9. Hofnung, "Au coeur de la DGSE."
10. Mas, "La coopération entre services de renseignement."
11. Silberzahn, *Au coeur du secret*, 40 (author's translation).
12. Corbin de Mangoux, "Les mutations du renseignement." See also Lander, "International Intelligence Cooperation."
13. Brenner and Parmentier, *Reconcilable Differences*, 1.
14. Raviv, "PRISM."
15. Marion, *La mission impossible*, 69.
16. Mermet in Bauer and Dupuis-Danon, *Les guetteurs*, 86. This was confirmed by an independent source. Author's private information, 2023.
17. Guillaume Dasquié, "11 septembre 2001: Les Français en savaient long," *Le Monde*, December 27, 2007; Djaffar, "Que savaient les services de renseignement?"; Voger, *Je ne pouvais rien dire*, 160–62.
18. National Commission on Terrorist Attacks upon the United States, *9/11 Report*, 254–77; Marrin, "9/11 Terrorist Attacks."
19. National Security Agency, "(U) Reflections from an American in Paris."
20. National Security Agency, " (U) Hostage Support."
21. Jacques Follorou, "Surveillance: La DGSE a transmis des données à la NSA américaine," *Le Monde*, October 30, 2013.
22. Jean-Yves Le Drian in Assemblée Nationale, Commission de la Défense Nationale et des Forces Armées, *Compte rendu 17*, 3.
23. Toreau, "Le renseignement français dans la lutte contre l'islamisme armé," 449n2066.
24. Patricia Tourancheau, "Guantanamo: Les auditions pipées des services secrets," *Libération*, July 5, 2006.
25. Vincent Nouzille, "Comment Macron mène ses guerres secretes," *Le Figaro*, September 25, 2020.
26. Vincent Lamigeon, "Gina Haspel, ex-directrice de la CIA: 'La DGSE est dans le top-3 mondial,'" *Challenges*, June 24, 2022, https://www.challenges.fr/entreprise/defense/gina-haspel-ancienne-directrice-de-la-cia-la-dgse-est-dans-le-top-3-mondial_818378.

27. Rocard in Guisnel and Korn-Brzoza, *Au service secret de la France*, 457.
28. Mermet in Bauer and Dupuis-Danon, *Les guetteurs*, 86.
29. Silberzahn, *Au coeur du secret*, 171–72.
30. Hofnung, "Au coeur de la DGSE." Bajolet served as ambassador to Bosnia-Herzegovina at the time and likely would have gotten access to more information on the case as an ambassador to Iraq (September 2003 to August 2006) or possibly even later on when he led the agency.
31. On the French side, see Assemblée Nationale, Commission des Affaires Étrangères, *Rapport en conclusion des travaux*, 22. On the US side, see John McLaughlin, cited in Dana Priest, "Help from France in Key Covert Operations," *Washington Post*, July 3, 2005.
32. Sénat, Commission des Affaires Étrangères, de la Défense et des Forces Armées, *Rapport d'information sur "Ukraine,"* 21–22. See also Bajolet in Hofnung, "Guerre en Ukraine."
33. National Security Agency, "CLOSE ACCESS SIGAD"; National Security Agency, "Global SIGINT Highlights." For a more detailed explanation, see "Wikileaks Published Some of the Most Secret NSA Reports."
34. Barbier, "Espionnage et cybersécurité."
35. National Security Agency, "Visit Précis"; Jacques Follorou, "Les confessions d'un maître de l'espionnage français," *Le Monde*, September 3, 2016; Barbier, "Espionnage et cybersécurité."
36. Stimson, *On Active Services in Peace and War*, 188.
37. Federal Foreign Office, "Germany and France."
38. Silberzahn, *Au coeur du secret*, 301–2; Silberzhan, "Les Mutations de la DGSE," 17.
39. "A Unique Note from the BND About European SIGINT Alliances," Electrospaces, July 31, 2020, https://www.electrospaces.net/2020/07/a-unique-note-from-bnd-about-european.html.
40. Mermet in Bauer and Dupuis-Danon, *Les guetteurs*, 84; Jean Guisnel, "Espionnage: Les français aussi écoutent leurs allies," *Le Point*, June 6, 1998, 60–64.
41. AN, *Rapport sur le renseignement par l'image*, 100; AN, *Rapport relatif à l'activité de la délégation parlementaire au renseignement pour l'année 2015*, 57.
42. Jacques Follorou, "La France espionnée avec ses propres moyens," *Le Monde*, May 30, 2015.
43. Barbier, "Espionnage et cybersécurité." The idea is also mentioned by French politician Bruno Le Maire, currently France's minister of the economy, in Bruno Le Maire, "Pour une défense européene," *Le Monde*, June 21, 2008.
44. "Der elektronische Austausch von hochsensiblen Daten erleichtert die Industriespionage auch bei kleinerenFirmen," *Nürnberger Nachrichten*, June 23, 1998.
45. Jacques Follorou, "Les soupçons d'écoute de Fabius posent la question des dérives de l'espionnage allemand," *Le Monde*, November 13, 2015.
46. Deutscher Bunderstag, *Stenografisches Protokoll der 39*, 34, 45.
47. See Gomis, "Franco-British Defence and Security Treaties."
48. Mermet in Bauer and Dupuis-Danon, *Les guetteurs*, 84.
49. Nasiri, *Inside the Global Jihad*, 288–91.
50. Vincent Jauvert, "Comment la France écoute (aussi) le monde," *Nouvel obs*, July 1, 2015, https://www.nouvelobs.com/societe/20150625.OBS1569/exclusif-comment-la-france-ecoute-aussi-le-monde.html.

51. James Clark, "French Spies Listen in to British Calls," *Sunday Times*, January 23, 2000.
52. Martinet, *DGSE*, 261–67.
53. Chouet and Dewatre cited in Toreau, "Le renseignement français dans la lutte contre l'islamisme armé," 747, 778n3344.
54. Silberzahn, *Au coeur du secret*, 124.
55. Jean-Dominique Merchet, "Le renseignement français 'n'est pas à la fête' en Afrique," *L'Opinion*, September 11, 2023.
56. See, e.g., Notin, *DGSE*, 112–18.
57. Marion, *La mission impossible*, 144.
58. Dewatre in Toreau, "Le renseignement français dans la lutte contre l'islamisme armé," 160.
59. Chouet and Dewatre in Toreau, "Le renseignement français dans la lutte contre l'islamisme armé," 740; Waroux, *James Bond n'existe pas*, 164.
60. Notin, *La guerre de l'ombre*, location 10572.
61. AN, Commission de la Défense Nationale et des Forces Armées, *Compte rendu 56*, 8; AN, *Hearing of Erard Corbin de Mangoux*.
62. Cousseran and Hayez, *Leçons sur le renseignement*, 140.
63. "Front commun diplomatique contre Boko Haram," *Le Monde*, May 19, 2014.
64. Priest, "Help from France Key in Covert Operations."
65. Nouzille, *Erreurs fatales*, 174.
66. Faligot, Guisnel, and Kauffer, *Histoire politique*, 555–56; Servenay, "Terrorisme"; Toreau, "Le renseignement français dans la lutte contre l'islamisme armé," notes 3394–95.
67. For an argument emphasizing low politics, see Aldrich, "US-European Intelligence Co-operation," 131.
68. "14-Eyes Are 3rd Party Partners."
69. Jacobs, "Maximator," 660–61. On another SIGINT alliance between Belgium, Denmark, France, Germany, and the Netherlands, see Aldrich, *GCHQ*, 442–43.
70. AN, *Avis sur le projet de loi de finances pour 2017*, vol. 4, 13. On NATO intelligence cooperation, see AN, *Avis sur le projet de loi de finances pour 2011*, vol. 2, 20.
71. Treaty on the European Union, article 4-2. For academic takes, see Jeffreys-Jones, "Rise, Fall and Regeneration."
72. Neumann, "Member State Intelligence Support," 219–21.
73. Council of the European Union, "SIT-6577/07 Worst Case Scenarios." For context, see Arcos and Palacios, "Impact of Intelligence on Decision-Making."
74. Ikani, "Surprise, Revisited."
75. Author's observation as a participant at the ICE's inauguration, Paris, March 5, 2019.
76. Intelligence College in Europe, "The College."
77. Tuinier, "Explaining the Depth and Breadth"; Ben Jaffel, *Anglo-European Intelligence Cooperation*.

6

Cultural Representations

French political leaders have long expressed concern over what they see as the country's weak *culture du renseignement* (intelligence culture), especially in comparison to anglophone democracies. Justice Minister Jean-Jacques Urvoas once captured this sentiment by noting that "outside armed conflicts, so-called 'secret' services were long perceived to engage in perfidious and infamous missions. This is part of our national tradition. . . . Our history is full of memories in which intelligence is often associated with the idea of treachery, police surveillance, or unsavory operations."[1] For Urvoas, this historical baggage helps explain why France lacks the kind of public-facing intelligence culture found in countries like the United States and the United Kingdom. Yet this view is reductive, equating culture with public recognition. Culture is better understood as a set of practices that result from the interaction between human agency—intelligence officials, policymakers, citizens—and their organizational, political, sociocultural environment. It evolves as people and institutions adapt to new demands and norms.

The first and most basic expression of intelligence culture arises from the interaction between state institutions and intelligence practices. In France this became visible through the rise of dedicated services. As shown in chapters 1 and 2, institutionalization spurred the emergence of organizational and functional subcultures, such as those tied to HUMINT and operations, and domains such as domestic or foreign intelligence.

These subcultures reflect both structural adaptation to operational demands and more durable assumptions about mission focus and secrecy. Policymakers' interactions with agencies' leaders and outputs offer a second, more political window into intelligence culture. As chapters 1 and 3 demonstrate, these relations have often been marked by distance—even disdain—prompting figures such as DG Pierre Lacoste, Prime Minister François Fillon (2007–12), and more recently DG Bernard Émié, to claim that France lacks an intelligence culture.[2] This misrepresents the situation. France has never lacked such a culture; rather, its political culture of intelligence has been defined by systematic disinterest and elite disengagement.[3] In the past two decades, shifts in attitudes and discourse have visibly challenged this claim.

A third dimension of intelligence culture lies in public representation. Long before formal institutionalization, intelligence existed as a sociocultural object, expressed in language and images. Fictional portrayals matter: Secrecy creates a knowledge gap that fiction helps to fill. Spies occupy a space of imagination that exceeds their real institutional footprint.[4] This chapter focuses on this third—more public and popular—dimension and traces how political and organizational dynamics shape and are shaped by cultural representations.[5] This is important because portrayals illuminate shifting values and assumptions about intelligence.

To map the variety of representations of foreign intelligence in France, this chapter examines three interlinked discourses.[6] The first two sections explore fiction: literature and screen portrayals of spies as heroes or antiheroes. Entertainment, rather than accuracy, drives these portrayals. A second discourse comes from journalism and academia. These professions share an interest in authenticity but diverge in methodology and audience. They are key sources throughout this book, and their relationship with the DGSE is explored here. The third discourse comes from intelligence professionals themselves. Insiders shape public representations through memoirs, interviews, public speaking, and curated appearances. The DGSE now engages actively in image management, collaborating with fiction creators, journalists, and researchers and using institutional websites and social media to project a preferred narrative. This insider discourse often appears more authoritative due to firsthand experience. However, insiders' access—restricted by the need to know—does not guarantee their accounts are unbiased. They might select stories that do not represent broader trends (selection bias), attribute positive outcomes to activities they were involved in (self-serving bias), or craft stories that feel coherent and compelling but are not entirely accurate or objective (narrative bias). "Firsthand" does not mean objective. These narratives, while signaling evolving espoused values such as professionalism and public engagement, often reinforce enduring assumptions about the operational nature of intelligence and the centrality of secrecy.

These discourses—and the images they construct—raise questions about the role of intelligence in democratic societies and the blurred lines between fiction and reality. In the past decade the DGSE has become more deliberate in shaping its image, not only through exchanges with showrunners but also through exhibitions (often focused on the Resistance), press releases, media interviews, and digital outreach. These efforts have helped craft a more favorable image of the DGSE, improving public support. Optimists could note that this marks a shift in the agency's public strategy, reflecting broader adaptation to democratic expectations and reputational demands. More skeptical voices argue that this curated visibility creates an illusion of transparency. In practice, DGSE communications remain limited, and public access to information on its activities—past or present—is still highly restricted. This gap between surface openness and persistent opacity reveals the limits of cultural adaptation: Visible artifacts (e.g., structures and public speech) may evolve, but underlying assumptions about executive authority and secrecy endure.

Writing About Spies

The long-standing suspicion of spies in France has deep historical and political roots.[7] This attitude is reflected in the word's etymology. Contemporary French language dissociates the term "intelligence" (which refers to mental acuity) from *renseignement*. In the seventeenth century the plural form *intelligences* referred to secret negotiations. The word took a more negative meaning, associated with treason in the late eighteenth and early nineteenth centuries (*intelligence avec l'ennemi*). The French word for spy (*espion*) stems from *épier*, which initially meant to betray and now means to observe attentively.[8]

French literature has long conveyed this negative image. Leading French novelists of the eighteenth and nineteenth centuries such as

Marie-Henri Stendhal, Honoré de Balzac, and Victor Hugo spared no words for spies—a dreadful vocation according to Balzac.[9] This negative image was reinforced by scandals that crystallized French disdain for the spy business. In his open letter titled "*J'accuse . . . !* (see figure 6.1), French novelist Émile Zola accused the French government of anti-Semitism and condemned the imprisonment of French army officer Alfred Dreyfus for espionage (see chapter 1). Well into the twentieth century, the spy continued to be a vile figure, epitomized by the pejorative term *barbouze* (used to refer to undercover operatives). Meanwhile, across the Channel, authors such as William Le Queux (a dual French-English citizen), Rudyard Kipling, and Arthur Conan Doyle wrote much more positively about spies.[10] These literary differences underscore broader cultural divides: While anglophone narratives often celebrated espionage as a patriotic duty, French representations cast it as morally dubious—a reflection of deeper assumptions about secrecy, honor, and statecraft.

In France these prejudices fed popular misconceptions about intelligence work. Former DGSE leaders Jean-Claude Cousseran (DG from 2000 to 2002) and Philippe Hayez (who served from 2000 to 2006, including as deputy director for collection and analysis) link this tropism to the sociology of military institutions and a sense of honor that left little space for intelligence practices to be viewed as legitimate and thrive. This skepticism was not uniquely French. In his memoir, Henry Stimson—who served as US secretary of state and secretary of war—famously wrote that "gentlemen do not read each other's mail."[11] In France political and intellectual elites kept intelligence services at arm's length. This detachment perpetuated negative assumptions and limited early institutional adaptation.[12]

Attitudes toward intelligence shifted during World War II. In parallel, the emergence of the spy novel—a genre that frequently plays with or strives for authenticity—diversified the range of narratives about intelligence.[13] The experience of the war and Resistance stories—not least Joseph Kessel's seminal 1943 book *L'armée des ombres* (The army of shadows)—provided an impetus to portray the spy as a hero. Starting in 1949, Jean and Josette Bruce's OSS 117 book series sold widely, marking the "golden age" of popular spy novels in France in the 1950s and early 1960s.[14] The hero, Hubert Bonisseur de La Bath, is an American colonel of French descent who worked for the Office of Strategic Services (OSS)

Cinq Centimes

L'AURORE

Littéraire, Artistique, Sociale

Directeur ERNEST VAUGHAN

JEUDI 13 JANVIER 1898

J'Accuse...!

LETTRE AU PRÉSIDENT DE LA RÉPUBLIQUE

Par ÉMILE ZOLA

LETTRE A M. FÉLIX FAURE

Président de la République

Monsieur le Président,

Figure 6.1: Front page of the newspaper *L'Aurore*, January 13, 1898, featuring Émile Zola's open letter to the president of France, "J'accuse," which denounced the conviction and sentencing of Alfred Dreyfus. *Wikimedia Commons*

and later the CIA. Here the French public was offered a more palatable version of the spy, one aligned with postwar Western ideals but still external to French institutions.

From the mid-1960s onward, the success of these stereotypical spy novels started to decline, possibly due to readers' fatigue and the success of James Bond. The genre of the spy novel evolved toward pulp and political fiction through the pen of Gérard de Villiers and his aristocratic hero Malko Linge, also known as *Son Altesse Sérénissime* (SAS; His Serene Highness). With two hundred novels and over one hundred million copies sold from 1965 to today, the SAS book series has been a global hit.[15] In France, de Villiers reportedly maintained close contact with parts of the political elite and the DGSE as an "honorable correspondent."[16] De Villiers's novels develop an unsophisticated view of intelligence and human drama, mixed with sex scenes and an ability to write about—and sometimes anticipate—international crises.[17] Notably, neither the OSS 117 nor SAS series features a French protagonist. Instead, authors imagined their heroes as American or Austrian. This recurring displacement suggests a discomfort, a lack of cultural appetite, to center French intelligence within heroic narratives.[18]

A third wave of spy fiction emerged in the 1970s, moving away from some of the excesses of Malko Linge. Gilles-Maurice Dumoulin's hero—Vic St Val—is French but denationalized in the sense that he works as an intelligence officer for the United Nations. St Val does not fight against communists from the Eastern Bloc or dictators from the Global South but instead polluting industries and advertising magnates.[19] Overall, despite some variation, the figure of the spy in this body of literature is always an unabashedly pro-Western man of action, not an intellectual or bureaucratic mastermind like John le Carré's George Smiley.[20] French authors have tended to romanticize intelligence activities, emphasizing covert action.[21] French spy fiction thus lacks the complexity and ambiguity that characterizes some of the best novels in the genre.[22] This aesthetic preference reflects enduring assumptions that favor the tactical and clandestine over the intellectual and bureaucratic.

Spies on Screen

Representations of the spy figure in movies and television shows have oscillated between the hero and antihero archetypes. Several cinematic adaptations dominated the field during the second half of the twentieth century. They include a series of OSS 117 movies from the mid-1950s to the early 1970s as well as a masterful adaptation of *L'armée des ombres*.[23] On the antihero side, comedies dominated the production. Movies like *Les barbouzes* (released in English as *The Great Spy Chase*), *Le Monocle rit jaune* (The Monocle laughs yellow), *Le magnifique* (released in English as *The Man from Acapulco*), and *L'Opération Corned Beef* portray incompetent and ridiculous intelligence officers.[24] More recently, filmic adaptations of the OSS 117 series, starring Oscar-winner Jean Dujardin, portray an arrogant, incompetent, and racist French spy entangled in post-colonial intrigue.[25] The OSS 117 screenwriter, Jean-François Halin, also wrote the television show *Au service de la France* (released in English as *A Very Secret Service*), which mocks espionage, French chauvinism, and imperial legacies, using absurdist humor.[26]

Whether the story feature heroes or antiheroes, they consistently depict intelligence through the prism of covert action, with bureaucratic and analytical dimensions either omitted or ridiculed. *Au service de la France*, for instance, satirizes the weight of procedures and intra-agency rivalries with surreal effect. Whether reverent or mocking, these depictions reflect persistent assumptions about the nature of intelligence, particularly its entwinement with state power, colonial nostalgia, and masculine bravado.

In the post-9/11 era, screen portrayals have shifted toward greater realism, often focusing on the role of intelligence in countering terrorism. The success of the television series *Le bureau des légendes* (released in English as *The Bureau*), which follows DGSE officers under nonofficial cover in contemporary geopolitical hot spots, best illustrates this trend. *Le bureau des légendes*'s effort to align fiction to facts, and its exceptional access to the DGSE, signals a partial convergence between institutional image management and cultural production. This raises questions about the place of spy fiction in shaping public representations of intelligence and the evolving relationship between government agencies and the cultural industries. The show functions not only as entertainment but also as a discourse that has contributed to shift values associated to foreign intelligence toward strategic purpose, professionalism, and modernity, even as certain deeper traits about secrecy and operational bravado remain largely intact. The next section examines how the DGSE has sought to project its image through a variety of channels, including its growing ties to this industry.

Public Communication and Outreach

In the early 1990s the French political elite began to recognize the importance of intelligence in foreign and security policy. Key figures within the DGSE saw this as an opportunity to shape the service's public image, marking the start of a slow shift toward public communication and outreach.[27] DG Claude Silberzhan gave interviews to French daily *Le Monde* at the start and end of his tenure.[28] In 1991 he opened the doors of the DGSE headquarters to French public television for the first time, leading to the production of a short documentary.[29] It would take over a decade before the agency repeated the experiment, granting access for a longer documentary that followed its officers at work.[30]

In the mid-2000s various factors combined to bring the agency out of the shadows. Tackling the terrorist threat—which was now at the top of the political agenda—required a well-funded and efficiently organized intelligence community. Reforms progressively transformed intelligence into a matter of public policy.[31] Public expectations for transparency in a digital age defined by wide access to information underlined the need for a more deliberate and visible communication strategy. The core challenge was to communicate about the agency's missions in a controlled manner, fostering a positive image that could attract talent and legitimize activities while maintaining a veil of secrecy over much of them. The DGSE's communication campaign targeted two key audiences: policymakers and broader society.[32]

The nomination of the agency's first-ever communications officer in 2010 marked a turning point in the consolidation of the agency's public communications. DG Bernard Bajolet, who led the agency at the time, explains this effort was necessary "to show the role of intelligence in securing France and French people."[33] In one of his first public appearances, the communications officer explained, "Our role and the evolution of society must encourage us to open our doors and explain our mission and actions to the public."[34] The agency now has a communications cell attached to the DG's office and is also responsible for managing its relations with Parliament. This formalization of outreach reflects a form of institutional adaptation, a shift not only in structure but in espoused values about public engagement. The rest of this chapter focuses on the DGSE's communication efforts through collaborations with the entertainment industry, exhibitions, academic outreach (largely beyond the remit of the communications unit), and its online presence through a dedicated website and social media.[35] These initiatives have helped craft a more modern, accessible image of the DGSE, captivating a public eager to explore the secret world of espionage.

Liaising with the Entertainment Industry

One of the first times the DGSE advised the production of a movie was for Philippe Haim's *Secret défense* (2008). The film borrows the style and themes of American spy action movies at the peak of the so-called war on terrorism.[36] It did not achieve much critical or commercial success, but it showed that the DGSE was ready to engage with moviemakers.[37] After this initial attempt, the agency confirmed its interest in supporting "serious" representations of its work—to borrow the adjective used by its communications officer—by collaborating with the production team of the television show *Le bureau des légendes*.[38]

Le bureau des légendes provided a unique opportunity for the DGSE to improve its image. Showrunner Eric Rochant's taste for realistic spy fiction had already caught the attention of the DGSE, which reportedly used his 1994 film *Les patriotes* as a part of its training program. This may have facilitated his initial request for support from the agency. This request came at a time when the DGSE's public and internal image was tarnished by the failed operation to rescue Denis Allex and prevent a series of terrorist attacks in France (see chapters 3 and 4). In this context, the agency—and arguably the French public—sought a more compelling, affirmative narrative of national intelligence power.

After meeting with Rochant, DGSE leaders decided to trust the producer and showrunner, a decision reportedly endorsed by President François Hollande.[39] A memorandum of agreement established the framework: The production company of *Le bureau des légendes* would respect officers' anonymity (a legal requirement), avoid discussions of ongoing operations, and share draft scripts with the agency.[40] In return, *Le bureau des légendes*'s team was allowed to visit the agency's headquarters and meet real-life officers who talked about their work and offered advice on the plot. The presence of the show's set designer during a visit to the DGSE headquarters in Paris also facilitated the representation of the interior of the agency in the television show.[41] The production was also allowed to use the agency's official logo and to film external shots of its headquarters. This access enhanced the show's visual credibility and narrative realism. The arrangement marked a new stage in the DGSE's institutional adaptation, one that carefully balanced strategic cultural engagement with discretion.

Le bureau des légendes follows the life of a fictional DGSE unit coordinating nonofficial cover officers deployed in international hot spots. The series depicts a bureaucratic milieu of ordinary-looking people who struggle to balance life and work commitments and chitchat during lunch breaks.[42] The story presents competent professionals who master foreign languages and are resourceful in difficult situations. Their missions, however, are not ordinary, even in the context of a foreign intelligence service. Working under nonofficial cover is the tip of the spear and exposes the protagonists to unusually high levels of risk and violence. Unlike the characters, the plot is often unrealistic and tends to depict forms of heroism that borrow from the archetype of the spy as an action hero. Despite these elements of fantasy, the show's ambition to humanize officers and confront them with contemporary international crises makes it feel realistic. The format is very appealing.

The proximity between *Le bureau des légendes* and the DGSE is a subject of debate. On one hand, direct contact with the DGSE has reinforced the show's verisimilitude, giving it a sense of authenticity that supported its marketing.[43] From this perspective, the show has an educational value, even though it offers no real insight into contemporary intelligence activities. It helped to convey espoused values such as competence and duty without touching underlying assumptions about intelligence power and secrecy. On the other hand, critics worry that proximity between the production team and the DGSE has—at least indirectly—imposed limits on fiction and consequently on representations of intelligence in public debate.[44] By presenting intelligence officers as everyday men and women, the show reduces room for critical inquiry. Yet, as researcher Pauline Blistène points out, the plot does not reflect particularly well on the DGSE, especially when one of its most seasoned field officers betrays his country to save his lover. This and the overall quality of the scenario suggest that even if the DGSE was able to leverage this show as a means of influence, its authors kept a healthy degree of independence.[45]

Le bureau des légendes achieved significant commercial and critical acclaim, reshaping public perceptions of the DGSE. In the words of DG Émié, the show has been "a formidable vector of influence, reputation and recruitment" for the agency, cultivating its image both internally and externally. Externally, *Le bureau des légendes* conveyed the image of a modern service, far away from the *barbouzes* of the Cold War. In a telling example, Émié explains that when he first met Mike Pompeo on the seventh floor of the CIA headquarters in Langley, the director's first words were "Hi, Bernard! Here's the chief of *The Bureau*!"[46] Internally, the show also received wide acclaim from officers when it premiered at the headquarters. Posters of *Le bureau des légendes* have even been spotted on the walls of the DGSE offices.[47] For DG Bajolet, the show helped to restore officers' sense of professional pride and enabled them to communicate about their work life with family.[48] Remarkably, the DGSE achieved this reputational success without direct financial investment in the production. This success caught the attention of the Defense Ministry, which launched a "mission cinema" initiative to foster a dialogue between other parts of the ministry and the audiovisual industry.[49]

Le bureau des légendes shows that fiction can have significant effects on intelligence agencies, not least as a vector of public communication. This raises intriguing questions. Can and should fiction pretend to inform citizens?[50] Some French practitioners recognize that the show familiarizes its audience with intelligence.[51] Yet the audience might feel it has learned much more about the DGSE, even though the plot does not focus on the core business of producing intelligence for policymakers. The show does not provide information about actual DGSE activities. Blistène concludes that *Le bureau des légendes*'s focus on the ordinary aspects of intelligence offers a "simulacrum of transparency." Through its support of fictional communication, the DGSE projects a compelling narrative but continues to dissimulate secret intelligence activities behind a cultural facade.[52]

Curating the Agency's History

The DGSE's communication strategy has also sought to capitalize on its past. In 2011 the agency recruited a heritage curator to modernize its archival system and transfer declassified papers to the Service Historique de la Défense (Defense Historical Service) and the French National

Archives. This was followed by the establishment of an archival commission in 2013 to facilitate researchers' access to historical documents. Most of the archives that are publicly available on France's foreign intelligence agency relate to World War II and France's wars in Indochina and Algeria.[53] The only exception is a box of DGSE reports on the Rwandan Civil War (1990–94), following the work of a commission of inquiry established by President Hollande.

Yet the historical record remains thin. Public archives—the cornerstone of any rigorous history of government intelligence—are fragmentary. A 2020–21 controversy over the reinterpretation of national defense secrecy likely further complicated access. While French law mandates the release of classified documents after fifty years, a government directive now requires each classified document to be reviewed individually by the administrative authority that limited its access at the time. This effectively blocks automatic declassification. Researchers fear that this change marks a step backward, undermining efforts to write comprehensive histories of French intelligence.[54]

In parallel, the DGSE has pursued a carefully curated effort to communicate its history and activities through exhibitions. In 2016 and 2017 the Musée des Armées hosted an exhibition titled *Guerres secrètes* (Secret wars), which covered the institutionalization and evolution of French (but also American, British, and Soviet) intelligence services and activities throughout the twentieth century. The exhibition, organized by the French Ministry of Armed Forces, borrowed artifacts from a broad range of lenders, including the DGSE.[55] This marked the first time the DGSE exhibited some of its artifacts and documents to promote public understanding of its work.[56]

Since then, the agency has contributed to at least two additional exhibitions. In 2020 and 2021 the Cité des Sciences et de l'Industrie (Paris's science museum) hosted an exhibition titled *Espions* (Spies), inspired by the *Le bureau des légendes* and developed in partnership with core members of the French intelligence community, including the DGSE. The exhibition presented the community and the range of activities its officers engage in, in a more contemporary setting, confronting its visitors with a set of cases, such as the controversy on the presence of weapons of mass destruction in Iraq.[57] In the summer of 2022 the Musée de l'Ordre de la Libération hosted an exhibition on Charles de Gaulle's secret agents of

1940–44. The DGSE, which celebrated the eightieth anniversary of the BCRA and its own fortieth, was a key institutional partner.[58]

Under the leadership of DG Émié, a significant part of the DGSE's public communications focused on its ties to the Resistance during World War II. The agency used this theme to reinforce the sense of organizational identity and belonging of DGSE officers. This link is illustrated on the walls of the DGSE headquarters, where the portraits of four members of the Bureau Central de Renseignement et d'Action represent the current agency's core values: loyalty, exigency, discretion, and adaptability. For decades, the DGSE's main amphitheater was named after Col. (later Gen.) Louis Rivet, who led the Service de Renseignement from 1936 to 1944, walking a fine line to maintain some autonomy for French intelligence under Vichy.[59] The DGSE is understandably keen to anchor new recruits in the lineage of past heroes. Each new cohort of officers is now named after a BCRA officer who died for France. DGSE military units have even been authorized to wear the green fourragère of the Ordre de la Libération, established by de Gaulle to honor fighters who distinguished themselves in the fight to liberate France. New recruits also receive a numbered insignia bearing the Cross of Lorraine (see figure 6.2), the symbol of Free France during World War II—a ritual that anchors their service in a mythic lineage of sacrifice and national duty.[60]

This narrative draws a parallel between DGSE officers and wartime heroes. Though the broader contribution of the Resistance to the war effort remains debated, there is no doubt that *résistants* were heroic, and some DGSE officers similarly risk their lives in service. Yet many *résistants* were also controversial figures, espousing extreme beliefs from either end of the political spectrum—ranging from far-left partisans to far-right militants. As chapter 1 showed, the DGSE's institutional roots are complex. They include Vichy-era officers who—controversially—served under Nazi occupation. The DGSE's narrative tends to simplify its history, constructing a mythos that emphasizes heroism and national duty while downplaying moral ambiguity and institutional hybridity.

This approach is not unique. The CIA, for instance, displays a statue of Nathan Hale in its garden—a failed spy who probably never uttered his famous last words: "I only regret that I have but one life to lose for my country."[61] These foundational myths serve a purpose. For the DGSE, the Resistance link legitimizes a particular self-image—one that privileges

Figure 6.2: Affiliation insignia of the BCRA-DGSE.
© *Musée de l'Ordre de la Libération*

operations over analysis. This selective memory anchors assumptions about identity, sacrifice, and loyalty. Academics have an important role to play in deconstructing such myths and offering alternative lenses through which the public can understand the work and limits of intelligence.

Academic Outreach

For Adm. Pierre Lacoste, who led the agency in the mid-1980s, the lack of reliable information on intelligence in the public space fed misperceptions and prevented "reflection on the role and place of intelligence in modern society."[62] In the absence of access to information and rigorous research on intelligence, fiction, sensationalist media coverage, and (disgruntled) former employees dominated the public debate on intelligence.

These sources are partial and skewed public understanding, leaving space for myth and fantasy to flourish.[63]

To address this gap, Lacoste launched a research seminar on the French culture of intelligence at the University of Marne-la-Vallée in 1995. Though French scholars had published some research on intelligence before, this seminar provided the first platform for practitioners and researchers to reflect together on the place of intelligence in French society and institutions. The initiative empowered a generation of researchers who made seminal contributions to the academic study of intelligence in France.[64] While this academic work has advanced public knowledge, its scale and visibility remain modest, especially compared to the Anglo-American context. Ultimately, the public impact of intelligence scholarship, whether in France or the United States, cannot compete with the cultural reach of novels, movies, and television shows.

In 2017 the DGSE established a unit called Interaxions to tap into networks of experts in various disciplines and sectors, including academia, think tanks, and research institutes in France and abroad. Interactions with these outsiders take multiple forms, ranging from closed seminars and roundtable discussions to symposia and conferences.[65] A handful of these events have led to publications on topics ranging from "Islam After Daesh" to the rise of radical Islam in West Africa and the future security role of the western Balkans.[66] These publicly available reports offer a limited yet revealing window into the agency's interests and outreach strategy. While they have not altered the public image of the DGSE, they reflect a form of controlled adaptation signaling openness without conceding operational transparency.

Online Presence

The first official DGSE web page appeared in 2007.[67] For a decade, the agency's online presence was minimal. A handful of pages provided basic information about the missions of the agency and how to apply for a position. Even after the DGSE hired its first communications officer, who considered the agency's website "an essential component" in the agency's effort to support "an intelligence culture,"[68] it took several years to modernize its online presence. In the mid-2010s DGSE recruiters appeared on

LinkedIn, where they created a company profile. The agency launched its YouTube channel in 2018, releasing a handful of recruitment videos. More recently, it started to interact with well-established YouTubers to reach a broader audience of potential recruits.[69] The agency also organizes an annual online cryptanalysis competition. In 2019 the "Challenge Richelieu"—an invitation to decode a lengthy document—was posted on the website of the Ministry of Armed Forces.[70] The following year, the challenge was named after Brigitte Friang, a BCRA member.[71]

The DGSE does not have an account on X (formerly Twitter). The agency's communications officer explains that developing a social media presence presupposes "topicality and interactions." It risks "feeding the fantasy machine or having someone reveal an ongoing operation."[72] These concerns stand in stark contrast with agencies such as the CIA, whose first tweet in 2014 playfully stated, "We can neither confirm nor deny this is our first tweet." Given the level of public imagination sparked by *Le bureau des légendes*, such caution seems overly rigid, yet it reflects a deeper institutional unease with public communication, which remains shaped by a top-down logic of authority and control. Despite this institutional caution, DG Émié became the first DGSE leader with a public account on X (@BernardEmie). Most of his posts during his tenure were related to the memory of the Resistance as well as to the government's defense and security policy. The account also includes more personal touches reflecting on Émié's experience as an ambassador. For instance, the DG posted photos of himself with British royalty following Queen Elizabeth II's passing and King Charles III's coronation. These personal posts suggest that Émié's social media presence operated independently of the agency's broader communication strategy. This underscores the uneven nature of the DGSE's adaptation in projecting its institutional voice—showing how communication remained closely tied to the director's discretion rather than governed by a consistent institutional strategy.

The latest step in expanding the DGSE's online presence came in 2021, when it moved its website from the Ministry of Armed Forces domain to a stand-alone platform.[73] The new site features a sleek design and—reflecting what appears to be a key narrative priority—includes a dedicated section on the agency's "filiation" with the Resistance. This move further illustrates how the DGSE curates its identity through tightly controlled symbols that affirm selective historical roots and legitimize a specific view of its institutional role.

Public Use of Intelligence

Would it be reasonable for French citizens to expect more substantive communication from the DGSE? Officially, the DGSE does not communicate about its operations. As a former director stated, its mission is to "inform government and not to inform or orient the public."[74] Yet, in at least two recent cases, policymakers publicly used DGSE intelligence to justify their decisions.

In September 2013 the Elysée decided to declassify a national intelligence synthesis on Syrian chemical attacks following the refusal by the United Kingdom and the United States to conduct air strikes in Syria. The DGSE was able to recover multiple sources of evidence that the Syrian regime had used chemical weapons on its population.[75] The declassified report, based on intelligence from the DGSE, provides background on the history, nature, delivery means, and command and control of Syria's chemical program before confirming a chemical attack on April 21, 2013, in the outskirts of Damascus. The document even refers to the analysis of biomedical samples gathered "in conditions verified by our services," which confirm the use of sarin gas. The subsequent evaluation pins responsibility on the Syrian regime and discusses its intentions: to secure strategic sites and control the capital.[76] Reflecting on the decision years later, Hollande explained:

> When the use of chemical weapons by the Syrian regime was revealed, a controversy arose over the veracity of the use and the perpetrator. It was crucial for us to demonstrate that our information was reliable—and it was corroborated by others. In my opinion, it was undoubtedly necessary to tell the French to avoid repeating the episode of the second Iraq war and work towards the legitimacy of an intervention. I therefore decided to make this information public.[77]

A more recent case illustrates a similar trend. DG Émié appeared alongside the minister of armed forces to present the DGSE's assessment of jihadist threats in the Sahel and the Levant, using imagery to support his key points and warning of potential attacks in Europe. He also presented a video of terrorist leader Iyad Ag-Ghaly filmed "by a human source working very closely to the terrorist chiefs."[78]

These two episodes do not signal a shift toward systematic public disclosure. In both cases, senior political figures (a minister and the president) took the lead. If anything, these examples show that France's senior policymakers have now become sufficiently acculturated to the DGSE's capabilities to use them strategically when it suits their purpose. The DGSE's public silence during the lead-up to and escalation of Russia's war in Ukraine further highlights its continued adherence to a model of discretion, distancing it from the more visible public role embraced by its American and British counterparts.[79] This restraint reflects not just political caution but also enduring assumptions about secrecy and the very purpose of foreign intelligence—assumptions that continue to constrain the DGSE's role.

Conclusion

The oft-repeated claim that France lacks an intelligence culture is inaccurate. Cultural, public, and political representations of intelligence all contribute to shaping a national intelligence culture. The French people have long been exposed to various narratives about France's foreign intelligence service. While it is true that the spy figure has often been portrayed with disdain or ridicule in novels and on screens, a more heroic narrative has coexisted since at least World War II. Since the 2000s the DGSE has made significant efforts to engage with selected outsiders and promote a positive image of itself. Today France's most senior policymakers are familiar with the DGSE to the extent that they occasionally use its intelligence to publicly support difficult security decisions. These selective disclosures signal a greater willingness to leverage intelligence as a tool of strategic communication.

Public opinion polls over the past two decades suggest a strong level of public trust in the DGSE. The prominent role of intelligence in counterterrorism has likely helped to legitimize the agency in the public eye. Polls indicate a clear increase in public awareness and positive recognition of the DGSE, with 47 percent of the respondents claiming to know about the agency in 2003–4, 57 percent in 2005, and 67 percent in 2010. In the 2010 poll, the foreign intelligence service received a 75 percent positive rating.[80] By 2018, 77 percent of French people reported having heard of the DGSE, and within this group 89 percent expressed trust in the agency. Citing these numbers, DG Émié concluded that French people "know and appreciate" the agency.[81]

Yet these polls only capture the surface of cultural acceptance. Intelligence culture is not monolithic, and conflicting representations of France's foreign intelligence service coexist. These discourses reflect the layered nature of cultural adaptation, where new practices and values emerge, but deeper assumptions about intelligence power and secrecy evolve more slowly. Historians have strongly opposed recent restrictions on declassification. Civil liberties groups have mobilized against DGSE monitoring of Internet communications, especially in the wake of the Edward Snowden revelations.[82] These criticisms show that institutional legitimacy is not static but instead continually negotiated and that the boundaries of acceptable intelligence practice remain contested.

The agency's public communication efforts, alongside fiction, scholarship, and journalism, shape how intelligence is represented and understood. Despite their limits and imperfections, these varied perspectives are a hallmark of democratic life. The representations they produce are partial, shedding selective light on what the DGSE is, does, and represents. Yet it is precisely this diversity of representations that sustains a necessary public conversation about the role and limits of intelligence in a liberal democracy.

Notes

1. Jean-Jacques Urvoas in AN, Commission des Lois Constitutionelles, de la Législation et de l'Administration Générale de la République, *Rapport sur le project de loi relatif au renseignement*, 81 (author's translation).
2. Lacoste, *Un amiral au secret*, 205; Lacoste, "Pratique du pouvoir et renseignement," 29; Fillon, "Installation de l'académie du renseignement," 9; Bernard Émié in Elouarghi, Foenkinos, and Marjany, "Bernard Émié."
3. Jackson, "Pierre Bourdieu," 162–71; McGowan, "Balancing Act," 23–25.
4. Blistène, "Le secret comme ordinaire," 115.
5. For a similar triptych on intelligence culture, see Ferro, "Responsables politiques français et renseignement," 1.
6. See the seminal work by Blistène, "Voir et faire voir le secret de l'état," 357–68.
7. Ferro, "Les services de renseignement français," 1–2.
8. Becker, "Spy Who Couldn't Possibly Be French," 70–71.
9. Cousseran and Hayez, *Leçons sur le renseignement*, 64–65.

10. Becker, "Spy Who Couldn't Possibly Be French," 77.
11. Stimson, *On Active Services in Peace and War*, 188.
12. Forcade and Laurent, *Secrets d'état*, 11; Laurent, "Is There Something Wrong with Intelligence in France?," 299.
13. Oudet, "Le roman d'espionnage."
14. Neveu, "Trente ans de littérature," 52.
15. Ariane Chemin and Judith Perrignon, "Gérard de Villiers, itinéraire d'un réac," *Le Monde*, November 24, 2013.
16. Robert F. Worth, "The Spy Novelist Who Knows Too Much," *New York Times*, January 30, 2013; Lacoste, *Un amiral au secret*, 111–12; Franquebalme, *Son Altesse Sérénissime*.
17. Worth, "Spy Novelist Who Knows Too Much"; Blistène, "Sea, Sex, and Spies," 327–42.
18. Becker, "Spy Who Couldn't Possibly Be French," 85–86.
19. Neveu, "Trente ans de littérature," 56.
20. On George Smiley, see Blistène and Van Puyvelde, "A Delicate Truth," 194.
21. Ferro, "Les services de renseignement français," 5.
22. Blistène, "Fictions du secret, secrets de la fiction," 133–34.
23. Jean Sacha, *OSS 117 n'est pas mort* (1956); Andre Hunebelle, *OSS 117 se déchaîne* (1963); Pierre Kalfon, *OSS 117 prend des vacances* (1970); Jean-Pierre Melville, *Army of the Shadows* (1969).
24. Georges Lautner, *Les barbouzes* (1964); Georges Lautner, *Le Monocle rit jaune* (1964); Philippe de Broca, *Le magnifique* (1973); Jean-Marie Poir, *L'Opération Corned Beef* (1991).
25. Michel Hazanavicus, *OSS 117: Le Caire, nid d'espions* (2006), and *OSS 117: Rio ne répond plus* (2009).
26. Jean-François Halin, Claire Lemaréchal, and Jean-André Yerlès, *Au service de la France* (2015).
27. Pennetier, "Springtime of French Intelligence," 780–98.
28. "Un entretien avec le patron des services secrets M. Claude Silberzahn propose un plan de renforcement de la DGSE," *Le Monde*, January 31, 1990; Jacques Isnard, "L'Europe du renseignement se construit plus vite que l'Europe politique," *Le Monde*, March 31, 1993.
29. Meidinger, "L'espion du président."
30. Lorton and Motte, "Soldats de l'ombre."
31. Bajolet in Moinet, "Communiquer pour expliquer," 110; Laurent, "Les parlementaires face à l'état secret," 143–44; Chopin, "Intelligence Reform," 546–47.
32. Nicolas Wuest-Famôse in Lelièvre, "La communication web," 345.
33. Bajolet in Guisnel and Korn-Brzoza, *Au service secret de la France*, 516.
34. Wuest-Famôse, "Expliquer notre mission."
35. Bajolet in Moinet, "Communiquer pour expliquer," 111; Émié in Le Fur and Wasjman, "Les ambitions du renseignement."
36. On the historical relationship between the CIA and the entertainment industry, see Willmetts, *In Secrecy's Shadow*; Jenkins, *CIA in Hollywood*; and McCarthy, *Selling the CIA*.
37. Blistène, "La communication au secret," 141.

38. Wuest-Famôse in Lelièvre, "La communication web," 349; Blistène, "Voir et faire voir le secret de l'état," 185.
39. Guisnel, *Histoire secrète de la DGSE*, 42.
40. Blistène, "La communication au secret," 143–44.
41. Léna Lutaud, "La DGSE, meilleur agent infiltré au *Bureau des légendes*," *Le Figaro*, May 14, 2017; Vincent Nouzille, "La vraie vie des espions," *Le Figaro*, August 4, 2017; Trotignon, *Politique du secret*, 21–26.
42. Rochant, "Nous essayons de parler"; Blistène, "Le secret comme ordinaire," 116, 122, 126. On the different realisms of *The Bureau*, see Blistène, "*The Bureau* and the Realism of Spy Fiction," 231–49.
43. Oudet, "Un regard sur *Le bureau des légendes*"; Blistène, "La communication au secret," 106; Blistène, "Voir et faire voir le secret de l'état," 192.
44. Depending on the account, the agency suggested or requested minor changes on some aspects of the scenario. See Guisnel, *Histoire secrète de la DGSE*, 42–43; Blistène, "Voir et faire voir le secret de l'état," 263, 269.
45. Blistène, "Le secret comme ordinaire," 128, 269.
46. Bernard Émié in Le Fur and Wasjman, "Les ambitions du renseignement."
47. Guisnel, *Histoire secrète de la DGSE*, 58, 60.
48. Bajolet in Moinet, "Communiquer pour expliquer," 111.
49. Ministère des Armées, "La mission cinéma et industries créatives (MCIC) du ministère des armées," https://www.defense.gouv.fr/mission-cinema-industries-creatives-mcic-du-ministere-armees.
50. Chopin and Oudet, *Renseignement et sécurité*, 244–45.
51. Blistène, "Voir et faire voir le secret de l'état," 247.
52. Blistène, "Le secret comme ordinaire," 129; Blistène, "La communication au secret," 147.
53. Guisnel, *Histoire secrète de la DGSE*, 307–9.
54. Olivier Forcade, Sébastien-Yves Laurent, and Bertrand Warusfel, "Archives classées 'secret-défense,'" *Le Monde*, January 26, 2020; Forcade, Laurent, and Warusfel, "Archives et politiques du secret." See also Conseil d'État, Section du Contentieux, 10ème et 9ème Chambres Réunies, *Association des Archivistes Français*, 8.
55. Musée de l'Armée, "Guerres secrètes."
56. Martin Briens in Fondation Charles de Gaulle, *Défendre la France*, 280.
57. Cité des Sciences et de l'Industrie, "Espions."
58. Musée de l'Ordre de la Libération, "Les agents secrets du général."
59. Rivet, *Carnets du chef des services secrets*.
60. DGSE, "L'engagement en héritage"; Bajolet, "La DGSE, modèle français d'intégration," 6; Bernard Émié in Christophe Cornevin, "Le patron de la DGSE au *Figaro*: 'Aujourd'hui comme hier, nos agents sont en première ligne,'" *Le Figaro*, June 23, 2022.
61. Jeffreys-Jones, *Cloak and Dollar*, 19–20.
62. Lacoste, *Le renseignement*, 2.
63. Lacoste, "Pratique du pouvoir et renseignement," 29. The most comprehensive—though imperfect—history of French intelligence was produced by three journalists; see Faligot, Guisnel, and Kauffer, *Histoire politique*. More recently Jacques Follorou, Jean-Christophe Notin, Matthieu Suc, and Vincent Nouzille

have provided coverage on intelligence affairs. For a reflection on the role of some of these journalists, see Michalon and Puybareau, "Secret d'état et secret des sources," 227–62. Former DGSE officers who have published memoirs include Alain Chouet, Jean-Marc Gadoullet, Thierry Jouan, Jean-François Lhuillier, Pierre Martinet (sentenced in 2006 to a fifteen-month suspended prison sentence and fined €5,000 for his book *Un agent sort de l'ombre*), Pierre Siramy (alias Mauriace Dufresse, sentenced to a two-month suspended sentence and fined €5,000 for naming two officers), Richard Volange, and François Waroux.

64. Forcade, *La république secrète*; Laurent, *Politiques de l'ombre*; Soutou, Frémaux, and Forcade, *L'exploitation du renseignement*; Warusfel, *Contre-espionnage*.
65. Author's observation as a participant, 2018. See also Van Puyvelde, "Academic-Practitioner Relationship," 188–90.
66. Ministère des Armées, "Interaxions."
67. Internet Archive, Wayback Machine.
68. Wuest-Famôse in Lelièvre, "La communication web," 106, 348.
69. DGSE, "@DGSEgouv"; Underscore, "J'ai été contacté par la DGSE."
70. For a solution to the challenge and some explanations, see Redouane, "Writeup of the Richelieu Challenge."
71. DGSE, "Opération 'Brigitte Friang.'"
72. Wuest-Famôse in Lelièvre, "La communication web," 197.
73. Internet Archive, www.defense.gouv.fr/dgse/. For the DGSE website, see https://www.dgse.gouv.fr.
74. Bajolet in Moinet, "Communiquer pour expliquer," 112.
75. Author's observation, DGSE exhibition, September 2023.
76. Government of France, "Synthèse nationale de renseignement déclassifié."
77. François Hollande in Vadillo and Papaemmanuel, *Les espions de l'Elysée*, 163.
78. Elise Vincent, "Au Mali, les djihadistes 'réfléchissent à des attaques en Europe,' selon le patron de la DGSE," *Le Monde*, February 3, 2021. For the video, see François, "Quand la DGSE dévoile."
79. Dylan and Maguire, "Secret Intelligence and Public Diplomacy," 33–74; Van Puyvelde, "Médiatisation du renseignement."
80. Ferro, "Les services de renseignement francais," 7.
81. Émié in Le Fur and Wasjman, "Les ambitions du renseignement."
82. Tréguer, "Intelligence Reform and the Snowden Paradox," 21–24.

7

Legacy, Impact, and Future

This book has argued that although inertia remains a feature of the DGSE's institutional life, adaptation has, on balance, prevailed. Three forces have driven the DGSE's adaptation in the past decades: the prominence of the terrorist threat, sustained political backing, and informed leadership. Together they have enabled the agency to secure increased funding, enhance and expand its workforce and technical capacities, and strengthen its integration and influence in the French administration and policymaking apparatus.

The agency's core missions have remained stable for decades and are institutionally embedded. They are unlikely to shift significantly, even as changes in the threat landscape and political alternance will continue to demand further adaptation. Building on the three core drivers that explain adaptation, this conclusion explores the DGSE's current posture and future trajectory. It weighs the impact of the contemporary threat landscape, probes the evolving intelligence-policy relationship, and considers the potential outcomes of the agency's latest reform. The book now ends with a discussion of the agency's growing public profile and oversight, two crucial markers of adaptation in a liberal democracy.

A Multifaceted Threat Landscape

At the turn of the twenty-first century, major terrorist attacks in France and elsewhere in the Western world acted as a wake-up call, prompting French leaders to pay closer attention to their intelligence community. The prolonged period during which terrorism dominated the foreign and security policy agenda provided a consistent environment for the DGSE to pursue its adaptation. The agency has gradually become integrated into the French administration and decision-making machinery. This position is now firmly entrenched, and shifts in the threat environment are unlikely to weaken it.

The prominence of the terrorist threat drove much of the agency's adaptation in the past decades. As France continues to pursue global ambitions, the DGSE now faces a longer list of requirements. The return of war in Europe following Russia's invasion of Ukraine and the increasingly uninhibited use of covert action by great and small powers also pose obvious challenges.[1] This multifaceted threat landscape is likely to stretch intelligence agencies' resources, thus forcing prioritization.[2] At the same time, this situation all but ensures the continuing relevance of the DGSE in supporting and enacting policy.

Where will the DGSE focus its efforts? France's influence in Africa, anchored in historical ties and geographic proximity, is under increasing challenge from Russia and China but also the United States and Israel. Competition is evident in places such as Djibouti, a former French colony rich in mineral resources and strategically located.[3] The DGSE's decades of experience in Africa remain an asset that French policymakers and the agency are unlikely to abandon. The enduring weight of history and geographic proximity make a continuing focus on France's African sphere of influence very likely.

The war in Ukraine has drawn renewed attention to Eastern Europe. Shortly before the onset of Russia's 2022 invasion, according to DG Bernard Émié, the DGSE gathered precise technical intelligence comparable to that of its American counterparts. The divergence lay in analysis: While the DGSE assessed that Russia would not initiate a conflict while high-level diplomatic negotiations were ongoing, the CIA anticipated imminent Russian action, and US policymakers decided to disclose that intelligence to rally allies and dissuade aggression. Ultimately, the Russians defied French and other Western European officials' expectations, but the French had accurately assessed their readiness for conflict.[4] This case underscores the complexity of intelligence analysis: Leadership psychology, political context, and organizational culture complicate interpretation.[5] Intelligence failures are often inevitable, and successes, though harder to see, are not absent. More than a year after Russia's full-scale invasion, media reports revealed that the French community had anticipated the Wagner mutiny in Russia.[6]

Although the DGSE has redirected some resources toward China and the Indo-Pacific region, where France has overseas territories, it has not fully pivoted in that direction.[7] Resource constraints and ongoing commitments in Europe and Africa make such a shift unlikely in the near term.

Intelligence-Policy Nexus

The structures established in the 2000s to strengthen the intelligence-policy nexus—the CNRLT, the intelligence council, and the DPR—are here to stay. Steady investments in the DGSE also appear to be holding firm and can be expected to continue in the medium term as the agency completes its move to its new headquarters.

Currently President Macron maintains a close relationship with the director general. DG Lerner's career at the Ministry of the Interior and background as a graduate of France's top public administration school confirm the trend of the past three decades. DGSE leadership now attracts prominent figures from the French administrative elite, not only at the DG level but also below. The agency's integration into the fabric of the French state will guarantee its sustained support and influence.

The most serious challenge to the intelligence-policy relationship may come not from within the agency but instead from political shifts. How would the agency respond to the rise to power of an extremist party? French civil servants are duty bound to implement the legitimate directives of the elected government, but their ultimate allegiance remains to the republic's constitutional values. This could create significant friction with and within the DGSE and the broader French intelligence community, particularly given the ambiguous stances toward Russia taken by both the Rassemblement National (France's far-right party) and the far-left La France Insoumise. These stances risk undermining the response to what remains a clear and present danger to European stability: Russia. Such a scenario is likely to test the very meaning of loyalty, a core value of the DGSE.

Reform and Its Aftermath

The DGSE presents itself as an integrated agency with a strong emphasis on operations, a trend that is likely to continue. However, integration has often been more nominal than real. The 2022 reform, which established several mission centers and merged key directorates, aims to focus the agency's efforts more effectively. It is too early to determine whether recent changes will have a positive impact. One measure of the success of the previous DGSE reform was that it dated back to DG Silberzahn's mandate more than thirty years ago. Criticisms of the latest reform have yet to become public, but the experiences of other countries suggest that challenges will arise, if they have not already. Norway's intelligence community, though much smaller, found that its shift to mission centers dispersed expertise, leading it to revert to a more traditional structure.[8] In the United States, Director John Brennan's modernization of the CIA—which also included the establishment of mission centers—created much confusion and noise.[9]

The DGSE has long prioritized operations over analysis, a preference rooted in its origins and reinforced by organizational culture. Chapter 1 traced this cultural trait back to the agency's origins during World War II. The DGSE's own communications reaffirm this heritage (chapter 6) and publicly acknowledge the limited career opportunities it offers for those who wish to pursue a career in analysis (chapter 4). While the 2022 reform elevated analysis institutionally, it remains unclear whether this will lead to lasting cultural change. Meaningful reform would require a distinct career path for analysts, which could challenge the agency's long-standing emphasis on staff versatility and integration.

Continuing funding will be crucial for the DGSE to pursue its adaptation to technological change. This is a costly but essential endeavor, particularly as emerging technologies such as artificial intelligence and quantum technology become increasingly central to intelligence operations. The agency already uses machine learning to process the vast quantities of data it collects or purchases, enabling analysts to focus on specific areas of interest.[10] However, investing in AI alone is not enough. Success in digital transformation depends on integrating these capabilities with other emerging technologies, nontechnical capabilities such as agent-handling methods and critical thinking, and established procedures.

This last point brings us to the question of human resources. The DGSE is larger and recruitment much more diverse and competitive than it was back in 1982. Yet significant challenges remain. The agency reportedly loses between five hundred and seven hundred personnel each year, around 10 percent of its workforce.[11] This turnover is often attributed to better salaries and working conditions in the private sector, particularly in technical roles. However, the problem is broader: Newer generations feel less committed to a single career and expect greater flexibility in their work conditions.[12] While the DGSE has found ways to accommodate this demand, the nature of intelligence work and the constraints of civil service rules will continue to impose significant limits to recruitment, retention, and promotion.

Intelligence and the People

The DGSE enjoys broad public support and a far more favorable image than in its early years. Even major intelligence failures, such as the 2015 Paris attacks, have not significantly tarnished this image. The popular television series *Le bureau des légendes* has crystallized this shift in public and political attitudes toward intelligence but certainly not caused it. The prominence of the terrorist threat and the important role intelligence agencies play in countering it provide a much more plausible explanation.

Domestically, the DGSE has taken steps toward greater openness. Under DG Émié, public messaging emphasized its heritage of resistance and sacrifice. In 2024 a book of authorized interviews and a documentary presented a more diverse picture of agency life.[13] Still, public communication remains limited, especially compared to the growing number of Western agencies that now consider the public one of their key consumers.[14] French decision-makers' reluctance to adopt a more open approach and produce intelligence for public consumption may not endure, as open information environments increasingly shape legitimacy and influence.

Greater openness creates opportunities to engage with societal actors and leverage their strengths. This was a key idea behind the establishment of Interaxions, the DGSE's think tank. However, the ambition and scope of this and similar initiatives remain limited by an institutional culture still centered on secrecy and operations. This inward focus limits opportunities to draw on external expertise, where much relevant knowledge and capabilities lie.[15]

As a public policy issue, intelligence demands oversight and a degree of transparency to ensure it serves the public interest. French oversight procedures have evolved to define clear roles for the CNCTR and the parliamentary delegation to intelligence. As the DPR gains experience and improves its reporting, it will likely address a wider range of policy issues. In the United Kingdom, the parliamentary Intelligence and Security Committee has produced detailed reports on topics such as workforce diversity within the intelligence community, procurement, and international partnerships.[16] Although it seems unthinkable at present, the DPR could eventually develop an operational oversight role inspired by the one played by the congressional intelligence committees in the United States. Practitioners are likely to resist such ideas, concerned that increased oversight might entangle intelligence activities in partisan politics. France's other key oversight body—the CNCTR—is now considering whether a legislative review is needed to adapt its role following rulings of the European Court of Human Rights, a sign that legal adaptation is still underway.[17]

The DGSE's future will be shaped by a shifting threat landscape and changing political conditions. Like all intelligence agencies, it will adapt by necessity and design. But intelligence cannot be reformed through a single decision or dramatic moment. It evolves through incremental change, negotiated legitimacy, and persistent tension between secrecy and accountability.

Notes

1. Lledo-Ferrer and Van Puyvelde, "Assassination."
2. Bertrand in Notin, *DGSE*, 124.
3. Hofnung, "Le renseignement francais en Afrique," 7.
4. Gustafson et al., "Intelligence Warning in the Ukraine War," 404; Émié, in Notin, *DGSE*, 18.
5. Betts, "Analysis, War, and Decision," 61.

6. Jean-Dominique Merchet, "Mutinerie de Wagner," *L'Opinion*, July 26, 2023.
7. Émié, in Notin, *DGSE*, 12.
8. Stenslie, "Innovation, Openness, and the Future of Intelligence."
9. See, e.g., David Ignatius, "Will John Brennan's Controversial CIA Modernization Survive Trump?," *Washington Post*, January 17, 2017; Slick, "Measuring Change at the CIA."
10. Frédéric (imagery interpret), in Notin, *DGSE*, 63.
11. Girard, "Maître espion," 38.
12. Central Intelligence Agency, *Emerging Trends*, 49.
13. Notin, *DGSE*.
14. For a list, see Harr Vaage and Stenslie, "How Good Is Norwegian Intelligence?," 969.
15. Zegart, "Open Secrets."
16. UK Parliament, *Diversity and Inclusion*; UK Parliament, *International Partnerships*; UK Parliament, *GCHQ Accommodation Procurement.*
17. "France's Intelligence Watchdog Looks to Britain."

Bibliography

Primary Sources

Académie du Renseignement. *La communauté française du renseignement.* Services du Premier Ministre, 2018.

Archives Nationales, Pierrefite-sur-Seine. Box 20210031/10: Direction des Opérations, Service Missions. "Mission effectuée en mai 1992 auprès du FPR." April 20, 1998.

Archives Nationales, Pierrefite-sur-Seine. Box 20210031/10: Direction Générale de la Sécurité Extérieure. "Note de renseignement No. 4420/T, Libye-Ouganda: Livraison d'armes chimiques." July 6, 1990.

Archives Nationales, Pierrefite-sur-Seine. Box 20210031/10: Direction Générale de la Sécurité Extérieure. "Note de renseignement. Rwanda-Libye. Cooperation Rwando-Libyenne." August 5, 1993.

Assemblée Nationale, Commission d'Enquête Chargée de Faire la Lumière sur les Dysfonctionnements ayant Conduit aux Attaques Commises à la Préfecture de Police de Paris le Jeudi 3 Octobre 2019. *Compte rendu 11.* December 4, 2019.

Assemblée Nationale, Commission d'Enquête Chargée de Faire la Lumière sur les Dysfonctionnements ayant Conduit aux Attaques Commises à la Préfecture de Police de Paris le Jeudi 3 Octobre 2019. *Compte rendu 26.* January 28, 2020.

Assemblée Nationale, Commission d'Enquête Chargée de Faire la Lumière sur les Dysfonctionnements ayant Conduit aux Attaques Commises à la Préfecture de Police de Paris le Jeudi 3 Octobre 2019. *Compte rendu 31.* January 30, 2020.

Assemblée Nationale, Commission d'Enquête Chargée de Faire la Lumière sur les Dysfonctionnements ayant Conduit aux Attaques Commises à la Préfecture de Police de Paris le Jeudi 3 Octobre 2019. January 29, 2020.

Assemblée Nationale, Commission d'Enquête Relative aux Moyens Mis en Oeuvre par l'État pour Lutter contre le Terrorisme depuis le 7 Janvier 2015. *Tome 2: Comptes rendus des auditions.* July 5, 2016.

Assemblée Nationale, Commission d'Enquête sur le Fonctionnement des Services de

Renseignement Français dans le Suivi et la Surveillance des Mouvements Radicaux armés. May 24, 2013.

Assemblée Nationale, Commission de la Défense Nationale et des Forces Armées. *Avis sur le projet de loi de finances pour 2006*. October 12, 2005.

Assemblée Nationale, Commission de la Défense Nationale et des Forces Armées. *Avis sur le projet de loi de finances pour 2007*. October 12, 2006.

Assemblée Nationale, Commission de la Défense Nationale et des Forces Armées. *Avis sur le projet de loi de finances pour 2011*. Vol. 2. October 14, 2010.

Assemblée Nationale, Commission de la Défense Nationale et des Forces Armées. *Avis sur le projet de loi de finances pour 2022*. Vol. 2. October 20, 2021.

Assemblée Nationale, Commission de la Défense Nationale et des Forces Armées. *Avis sur le projet de loi de finances pour 2024*. Vol. 2. October 26, 2023.

Assemblée Nationale, Commission de la Défense Nationale et des Forces Armées. *Avis sur le projet de loi relatif au renseignement*. March 31, 2015.

Assemblée Nationale, Commission de la Défense Nationale et des Forces Armées. *Compte rendu 13*. October 28, 2009.

Assemblée Nationale, Commission de la Défense Nationale et des Forces Armées. *Compte rendu 17*. November 18, 2015, 1–9.

Assemblée Nationale, Commission de la Défense Nationale et des Forces Armées. *Compte rendu 36*. February 21, 2018.

Assemblée Nationale, Commission de la Défense Nationale et des Forces Armées. *Compte rendu 47*. February 5, 2013.

Assemblée Nationale, Commission de la Défense Nationale et des Forces Armées. *Compte rendu 49*. March 25, 2015.

Assemblée Nationale, Commission de la Défense Nationale et des Forces Armées. *Compte rendu 56*. February 20, 2013.

Assemblée Nationale, Commission de la Défense Nationale et des Forces Armées. *Hearing of Erard Corbin de Mangoux*. February 20, 2013.

Assemblée Nationale, Commission de la Défense Nationale et des Forces Armées. *Hearing of Jean-François Ferlet*. March 8, 2018.

Assemblée Nationale, Commission de la Défense Nationale et des Forces Armées. *Hearing of Laurent Nuñez*. February 9, 2021.

Assemblée Nationale, Commission de la Défense Nationale et des Forces Armées. *Projet de Loi de Finances pour 2008*. October 11, 2007.

Assemblée Nationale, Commission de la Défense Nationale et des Forces Armées. *Projet de loi de finances pour 2009*. October 16, 2008.

Assemblée Nationale, Commission de la Défense Nationale et des Forces Armées. *Projet de loi de finances pour 2010*. October 14, 2009.

Assemblée Nationale, Commission de la Défense Nationale et des Forces Armées. *Rapport d'information en conclusion d'une mission d'information sur la cyberdéfense*. July 4, 2018.

Assemblée Nationale, Commission de la Défense Nationale et des Forces Armées. *Rapport d'information en conclusion des travaux d'une mission d'information sur les conséquences pour la France des attentats du 11 septembre 2001*. December 12, 2001.

Assemblée Nationale, Commission de la Défense Nationale et des Forces Armées. *Rapport sur la proposition de loi visant à la prise en charge et a la reparation des conséquences des essais nucléaires francais*. June 9, 2021.

Assemblée Nationale, Commission des Affaires Étrangères. *Avis sur le projet de loi de finances pour 2017*. Vol. 4. October 13, 2016.

Assemblée Nationale, Commission des Affaires Étrangères. *Avis sur le projet de loi de finances pour 2021*. October 9, 2020.

Assemblée Nationale, Commission des Affaires Étrangères. *Rapport en conclusion des travaux d'une mission d'information sur la coopération internationale pour lutter contre le terrorisme*, Rapport 1716. July 6, 2004.

Assemblée Nationale, Commission des Affaires Étrangères. *Rapport sur la proposition de résolution no. 2382*. October 18, 2005.

Assemblée Nationale, Commission des Affaires Étrangères. *Renseignement et prospective de défense: Des moyens à la hauteur de nos ambitions?* 2021.

Assemblée Nationale, Commission des Affaires Étrangères, de la Défense et des Forces Armées. *Rapport d'information sur l'environnement et la prospective de la politique de défense*. November 24, 2021.

Assemblée Nationale, Commission des Affaires Étrangères, de la Défense et des Forces Armées. *Le renforcement des forces spéciales françaises, avenir de la guerre ou conséquence de la crise?* May 13, 2014.

Assemblée Nationale, Commission des Finances, de l'Économie Générale et du Contrôle Budgétaire. *Compte rendu 8*. October 24, 2006.

Assemblée Nationale, Commission des Finances, de l'Économie Générale et du Contrôle Budgétaire. *Rapport sur le projet de loi de finances pour 2018*. October 12, 2017.

Assemblée Nationale, Commission des Finances, de l'Économie Générale et du Plan. *Rapport d'information en conclusion des travaux de la mission d'évaluation et de contrôle sur le service de l'état à l'étranger*. July 5, 2006.

Assemblée Nationale, Commission des Finances, de l'Économie Générale et du Plan. *Rapport sur le renseignement par l'image*. July 4, 2001.

Assemblée Nationale, Commission des Lois Constitutionnelles, de la Législation et de l'Administration Générale de la République. *Rapport relatif à la prévention d'actes de terrorisme et au renseignement*. May 20, 2021.

Assemblée Nationale, Commission des Lois Constitutionelles, de la Législation et de l'Administration Générale de la République, *Rapport sur le project de loi relatif au renseignement*, April 2, 2015.

Assemblée Nationale, Délégation Parlementaire au Renseignement. *Rapport relatif à l'activité de la délégation parlementaire au renseignement pour l'année 2012*. April 30, 2013.

Assemblée Nationale, Délégation Parlementaire au Renseignement. *Rapport relatif à l'activité de la délégation parlementaire au renseignement pour l'année 2014*. December 18, 2014.

Assemblée Nationale, Délégation Parlementaire au Renseignement. *Rapport relatif à l'activité de la délégation parlementaire au renseignement pour l'année 2015*. February 25, 2016.

Assemblée Nationale, Délégation Parlementaire au Renseignement. *Rapport relatif à l'activité de la délégation parlementaire au renseignement pour l'année 2018*. April 11, 2019.

Assemblée Nationale, Délégation Parlementaire au Renseignement. *Rapport relatif à l'activité de la délégation parlementaire au renseignement pour l'année 2019–2020*. June 11, 2020.

Assemblée Nationale. *Loi no. 91-646 relative au secret des correspondances émises par la voie des communications électroniques*. July 10, 1991.

Assemblée Nationale. *Loi no. 2015-912 relative au renseignement*. July 24, 2015.

Assemblée Nationale. *Loi no. 2015-1556 relative aux mesures de surveillance des communications électroniques internationales*. November 30, 2015.

Assemblée Nationale. *Loi no. 2007-1443 portant création d'une délégation parlementaire au renseignement*. October 9, 2007.

Assemblée Nationale, Commission des Affaires Étrangères. *Rapport d'information sur la réforme du corps diplomatique*. January 11, 2023.

Assemblée Nationale. *Loi relative à la programmation militaire pour les années 2014 à 2019 et portant diverses dispositions concernant la défense et la sécurité nationale*. December 18, 2013.

Assemblée Nationale, Mission d'Information de la Conférence des Présidents sur la Résilience Nationale. *Hearing of Laurent Nuñez*. December 8, 2021.

Assemblée Nationale, Mission d'Information sur les Moyens de Daech. *Rapport d'information*. July 13, 2016.

Assemblée Nationale, Office Parlementaire d'Évaluation des Choix Scientifiques et Technologiques. *Rapport sur le brouillage des communications électronqiues: Enjeux, limites, solutions*. November 10, 2016.

Assemblée Nationale. *Programmation militaire: Discussion d'un projet de loi adopté par le Sénat*. November 26, 2013.

Central Intelligence Agency. *Emerging Trends: The Future Workforce*. Center for the Study of Intelligence, 2012.

Central Intelligence Agency. "Intelligence Events Timeline: November 1, 1999." https://www.cia.gov/legacy/museum/senior-analytic-service-sas-established/.

"Centres de missions." Annuaire Service Public. August 9, 2023. https://lannuaire.service-public.fr/gouvernement/ecd1cc64-cad8-4484-851f-98ac010e082d.

Cité des Sciences et de l'Industrie. "Espions." https://www.cite-sciences.fr/fr/ressources/expositions-passees/espions/lexposition.

Code de la Défense. Article D. 3126-3. 2023.

Commission de Recherche sur les Archives Françaises Relatives au Rwanda et au Génocide des Tutsi. *La France, le Rwanda et le génocide des Tutsi (1990–1994): Rapport remis au Président de la République*. March 26, 2021.

Commission Nationale de Contrôle des Techniques de Renseignement. *Le cadre légal du renseignement*. 2023. https://web.archive.org/web/20230604223457/https://www.cnctr.fr/3_cadre_legal.html.

Commission Nationale de Contrôle des Techniques de Renseignement. *Le contrôle exercé par la CNCTR*. 2023. https://web.archive.org/web/20221025225942/https://www.cnctr.fr/4_controle.html.

Communications Security Establishment Canada. "SNOWGLOBE: From Discovery to Attribution." 2011. https://www.spiegel.de/media/6fff7917-0001-0014-0000-000000035683/media-35683.pdf\.

Conseil Constitutionnel. *Décision No. 2001-456 DC: Loi de finances pour 2002*. December 27, 2001.

Conseil d'État, Section du Contentieux, 10ème et 9ème Chambres Réunies. *Association des Archivistes Français et Autres*. No. 444865, 448763, June 16, 2021.

Coordination Nationale du Renseignement et de la Lutte contre le Terrorisme. *La stratégie nationale du renseignement*. Présidence de la République, July 2017.

Coordination Nationale du Renseignement et de la Lutte contre le Terrorisme. *La stratégie nationale du renseignement*. Présidence de la République, July 2019.

Council of the European Union. "SIT-6577/07 Worst Case Scenarios for the Narrower Middle East." July 12, 2017.

Deutscher Bunderstag. *Untersuchungsausschuss, Stenografisches Protokoll der 39. Itzung—vorlaufige Fassung, Zeugenvernehmung: Dr Urmann, Berlin*. March 5, 2015. https://wikileaks.org/bnd-nsa/sitzungen/39_01/WikiLeaks_Transcript_Session_39_01_from_German_NSA_Inquiry.pdf.

Direction des Ressources Humaines de l'Armée de Terre. *Instruction No. 731/DEF/RH-AT/BPMF/DS relative au domaine de spécialités renseignement et à la formation individuelle de spécialité du personnel militaire du domaine de spécialités renseignement*. May 21, 2015.

Direction Générale de la Sécurité Extérieure. "@DGSEgouv." YouTube, https://www.youtube.com/@DGSEgouv/about.

Direction Générale de la Sécurité Extérieure. "La chaîne décisionelle de projection de la menace de l'État Islamique." February 19, 2016. In Matthieu Suc, *Les espions de la terreur*. HarperCollins, 2018, 212.

Direction Générale de la Sécurité Extérieure. "L'engagement en héritage." https://www.dgse.gouv.fr/fr/nous-connaitre/notre-heritage.

Direction Générale de la Sécurité Extérieure. "Iraq: État des recherches sur les tubes en alluminium 7075-T6." February 5, 2003.

Direction Générale de la Sécurité Extérieure. "Opération 'Brigitte Friang,' prêts pour relever le défi?" October 23, 2020. https://www.dgse.gouv.fr/fr/la-dgse/nos-actualites/operation-brigitte-friang-prets-pour-relever-le-defi-0.

Direction Générale de la Sécurité Extérieure. *Propos sur la guerre du Golfe*. N.d. Consulted at DGSE Headquarters, Paris.

Direction Générale de la Sécurité Extérieure. *Rapport du jury sur le concours externe pour l'accès au corps des attachés de la direction générale de la sécurité extérieure: Session 2018*. 2019.

ElBaradei, Mohamed. "The Status of Nuclear Inspections in Iraq: 14 February 2003 Update." February 14, 2003. International Atomic Energy Agency.

European Parliament. "LIBE Committee Inquiry on Electronic Mass Surveillance of EU Citizens." https://www.europarl.europa.eu/committees/en/libe-committee-inquiry-on-electronic-mas/product-details/20130923CDT71796.

Federal Foreign Office. "Germany and France: Bilateral Relations." March 1, 2023. https://www.auswaertiges-amt.de/en/aussenpolitik/france/209418.

Fillon, François. "Installation de l'académie du renseignement." September 20, 2010. École Militaire, Paris.

Gouvernement Provisoire de la République Française. "Projet de décret portant création d'un Service de Documentation Extérieure et de Contre-Espionnage, 28 décembre 1945." In *Guerres secrètes*, edited by Christophe Bertrand, David Guillet, Carine Lachèvre, François Lagrange, and Emmanuel Ranvoisy, 71. Somogy, 2016.

Government of France. "Synthèse nationale de renseignement déclassifié: Programme chimique syrien; Cas d'emploi passés d'agents chimiques par le regime—Attaque chimique conduite par le régime le 21 août 2013." https://www.diplomatie.gouv.fr/IMG/pdf/Syrie_Synthese_nationale_de_renseignement_declassifie_le_02_09_2013_cle01b7e8.pdf.

Institut National de la Statistique et des Études Économiques. *Répartition des effectifs selon quelques grandes caractéristiques des agents de la fonction publique en 2018*. https://www.insee.fr/fr/statistiques/6528822.

Intelligence College in Europe. "The College." https://www.intelligence-college-europe.org/presentation/.

Interagency OPSEC Support Staff. *IOSS Intelligence Threat Handbook*. Interagency OPSEC Support Staff, 1996.

Internet Archive. Wayback Machine. August 29, 2024. http://web.archive.org/web/20240000000000*/https://www.defense.gouv.fr/dgse.

Ministre de la Défense. *Arrêté portant organisation de la direction générale de la sécurité extérieure*. December 21, 2012.

Ministre de la Défense. *Arrêté portant organisation de la direction générale de la sécurité extérieure*. March 10, 2015.

Ministre de la Défense. *Décret nº 82-306 portant création et fixant les attributions de la direction générale de la sécurité extérieure*. April 2, 1982.

Ministère de la Défense. "Réponse à une question parlementaire de M. Rivière Jérôme." *Journal officiel*, November 23, 2004.

Ministère de l'Économie, des Finances et de la Souveraineté Industrielle et Numérique. *Projet de loi de finances 2022*. https://www.budget.gouv.fr/files/uploads/extract/2022/PLF/BG/PGM/144/FR_2022_PLF_BG_PGM_144_JPE.html.

Ministère de l'Économie et des Finances. *Projet de loi de finances pour 2009: Annexes budgétaires*. https://www.budget.gouv.fr/sites/performance_publique/files/farandole/ressources/2009/pap/html/DBGPGMPRESPGMACTPGM144.htm.

Ministère des Armées. "Interaxions." Internet Archive Wayback Machine. http://web.archive.org/web/20201125203355/https://www.defense.gouv.fr/dgse/tout-le-site/interaxions.

Ministère des Armées. "La mission cinéma et industries créatives (MCIC) du ministère des armées." https://www.defense.gouv.fr/mission-cinema-industries-creatives-mcic-du-ministere-armees.

Ministère des Armées. "Réponse à une question parlementaire de M. Bastien Lachaud." *Journal officiel*, September 7, 2021.

Ministre des Armées. *Arrêté portant organisation de la direction générale de la sécurité extérieure*. December 4, 2002.

Ministre des Armées. *Arrêté portant organisation de la direction générale de la sécurité extérieure*. July 13, 2022.

Ministre des Armées. *Instruction No. 101000/ARM/CAB relative à la politique de lutte informatique et défensive du ministère des armées*. December 24, 2018.

Musée de l'Armée. "Guerres secrètes: L'exposition en ligne." April 27, 2020. https://www.musee-armee.fr/au-programme/expositions/detail/guerres-secretes-lexposition-en-ligne.html.

Musée de l'Ordre de la Libération. "Les agents secrets du général, 1940–1944." Press kit, 2022.

National Commission on Terrorist Attacks upon the United States. *9/11 Report*. W. W. Norton, 2004.

National Intelligence Council. *Iraq's Continuing Programs for Weapons of Mass Destruction*. NIE 2002-16HC. October 2002. https://nsarchive2.gwu.edu/NSAEBB/NSAEBB129/nie.pdf.

National Security Agency. "CLOSE ACCESS SIGAD." September 10, 2010. https://www.eff.org/files/2014/04/09/20131021-monde-close_access_sigads.pdf.

National Security Agency. "Global SIGINT Highlights." May 22, 2012. https://wikileaks.org/nsa-france/intercepts/WikiLeaks_NSA_Eavesdrops_Hollande_on_Greek_Exit.pdf.

National Security Agency. "Visit Précis: Bernard Barbier; Patrick Pailloux." April 12, 2013. https://cryptome.org/2013/10/nsa-hosts-fr-spies.pdf.

National Security Agency, SIGINT Liaison Officer in Paris. "(U) Hostage Support: Another Success Story." *SIDtoday*, February 1, 2005.

National Security Agency, SIGINT Liaison Officer in Paris. "(U) Reflections from an American in Paris." *SIDtoday*, September 30, 2005.

New Zealand Security Intelligence Service. "*Rainbow Warrior*: An NZSIS Perspective." October 1996.

Premier Ministre. *Décret no. 2014-474 pris pour l'application de l'article 6 nonies de l'ordonnance no. 58-1100 du 17 novembre 1958 relative au fonctionnement des assemblées parlementaires et portant désignation des services spécialisés de renseignement*. May 12, 2014.

Premier Ministre. *Décret no. 2015-386 fixant le statut des fonctionnaires de la DGSE*. April 3, 2015.

Premier Ministre. *Décret no. 2023-1039 modifiant les dispositions générales applicables aux fonctionnaires et aux agents contractuels de la direction générale de la sécurité extérieure*. November 15, 2023.

Présidence de la République. *Défense et sécurité nationale: Le livre blanc*. Odile Jacob / La Documentation Française, 2008.

Président de la République. *Décret no. 82-306 du 2 avril 1982 portant création et fixant les attributions de la direction générale de la sécurité extérieure*. April 4, 1982.

Président de la République. *Décret no. 92-523 portant création de la direction du renseignement militaire*. June 16, 1992.

Président de la République. *Décret no. 2009-1657 relatif au conseil de défense et de sécurité nationale et au secrétariat général de la défense et de la sécurité nationale*. December 24, 2009.

Président de la République. *Décret no. 2014-833 relatif à l'inspection des services de renseignement*. July 24, 2014.

Président de la République. *Décret no. 2017-1095 relatif au coordonnateur national du renseignement et de la lutte contre le terrorisme*. June 14, 2017.

Président de la République. *Décret no. 2022-983 relatif aux missions du coordonnateur national du renseignement et de la lutte contre le terrorisme dans le domaine des ressources humaines*. July 4, 2022.

Président de la République. *Décret 2023-295 portant nomination du directeur général de la sécurité extérieure*. December 20, 2023.

Sénat, Commission des Affaires Étrangères, de la Défense et des Forces Armées. *Rapport d'information no. 525 (2013–2014)*. May 13, 2014.

Sénat, Commission des Affaires Étrangères, de la Défense et des Forces Armées. *Rapport d'information sur "Ukraine: un an de guerre. Quels enseignements pour la France?"* February 8, 2023.

Sénat, Commission des Affaires Étrangères, de la Défense et des Forces Armées. *Rapport sur le projet de loi de finances pour 2023*. November 17, 2022.

Treaty on the European Union. Consolidated version. *Official Journal of the European Union* (2012).

UK Parliament, Intelligence and Security Committee. *Annual Report 2019–2021*. 2021.

UK Parliament, Intelligence and Security Committee. *Diversity and Inclusion in the UK Intelligence Community*. July 18, 2018.

UK Parliament, Intelligence and Security Committee. *GCHQ Accommodation Procurement: A Case Study*. November 19, 2020.

UK Parliament, Intelligence and Security Committee. *International Partnerships*. December 5, 2023.

United Nations Secretary-General. *Ruling on the* Rainbow Warrior *Affair Between France and New Zealand*. July 6, 1986.

Secondary Sources

Académie Française. "Renseignement."*Dictionnaire*, 9th ed. https://www.dictionnaire-academie.fr/article/A9R1764/.

Aid, Matthew. "French SIGINT: Part II." July 6, 2013. https://matthewaid.tumblr.com/post/54752805337/french-sigint-part-ii.

"Airgapped Network Threats." *Intellipedia*. https://archive.org/details/5691424-Intellipedia-Air-Gapped-Network-Threats.

Albertelli, Sébastien. *Les services secrets du Général de Gaulle: Le BCRA 1940–1944*. Perrin, 2020.

Aldrich, Richard. *GCHQ*. Harper, 2011.

Aldrich, Richard. "US-European Intelligence Co-operation on Counter-Terrorism: Low Politics and Compulsion." *British Journal of Politics and International Relations* 11, no. 1 (2009): 122–39.

Alexander, Martin. "'Did the Deuxème Bureau Work?': The Role of Intelligence in French Defense Policy and Strategy." *Intelligence and National Security* 6, no. 2 (1991): 293–333.

Allard, Olivier, and Yael Kreplak. "La méfiance au quotidien: Entretien avec un ancient officier de renseignement." *Traçés: Revue de sciences humaines*, no. 31 (2016): 171–93.

Arboit, Gérald. *Des services secrets pour la France: Du dépôt de la Guerre à la DGSE* (1856–2013). CNRS Editions, 2014.

Arboit, Gérald. "Les services spéciaux du temps de l'affaire Dreyfus." *Après-demain* 37, no. 1 (2016): 10–11.

Arboit, Gérald. *Napoléon et le renseignement*. Perrin, 2022.

Arcos, Ruben, and Jose-Miguel Palacios. "The Impact of Intelligence on Decision-Making: The EU and the Arab Spring." *Intelligence and National Security* 33, no. 5 (2018): 737–54.

Armor, Pierre. "La DGSE et ses nouveaux défis." *Après-demain*, no. 37 (2016): 20–23.

"L'art du renseignement: Analyse et combinaison des moyens." *Armées d'aujourd'hui*, no. 276 (2003): 38–43.

Attali, Jacques. *Verbatim II: Chronique des années 1981–1986; Deuxième partie 1983–1986*. Fayard, 1993.

"Babar: Espionage Software Finally Found and Put Under the Microscope." February 18, 2015. https://www.gdatasoftware.com/blog/2015/02/24270-babar-espionage-software-finally-found-and-put-under-the-microscope.

Bajolet, Bernard. "La DGSE, modèle français d'intégration." *ENA hors les murs*, no. 442 (2014): 6–9.

Bajolet, Bernard. "La DGSE, outil de réduction de l'incertitude?" *Revue défense nationale*, no. 766 (2014): 27–31.

Bajolet, Bernard. *Le soleil ne se lève plus à l'est*. Plon, 2018.

Barbier, Bernard. "Espionnage et cybersécurité." *Symposium CentraleSupelec*. June 2016. https://www.youtube.com/watch?v=s8gCaySejr4.

Bastide, Lauren. "Pierre Brochand, Directeur General de la DGSE." *Armées d'aujourd'hui*, no. 276 (2003): 10–11.

Bat, Jean-Pierre. *La fabrique des barbouzes: Histoire des réseaux Foccart en Afrique*. Nouveau Monde, 2015.

Bat, Jean-Pierre. *Les réseaux Foccart: L'homme des affaires secretes*. Nouveau Monde, 2018.

Bat, Jean-Pierre. "Le Secteur N (Afrique) et la fin de la guerre froide." *Relations internationales* 165, no. 1 (2016): 43–56.

Bat, Jean-Pierre. *Le syndrome Foccart*. Gallimard, 2012.

Bauer, Alain, and Marie-Christine Dupuis-Danon. *Les guetteurs*. Odile Jacob, 2018.

Bauer, Deborah. *Marianne Is Watching: Intelligence, Counterintelligence, and the Origins of the French Surveillance State*. University of Nebraska Press, 2021.

Becker, Anja. "The Spy Who Couldn't Possibly Be French." *Journal of Intelligence History* 1, no. 1 (2001): 68–87.

Bely, Lucien. *Espions et ambassadeurs au temps de Louis XIV*. Fayard, 1990.

Ben Jaffel, Hager. *Anglo-European Intelligence Cooperation: Britain in Europe, Europe in Britain*. Routledge, 2019.

Betts, Richard K. "Analysis, War, and Decision: Why Intelligence Failures Are Inevitable." *World Politics* 31, no. 1 (1978): 61–89.

Blistène, Pauline. "*The Bureau* and the Realism of Spy Fiction." *Open Philosophy*, no. 5 (2022): 231–49.

Blistène, Pauline. "La communication au secret: Comment la DGSE a remodelé son image publique." *Quaderni*, no. 106 (2022): 135–48.

Blistène, Pauline. "Fictions du secret, secrets de la fiction." *Inflexions* 47, no. 2 (2021): 133–40.

Blistène, Pauline. "Sea, Sex, and Spies: On Gérard de Villiers' Relations with the Covert World." *Intelligence and National Security* 39, no. 2 (2024): 327–42.

Blistène, Pauline. "Le secret comme ordinaire: *Le Bureau des Légendes* et la modification du regard." *A contrario* 26, no. 1 (2018): 115–33.

Blistène, Pauline. "Voir et faire voir le secret de l'état: Fonctions et enjeux de la fiction d'espionnage contemporaine." PhD thesis, Université Paris 1 Panthéon-Sorbonne, January 31, 2020.

Blistène, Pauline, and Damien Van Puyvelde. "A Delicate Truth: John le Carré, Spy Fiction and Intelligence." *Intelligence and National Security* 38, no. 2 (2023): 193–203.

Bourlet, Michael. "La section économique pendant la Première Guerre Mondiale." In *Naissance et évolution du renseignement dans l'espace européen (1870–1940)*, edited by Frédéric Guelton and Abdil Bicer, 117–35. Service Historique de la Défense, 2006.

Braud, Emmanuelle. "Le renseignement économique militaire en France à partir de 1916: Impératifs stratégiques et économie de guerre." *Revue historique des armées*, no. 42 (2006): 84–93.

Brenner, Michael, and Guillaume Parmentier. *Reconcilable Differences: U.S.-French Relations in the New Era*. Brookings Institution Press, 2002.

Bruce, James B., and Roger Z. George. "Intelligence Analysis: The Emergence of a Discipline." In *Analyzing Intelligence: Origins, Obstacles, and Innovations*, edited by Roger Z. George and James B. Bruce, 1–15. Georgetown University Press, 2008.

Bruneau, Thomas, and Florina Cristiana Matei. "Intelligence Reform in New Democracies: Factors Supporting or Arresting Progress." *Democratization* 18, no. 3 (2011): 602–30.

Bruyère-Ostells, Walter. "Outil militaire et politique africaine de la France depuis 1960: Tableau historiographique et perspectives de recherche." *Relations internationales* 165, no. 1 (2016): 3–22.

Capet, Philippe, and Adrien Revault d'Allonnes. "La cotation dans le domaine militaire: Doctrines, pratiques et insuffisances." In *L'évaluation de l'information*, edited by Philippe Capet and Thomas Delavallade, 125–44. Lavoisier, 2013.

Centre National des Resources Textuelles et Lexicales. "Renseignement." https://www.cnrtl.fr/etymologie/renseignement.

Champtiaux, Dominique. "Les opérations spéciales et les actions clandestines." *Hestia* (2014). https://hestia.hypotheses.org/112.

Chesnot, Christian, and Georges Malbrunot. *Mémoires d'otages*. J'ai lu, 2005.

Chirac, Jacques. *My Life in Politics*. Macmillan, 2011.

Chopin, Olivier. "Intelligence Reform and the Transformation of the State: The End of the French Exception." *Journal of Strategic Studies* 40, no. 4 (2017): 532–53.

Chopin, Olivier, and Benjamin Oudet. *Renseignement et sécurité*. Armand Colin, 2019.

Chouet, Alain. *Au coeur des services spéciaux*. La Découverte, 2013.

Corbin de Mangoux, Erard. "Les mutations du renseignement extérieur français." *Questions internationales*, no. 35 (2009): 29–33.

Cormac, Rory, Calder Walton, and Damien Van Puyvelde. "What Constitutes Successful Covert Action? Evaluating Unacknowledged Interventionism in Foreign Affairs." *Review of International Studies* 48, no. 1 (2022): 111–28.

Couderc, Agathe. "Renseignement technique et secret militaire: Le chiffre français pendant les premiers mois de la Grande Guerre." *Stratégique*, no. 105 (2014): 57–72.

Coudurier, Hubert. *Jean-Yves Le Drian, le glaive du président*. Plon, 2017.

Cousseran, Jean-Claude, and Philippe Hayez. *Leçons sur le renseignement*. Odile Jacob, 2017.

Cousseran, Jean-Claude, and Philippe Hayez. *Renseigner les démocraties, renseigner en démocratie*. Odile Jacob, 2015.

Dahl, Erik. "Missing the Wake-Up Call: Why Intelligence Failures Rarely Inspire Improved Performance." *Intelligence and National Security* 25, no. 6 (2010): 778–99.

Dahl, Kenneth. *New Security for New Threats: The Case for Reforming the Interagency Process*. Brookings Institution, 2007.

Dalloz, Jacques. *La France et le monde depuis 1945*. Armand Colin, 2002.

Davet, Gérard, and Fabrice Lhomme. *"Un président ne devrait pas dire ça. . . ."* Stock, 2016.

Davidson, J. Scott. "The *Rainbow Warrior* Arbitration Concerning the Treatment of the French Agents Mafart and Prieur." *International and Comparative Law Quarterly* 40, no. 2 (1991): 446–57.

Davies, Philip. "Ideas of Intelligence: Divergent National Concepts and Institutions." *Harvard International Review* 24, no. 3 (2002): 62–66.

De Gaulle, Charles. "Paris outragé Paris brisé Paris martyrisé mais Paris libéré." August 25, 1944. Video. https://www.ina.fr/video/I00012416.

De Marenches, Alexandre, and Christine Ockrent. *Dans le secret des princes*. Stock, 1986.

Desgrandchamps, Marie-Luce. "Soutien miliaire et aide humanitaire: Les ambiguïtés de la France au Biafra." *Relations internationales* 165, no. 1 (2016): 81–96.

"Des héros très discrets." *Armées d'aujourd'hui*, no. 276 (2003): 36–37.

De Villepin, Dominique. Address on Iraq. United Nations Security Council. February 14, 2003.

De Villepin, Dominique. *Mémoire de paix pour temps de guerre*. Grasset, 2016.

Dewerpe, Alain. *Espion: Une anthologie historique du secret d'état contemporain*. Gallimard, 1994.

"DGSE Reform: The DR Is Dead, Long Live the DR!" Intelligence Online, July 25, 2022.

Djaffar, Abou. "Que savaient les services de renseignement?" September 22, 2009. https://www.lemonde.fr/blog/aboudjaffar/2009/09/22/que-savaient-les-services-de-renseignement-le-10-septembre-2001/.

Dufourcq, Jean. "In memoriam: Amiral Pierre Lacoste." *Revue défense nationale*, no. 828 (2020): 13–16.

Durbin, Brent. *The CIA and the Politics of Intelligence Reform*. Cambridge University Press, 2017.

Dylan, Huw, and Thomas Maguire. "Secret Intelligence and Public Diplomacy in the Ukraine War." *Survival* 64, no. 4 (2022): 33–74.

Elouarghi, Sandra, Muriel Foenkinos, and Maïna Marjany. "Bernard Émié: 'Nous voulons diffuser en France l'indispensable culture du renseignement.'" *Émile* (2019). https://www.emilemagazine.fr/article/2019/6/25/bernard-emie-nous-voulons-diffuser-en-france-lindispensable-culture-du-renseignement.

Estévez, Eduardo. "Comparing Intelligence Democratization in Latin America: Argentina, Peru, and Ecuador Cases." *Intelligence and National Security* 29, no. 4 (2014): 552–80.

Evans, Martin. *Algeria: France's Undeclared War*. Oxford University Press, 2012.

Faligot, Roger. "France, SIGINT and the Cold War." *Intelligence and National Security* 16, no. 1 (2001): 177–208.

Faligot, Roger, Jean Guisnel, and Rémi Kauffer. *Histoire politique des services secrets français*. La Découverte, 2013.

Faure, Claude. *Aux services de la république: Du BCRA à la DGSE*. Fayard, 2004.

Ferro, Coline. "Responsables politiques français et renseignement." *Revue défense nationale*, no. 377 (2013): 1.

Ferro, Coline. "Les services de renseignement français à l'épreuve de l'ère communicationnelle." *Revue défense nationale*, no. 335 (2013): 1–7.

Finnegan, Terrence. *Shooting the Front: Allied Aerial Reconnaissance and Photographic Interpretation on the Western Front; World War I*. National Defense Intelligence College, 2006.

"Five Eyes, 9-Eyes and Many More." Electrospaces, January 22, 2014. http://electrospaces.blogspot.co.uk/2013/11/five-eyes-9-eyes-and-many-more.html.

Foccart, Jacques. *Tous les soirs avec de Gaulle: Journal de l'Élysée; Tome I—1965–1967*. Fayard, 1997.

Fondation Charles de Gaulle, *Défendre la France: L'héritage de de Gaulle à la lumière des enjeux actuels*. Nouveau Monde and Ministère des Armées, 2020.

Forcade, Olivier. "Jacques Foccart: Une vie politique." In *Jacques Foccart: Archives ouvertes (1858–1974); La politique, l'Afrique et le monde*, edited by Jean-Pierre Bat, Olivier Forcade, and Sylvain Mary, 9–21. Presses de l'Université Paris-Sorbonne, 2017.

Forcade, Olivier. "Le renseignement français dans la Première Guerre Mondiale." Paper presented at the international colloquium "Espionnage et Renseignement pendant la Première Guerre Mondiale," Paris, November 2014.

Forcade, Olivier. *La république secrète: Histoire des services spéciaux français de 1918 à 1939*. Nouveau Monde, 2008.

Forcade, Olivier, and Sébastien Laurent. *Secrets d'état: Pouvoirs et renseignement dans le monde contemporain*. Armand Colin, 2005.

"Force de l'ombre: Les opérationnels de la DGSE." *Armées d'aujourd'hui*, no. 276 (2003): 50–51.

"14-Eyes Are 3rd Party Partners Forming the SIGINT Seniors Europe." Electrospaces, September 16, 2017. https://www.electrospaces.net/2013/12/14-eyes-are-3rd-party-partners-forming.html.

"France's Intelligence Watchdog Looks to Britain to Contend with Human Rights Challenges." Intelligence Online, August 30, 2024.

François, Didier. "Quand la DGSE dévoile une vidéo tournée clandestinement au coeur d'Al-Qaida." Europe 1, February 2, 2021.

Franquebalme, Benoît. *Son Altesse Sérénissime Gérard de Villiers*. Plon, 2018.

Frémeaux, Jacques, and Bruno C. Reis. "French Counterinsurgency in the Era of the Algerian Wars, 1830–1962." In *Insurgencies and Counterinsurgencies: National Styles and Strategic Cultures*, edited by Beatrice Heuser and Eitan Shamir, 47–74. Cambridge University Press, 2016.

Gomart, Thomas. *Soldat de l'ombre*. Tallandier, 2020.

Gomis, Benoit. "Franco-British Defence and Security Treaties: Entente While It Lasts." Chatham House Papers, March 2011.

Goya, Michel. *Le temps des guépards: La guerre mondiale de la France de 1961 à nos jours*. Tallandier, 2022.

Gregory, Shaun. "France and the War on Terrorism." *Terrorism and Political Violence* 15, no. 1 (2003): 130–33.

Guisnel, Jean. *Histoire secrète de la DGSE*. Robert Laffont, 2019.

Guisnel, Jean, and David Korn-Brzoza. *Au service secret de la France*. La Martinière, 2014.

Guisnel, Jean, and Bernard Violet. *Les services secrets: Le pouvoir et les services de renseignements sous François Mitterrand*. La Découverte, 1988.

Gustafson, Kristian, Dan Lomas, Steven Wagner, Neveen Shaaban Abdalla, and Philip H. J. Davies. "Intelligence Warning in the Ukraine War, Autumn 2021—Summer 2022." *Intelligence and National Security* 39, no. 3 (2024): 400–419.

Handel, Michael I. "Leaders and Intelligence." *Intelligence and National Security* 3, no. 3 (1988): 3–39.

Harr Vaage, Brigt, and Stig Stenslie. "How Good Is Norwegian Intelligence?" *International Journal of Intelligence and CounterIntelligence* 36, no. 3 (2023): 968–79.

Hayez, Philippe. "'Renseignement': The New French Intelligence Policy." *International Journal of Intelligence and CounterIntelligence* 23, no. 3 (2010): 474–86.

Hofnung, Thomas. "Au coeur de la DGSE: Entretien avec Bernard Bajolet." *Politique Internationale* 153 (2016). https://politiqueinternationale.com/revue/n153/article/au-coeur-de-la-dgse.

Hofnung, Thomas. "Guerre en Ukraine: 'Seule la Chine a les capacités de modérer Poutine.'" *La croix*, March 29, 2022.

Hofnung, Thomas. "Le renseignement français en Afrique." *Revue études*, no. 9 (2019): 7–16.

Holeindre, Jean-Vincent, and Benjamin Oudet. *Intelligence Studies in France: History, Structure and Proposals*. IRSEM, 2018.

Horne, Alistair. *A Savage War for Peace: Algeria, 1954–1962*. Viking, 1977.

Hudson, Bob, David Hunter, and Stephen Peckham, "Policy Failure and the Policy-Implementation Gap: Can Policy Support Programs Help?" *Policy Design and Practice* 2, no. 1 (2019): 1 14.

"Humain trop humain." *Armées d'aujourd'hui*, no. 276 (2003): 44–47.

Ikani, Nikki. "Surprise, Revisited: An EU Performance Evaluation of the Arab Uprisings." In *Estimative Intelligence in European Foreign Policymaking*, edited by Christoph Meyer, Eva Michaels, Nikki Ikani, Aviva Guttmann, and Michael S. Goodman, 69–95. Edinburgh University Press, 2022.

"Interceptions invisibles: L'enjeu technique." *Armées d'aujourd'hui*, no. 276 (2003): 48–49.

Izambard, Antoine. *Trahison à la DGSE*. Stock, 2022.

Izambard, Antoine, and Franck Renaud, "La sécurité interne de la DGSE fait sa révolution." Intelligence Online, January 16, 2025.

Jackson, Peter. *France and the Nazi Menace: Intelligence and Policy-Making, 1933–1939*. Oxford University Press, 2000.

Jackson, Peter. "Pierre Bourdieu, the 'Cultural Turn' and the Practice of International History." *Review of International Studies* 34, no.1 (2008): 155–81.

Jackson, Peter, and Sébastien-Yves Laurent. *Intelligence in the Modern World: A History*. Bloomsbury, forthcoming.

Jackson, Peter, and Joseph Maiolo. "Strategic Intelligence, Counter-Intelligence and Alliance Diplomacy in Anglo-French Relations Before the Second World War." *Militärgeschichtliche Zeitschrift* 65, no. 2 (2006): 417–61.

Jacobs, Bart. "Maximator: European Signals Intelligence Cooperation, from a Dutch Perspective." *Intelligence and National Security* 35, no. 5 (2020): 659–68.

Jean-Luc. "Forces spéciales, forces clandestines: dissemblances, synergies, interopérabilité." *Revue Défense Nationale* 776, no. 1 (2015): 75–79.

Jeffreys-Jones, Rhodri. *Cloak and Dollar: A History of American Secret Intelligence*. Yale University Press, 2002.

Jeffreys-Jones, Rhodri. "Rise, Fall and Regeneration: From CIA to EU." *Intelligence and National Security* 24, no. 1 (2009): 103–18.

Jenkins, Tricia. *The CIA in Hollywood: How the Agency Shapes Film and Television*. University of Texas Press, 2016.

Kostine, Sergueï, and Eric Raynaud. *Adieu Farewell*. Robert Laffont, 2009.

Krotz, Ulirch, and Latharina Wolf. "Franco-German Defence and Security Cooperation." In *The Handbook of European Defence Policies and Armed Forces*, edited by Hugo Meijer and Marco Wyss, 440–58. Oxford University Press, 2018.

Lacoste, Pierre. *Un amiral au secret*. Flammarion, 1998.

Lacoste, Pierre. "Pratique du pouvoir et renseignement." *Matériaux pour l'histoire de notre temps*, no. 58 (2000): 29–32.

Lacoste, Pierre. *Le renseignement à la française*. Economica, 1998.

Lahaie, Olivier. "Pratiques du renseignement humain en France pendant la Grande Guerre: Permanences et évolutions." In *Espionnage et renseignement pendant la Première Guerre Mondiale*, edited by Olivier Forcade and Maurice Vaïsse, 123–44. La Documentation Française, 2017.

Lander, Stephen. "International Intelligence Cooperation: An Inside Perspective." *Cambridge Review of International Affairs* 17, no. 3 (2004): 481–93.

Laurent, Sébastien. "L'analyse: La resource cachée du renseignement." *Revue des deux mondes* (April 2016): 60–66.

Laurent, Sébastien. *Atlas du Renseignement*. Presses de Sciences Po, 2014.

Laurent, Sébastien. *Les espions français parlent*. Nouveau Monde, 2013.

Laurent, Sébastien. "Foccart au miroir du SDECE des années 1960: Entre 'pré carré' africain et guerre froide." In *Jacques Foccart: Archives ouvertes (1858–1974); La politique, l'Afrique et le monde*, edited by Jean-Pierre Bat, Olivier Forcade, and Sylvain Mary, 231–37. Sorbonne Université Presses, 2017.

Laurent, Sébastien. "The Free French Secret Services: Intelligence and the Politics of Republican Legitimacy." *Intelligence and National Security* 15, no. 4 (2000): 19–41.

Laurent, Sébastien. "Le gaullisme et la 'société du renseignement' sous la IVe et la Ve République." In Laurent, *Politiques du Renseignement*, 295–307.

Laurent, Sébastien. "Is There Something Wrong with Intelligence in France? The Birth of the Modern Secret State." *Intelligence and National Security* 28, no. 3 (2013): 299–312.

Laurent, Sébastien. "Les parlementaires face à l'état secret et au renseignement sous les IVe et Ve Républiques: De l'ignorance à la politisation." *Cahiers de la sécurité*, no. 13 (2010): 134–44.

Laurent, Sébastien. "Pierre Messmer et la gestion de crise: Le ministre des armées, la sécurité militaire et le SDECE (1960–1970)." In *Pierre Messmer: Au Croisement du militaire, du colonial et du politique*, edited by François Audigier, François Cochet, Bernard Lachaise, and Maurice Vaïsse, 225–37. Riveneuve 2012.

Laurent, Sébastien. *Politiques de l'ombre: État, renseignement et surveillance en France*. Fayard, 2009.

Laurent, Sébastien, ed. *Politiques du renseignement*. Presses Universitaires de Bordeaux, 2009.

Laurent, Sébastien. "Politisations et politique du renseignement sous la Ve République." In Laurent, *Politiques du renseignement*, 295–307.

Laurent, Sébastien-Yves. "Le contrôle parlementaire du renseignement (1971–2015): Les enjeux politiques d'une tardive banalisation." In *Mélanges en l'honneur de Bernard Lachaise*, edited by François Audigier and Sébastien-Yves Laurent, 372–96. Riveneuve, 2015.

Laurent, Sébastien-Yves. *État secret, état clandestin: Essai sur la transparence démocratique*. Gallimard, 2024.

Laurent, Sébastien-Yves. "Face aux 'services' (1981–1983): Une autre leçon pour la gauche au pouvoir?" *Histoire@Politique* 27, no. 3 (2015): 62–73.

Laurent, Sébastien-Yves. "La gouvernance supérieure du renseignement: Un défi culturel pour la technostructure d'état." In *Au coeur de l'état: Une histoire du*

secrétariat général de la défense et de la sécurité nationale, edited by Guillaume Denglos and Philippe Vial, 473–92. Nouveau Monde, 2023.
Laurent, Sébastien-Yves. *Le renseignement*. Humensis, 2024.
Lebourg, Nicolas, and Olivier Schmitt. *Paris–Moscou: Un siècle d'extrême droite*. Seuil, 2024.
Le Fur, Anne, and Patrick Wasjman. "Les ambitions du renseignement extérieur français." *Politique internationale* 163 (2019). https://politiqueinternationale.com/revue/n163/article/les-ambitions-du-renseignement.
Lelièvre, Arnaud. "La communication web des services de renseignement: Étude sémio-pragmatique." PhD thesis, Université Catholique de Louvain, February 2018.
Le Maire, Bruno. *Le ministre*. Grasset, 2004.
Le Page, Jean-Marc. *Les services secrets en Indochine*. Nouveau Monde, 2012.
Lewis, Peter. "French Intelligence Adapts to New World Order." *Jane's Intelligence Review* 12, no. 7 (2000): 13.
Lledo-Ferrer, Yvan, and Van Puyvelde, Damien. "Assassination: An Increasingly Uninhibited Instrument of Power." IRSEM Research Paper no. 100 (2020): 1–18.
Lonsdale, David J. "Intelligence Reform: Adapting to the Changing Security Environment." *Comparative Strategy* 31, no. 5 (2012): 430–42.
Lorton, Patrice, and Roger Motte. "Soldats de l'ombre," France 2, March 4, 2004, https://www.youtube.com/watch?v=wH3uvQTgoIw.
Maddrell, Paul. "Conclusion." In Maddrell et al., *Spy Chiefs*, 247–59.
Maddrell, Paul. "Introduction." In Maddrell et al., *Spy Chiefs*, 1–3.
Maddrell, Paul. "What Is Intelligence Leadership? Three Historical Trends." In Maddrell et al., *Spy Chiefs*, 5–42.
Maddrell, Paul, Christopher Moran, Ioanna Iordanou, and Mark Stout, eds. *Spy Chiefs: Volume 2*. Georgetown University Press, 2018.
Mahoney, James, and Kathleen Thelen. "A Theory of Gradual Institutional Change." *Explaining Institutional Change: Ambiguity, Agency, and Power*, edited by James Mahoney and Kathleen Thelen, 1–37. Cambridge University Press, 2009.
Manach, Jean-Marc. "Frenchelon: La carte des stations espion du renseignement français." Bug Brother, May 2014. https://www.lemonde.fr/blog/bugbrother/2009/06/16/frenchelon-la-carte-des-stations-espion-du-renseignement-francais/.
Marion, Pierre, *Mémoires de l'ombre*. Flammarion, 1999.
Marion, Pierre. *La mission impossible: À la tête des services secrets*. Calmann-Lévy, 1991.
Marrin, Stephen. "The 9/11 Terrorist Attacks: A Failure of Policy Not Strategic Intelligence Analysis." *Intelligence and National Security* 26, nos. 2–3 (2011): 182–202.
Martinet, Pierre. *DGSE: Un agent sort de l'ombre*. J'ai Lu, 2005.
Mas, Olivier. "La coopération entre services de renseignement." Talks with a Spy, March 8, 2019. https://www.youtube.com/watch?v=qQPVaefTM6Y.
McCarthy, David. *Selling the CIA: Public Relations and the Culture of Secrecy*. University Press of Kansas, 2018.
McGowan, Fraser. "Balancing Act: The Quintessential Problem of National Intelligence and the Evolution of the U.S. National Intelligence Council, 1979–1993." PhD thesis, Glasgow University, 2023.
Meidinger, Joseph. "L'espion du président." France 3 Alsace, October 8, 1991, https://www.ina.fr/ina-eclaire-actu/video/sxc09011461/claude-silberzahn-l-espion-du-president.

Merchet, Jean-Dominique. "Renseignement et capacité d'anticipation." In *Défendre la France: L'héritage de de Gaulle à la lumière des enjeux actuels*, edited by Fondation Charles de Gaulle, 269–85. Nouveau Monde and Ministère des Armées, 2020.

Michalon, Barthélémy, and Benjamin Puybareau. "Secret d'état et secret des sources: Comment des journalistes enquêtent-ils sur le renseignement en France?" *Cultures et Conflits* 114, nos. 2–3 (2019): 227–62.

Mireval, Damien. "Armées, sécurité et rébellions: Le rôle du renseignement et des actions spéciales dans les guerres du Tchad (1969–1990)." PhD Thesis, Bordeaux University, September 7, 2018.

Moinet, Nicolas. "Communiquer pour expliquer et pour rassurer." *Hermès* 76, no. 3 (2016): 107–15.

Monsieur X and Patrick Pesnot. *Les dessous de la Françafrique*. Nouveau Monde, 2008.

Moran, Christopher, Ioanna Iordannou, and Mark Stout, eds. *Spy Chiefs: Volume 1, Intelligence Leaders in the United States and United Kingdom*. Georgetown University Press, 2018.

Nart, Raymond, and Jacky Debain. *L'affaire Farewell vue de l'intérieur*. Nouveau Monde, 2015.

Nasiri, Omar. *Inside the Global Jihad*. Hurst, 2006.

Neumann, Daniel Rainer. "Member State Intelligence Support to EU Foreign Policymaking." PhD thesis, King's College London, 2025.

Neveu, Erik. "Trente ans de littérature d'espionnage en France 1950–1980." *Vingtième siècle*, no. 10 (1986): 51–66.

Notin, Jean-Christophe. *DGSE: La fabrique des agents secrets*. Tallandier, 2024.

Notin, Jean-Christophe. *La guerre de l'ombre des francais en Afghanistan*. Fayard, 2011.

Notin, Jean-Christophe. *Les guerriers de l'ombre*. Tallandier, 2017.

Nouzille, Vincent. *Erreurs fatales: Comment nos présidents ont failli face au terrorisme*. Fayard, 2017.

Nouzille, Vincent. *Les tueurs de la république*. Fayard, 2015.

Orren, Karen, and Stephen Skowronek. *The Search for American Political Development*. Cambridge University Press, 2004.

Oudet, Benjamin. "D'une stratégie à une 'politique publique' de renseignement: Changement et trajectoire de réformes en France; 1989–2020." PhD thesis, Poitiers University, 2021.

Oudet, Benjamin. "Interconnected in Practice and Insular by Nature? The Internationalisation of the French Intelligence Apparatus." *Romanian Intelligence Studies Review*, nos. 17–18 (2017): 81–92.

Oudet, Benjamin. "Un regard sur *Le bureau des legends*." *La revue des séries 1* (2021).

Oudet, Benjamin. "Le roman d'espionnage: Quand la fiction du secret vient au secours de la science politique." *La revue géopolitique*, October 4, 2017.

Paganini, Pierluigi. "Animal Farm APT and the Shadow of French Intelligence." Infosec Institute, July 8, 2015. https://resources.infosecinstitute.com/topic/animal-farm-apt-and-the-shadow-of-france-intelligence/.

Paiolle, Paul. *Services spéciaux (1935–1945)*. Robert Laffont, 1975.

Pannier, Alice, and Olivier Schmitt. *French Defence Policy Since the End of the Cold War*. Routledge, 2022.

Pennetier, Jean-Marc. "The Springtime of French Intelligence." *Intelligence and National Securtity* 11, no. 4 (1996): 780–98.

Pillar, Paul R. "Adapting Intelligence to Changing Issues." In *Handbook of Intelligence Studies*, edited by Loch K. Johnson, 148–62. Routledge, 2006.

Porch, Douglas. *The French Secret Services: A History of French Intelligence from the Dreyfus Affair to the Gulf War*. Farrar, Straus and Giroux, 1995.

Powell, Nathaniel. *France's Wars in Chad*. Cambridge University Press, 2020.

Programme Commun de Gouvernement de Gauche. *Propositions socialistes pour l'actualisation*. Flammarion, 1978.

Raviv, Dan. "PRISM: Parole à la défense; Entretien avec Michael Hayden." *Politique internationale*, no. 141 (2014). https://politiqueinternationale.com/revue/n141/grand-entretien/prism-parole-a-la-defense.

Redouane. "Writeup of the Richelieu Challenge." June 14, 2019. https://red0xff.github.io/writeups/richelieu_challenge_writeup/.

Renault, Clément. "Franco-British Cooperation, 1939–1944." PhD thesis, University of Glasgow, 2025.

Rivet, Louis. *Carnets du chef des services secrets, 1936–1944*. Edited by Olivier Forcade and Sébastien Laurent. Nouveau Monde, 2010.

Robert, Maurice. *Maurice Robert: "Ministre" de l'Afrique*. Seuil, 2014.

Rondot, Philippe. "Face aux menaces diffuses, le renseignement humain devrait pouvoir garder sa place." *Après-demain* 37, no. 1 (2016): 34–36.

Schein, Edgar H. *Organizational Culture and Leadership*. Jossey-Bass, 2010.

Schmidt, Vivien A. "Discursive Institutionalism: The Explanatory Power of Ideas and Discourse." *Annual Review of Political Science*, no. 11 (2008): 303–26.

Schweizer, Peter. "The Growth of Economic Espionage: America Is Target Number One." *Foreign Affairs* 75, no. 1 (1996): 12–14.

Seibold, Michael. "Intelligence Requirements at the Crossroads: The 1948 French Plan de Renseignement." *Intelligence and National Security* 30, no. 5 (2015): 723–43.

Shedd, Andrew. "Intelligence Reform: A Glass Half Full." *Studies in Intelligence* 68, no. 5 (2024): 49–52.

Silberzahn, Claude. *Au coeur du secret*. Fayard, 1995.

Silberzahn, Claude. "Les mutations de la DGSE après la crise du *Rainbow Warrior*." *Après-demain*, no. 37 (2016): 15–17.

Singh, Amitpal. "Morgan Marquis-Boire on Babar and Casper Malware." Citizen Lab, March 12, 2015. https://citizenlab.ca/2015/03/morgan-marquis-boire-on-babar-casper-malware/.

Siramy, Pierre. *25 ans dans les services secrets*. Flammarion, 2010.

Slick, Stephen. "Measuring Change at the CIA." *Foreign Affairs*, May 4, 2016. https://foreignpolicy.com/2016/05/04/measuring-change-at-the-cia/.

Soutou, Georges-Henri. "Le renseignement français des années 50 et 60: Modeste mais raisonnable." In *Combats: Hommage à Jules Maurin, Jean-François Muracciole et Frédéric Rousseau*, edited by Jean-François Murraciole and Frédéric Rousseau, 66–78. Michel Houdiard, 2010.

Soutou, George-Henri. "La stratégie du renseignement: Essai de typologie." *Stratégique*, no. 105 (2004): 23–42.

Soutou, Georges-Henri, Jacques Frémaux, and Olivier Forcade, eds. *L'exploitation du renseignement en Europe et aux États-Unis des années 1930 aux années 1960*. Economica, 2001.

Statista Research Department. "Importance Given to Cultural Life Among the

Population in France in 2018." *Statista*, December 9, 2022. https://www.statista.com/statistics/1034955/importance-given-to-culture-france/.

Stenslie, Stig. "New Requirements for Collaboration: From Need to Know to Need to Share." *Intelligence and National Security* 40, no. 7 (forthcoming 2025).

Stimson, Henry L. *On Active Services in Peace and War*. Harper, 1948.

Stout, Mark. "World War I and the Birth of American Intelligence Culture." *Intelligence and National Security* 32, no. 3 (2017): 378–94.

Suc, Matthieu. *Les espions de la terreur*. HarperCollins, 2018.

Taillat, Stéphane. "Signaling, Victory, and Strategy in France's Military Cyber Doctrine." War on the Rocks, May 8, 2019. https://warontherocks.com/2019/05/signaling-victory-and-strategy-in-frances-military-cyber-doctrine/.

Thelen, Kathleen. "Institutional Change in Advanced Political Economies." *British Journal of Industrial Relations* 47, no. 3 (2009): 471–98.

Tibère, Clément. "Fonds spéciaux." In *Dictionnaire du renseignement*, edited by Hugues Moutouh and Jérôme Poirot, 396–98. Perrin, 2018.

Toreau, Patrice. "Le renseignement français dans la lutte contre l'islamisme armé de la guerre du golfe (1990) à l'attentat du Bataclan (2015)." PhD thesis, Université Bordeaux-Montaigne, 2019.

Tréguer, Félix. "Intelligence Reform and the Snowden Paradox: The Case of France." *Media and Communication* 5, no. 1 (2017): 17–28.

Trotignon, Yves. "Les failles du renseignement français, ou le syndrome Shadok." The Conversation, December 9, 2015. https://theconversation.com/les-failles-du-renseignement-francais-ou-le-syndrome-shadok-51832.

Trotignon, Yves. *Politique du secret*. Presses Universitaires de France, 2018.

Tuinier, Pepijn. "Explaining the Depth and Breadth of International Intelligence Cooperation: Towards a Comprehensive Understanding." *Intelligence and National Security* 36, no. 1 (2021): 116–38.

Turpin, Frédéric. *Jacques Foccart: Dans l'ombre du pouvoir*. CNRS Editions, 2015.

Turpin, Frédéric. "Jacques Foccart, le conseiller politique." In *Les Gaullistes: Hommes et réseaux*, edited by François Audigier, Bernard Lachaise, and Sébastien Laurent, 185–96. Nouveau Monde, 2013.

Underscore. "J'ai été contacté par la DGSE." YouTube, March 30, 2023. https://www.youtube.com/watch?v=g_jEz6aF2b4.

"A Unique Note from the BND About European SIGINT Alliances." Electrospaces, July 31, 2020. https://www.electrospaces.net/2020/07/a-unique-note-from-bnd-about-european.html.

Vadillo, Floran. "L'administration à l'épreuve du politique: Politisation et personnalisation des services de renseignement et de sécurité de 1981 à 1995." *La revue administrative*, no. 366 (2008): 586–96.

Vadillo, Floran. "Les modalités du contrôle démocratique des services de renseignement." *Après-demain*, no. 37 (2016): 40–42.

Vadillo, Floran. "Personnalisation et pratiques du pouvoir dans le monde du renseignement et de la sécurité (II)." *Revue administrative* 63, no. 374 (2010): 189–95.

Vadillo, Floran, and Alexandre Papaemmanuel. *Les espions de l'Elysée: Le président et les services de renseignement*. Perrin, 2019.

Vaïsse, Maurice. *La grandeur: Politique étrangère du général de Gaulle, 1958–1969*. Fayard, 1998.

Van Puyvelde, Damien. "The Academic-Practitioner Relationship in France." In *The Academic-Pactitioner Divide in Intelligence Studies*, edited by Rubén Arcos, Nicole K. Drumhiller, and Mark Phythian, 179–95. Rowman & Littlefield, 2022.

Van Puyvelde, Damien. "French Paramilitary Actions During the Algerian War of Independence, 1956–1958," *Intelligence and National Security* 36, no. 6 (2021): 898–909.

Van Puyvelde, Damien. "Médiatisation du renseignement et guerre en Ukraine." *Brève stratégique*, no. 37 (March 30, 2022).

Villatoux, Marie-Catherine. "Le renseignement aérien dans la grande guerre." *Mémoire et verité*, no. 6 (2017): 33–48.

Voger, Paul-Louis. *Je ne pouvais rien dire: Contre-espionnage, antiterrorisme, un ancien espion raconte*. L'Archipel, 2018.

Von Bülow, Mathilde. "Myth or Reality? The Red Hand and French Covert Action in Federal Germany During the Algerian War, 1956–1961." *Intelligence and National Security* 22, no. 6 (2007): 787–820.

Von Bülow, Mathilde. *West Germany, Cold War Europe and the Algerian War*. Cambridge University Press, 2016.

Walsh, Patrick. *Intelligence Leadership and Governance: Building Effective Intelligence Communities in the 21st Century*. Routledge, 2021.

Warner, Michael. *The Rise and Fall of Intelligence*. Georgetown University Press, 2014.

Warner, Michael, and J. Kenneth McDonald, *US Intelligence Community Reform Studies Since 1947*. Center for the Study of Intelligence, 2005.

Waroux, François. *James Bond n'existe pas*. Mareuil, 2017.

Warusfel, Bertrand. *Contre-espionnage et protection du secret: Histoire, droit et organisation de la sécurité nationale en France*. Lavauzelle, 2000.

"Wikileaks Published Some of the Most Secret NSA Reports So Far." Electrospaces, June 26, 2015. https://www.electrospaces.net/2015/06/wikileaks-publishes-some-of-most-secret.html.

Willmetts, Simon. *In Secrecy's Shadow: The OSS and the CIA in Hollywood Cinema, 1941–1979*. Edinburgh University Press, 2016.

Wuest-Famôse, Nicolas. "Expliquer notre mission et notre action." Europe 1, September 15, 2010. https://www.europe1.fr/societe/Expliquer-notre-mission-et-notre-action-131610.

Zegart, Amy. "Open Secrets: Ukraine and the Next Intelligence Revolution." *Foreign Affairs*, December 20, 2022. https://www.foreignaffairs.com/world/open-secrets-ukraine-intelligence-revolution-amy-zegart.

Zegart, Amy. "September 11 and the Adaptation Failure of U.S. Intelligence Agencies." *International Security* 29, no. 4 (2005): 78–111.

Zegart, Amy. *Spying Blind: The CIA, the FBI, and the Origins of 9/11*. Princeton University Press, 2007.

Zervoudakis, Alexander. "L'adaptation des services de renseignement." In *L'armée française dans la guerre d'Indochine*, edited by Maurice Vaïsse, 199–234. Editions Complexe, 2000.

Index

Note: Illustrations are indicated by page numbers in *italics*.

About the Author

Damien Van Puyvelde is associate professor and head of the Intelligence and Security Research Group at Leiden University. He is the author of *Outsourcing US Intelligence* (Edinburgh University Press), coauthor of *Cybersecurity: Politics, Governance and Conflict in Cyberspace* (Polity), and coeditor of *Researching National Security Intelligence* and *Covert Action: National Approaches to Unacknowledged Intervention* (both with Georgetown University Press). He has held academic positions in the United States, the United Kingdom, and France, where he is also a research fellow at the Strategic Research Institute of the French Ministry of Armed Forces. His work on intelligence, technology, and security has been widely published, and he serves on the editorial boards of *Intelligence and National Security* and *Études françaises de renseignement et de cyber*.